Lecture Notes in Computer Science   14067

Founding Editors

Gerhard Goos
Juris Hartmanis

The series Lecture Notes in Computer Science (LNCS), including its subseries Lecture Notes in Artificial Intelligence (LNAI) and Lecture Notes in Bioinformatics (LNBI), has established itself as a medium for the publication of new developments in computer science and information technology research, teaching, and education.

LNCS enjoys close cooperation with the computer science R & D community, the series counts many renowned academics among its volume editors and paper authors, and collaborates with prestigious societies. Its mission is to serve this international community by providing an invaluable service, mainly focused on the publication of conference and workshop proceedings and postproceedings. LNCS commenced publication in 1973.

David Mohaisen · Thomas Wies
Editors

Networked Systems

11th International Conference, NETYS 2023
Benguerir, Morocco, May 22–24, 2023
Proceedings

Editors
David Mohaisen (ID)
University of Central Florida
Orlando, FL, USA

Thomas Wies (ID)
New York University
New York, NY, USA

ISSN 0302-9743   ISSN 1611-3349 (electronic)
Lecture Notes in Computer Science
ISBN 978-3-031-37764-8   ISBN 978-3-031-37765-5 (eBook)
https://doi.org/10.1007/978-3-031-37765-5

This Springer imprint is published by the registered company Springer Nature Switzerland AG
The registered company address is: Gewerbestrasse 11, 6330 Cham, Switzerland

Preface

This volume contains the papers accepted at the 11th edition of the International Conference on Networked Systems (NETYS), which was held from May 22–24, 2023 in Benguerir (Morocco). NETYS aims to bring together researchers and engineers from the theory and practice of distributed and networked systems. The scope of the conference covers all aspects related to the design and development of these systems.

For this edition, we received 31 submissions. Each submission was single-blind reviewed by at least three members of the Program Committee, which consisted of 35 international experts spanning all relevant fields related to networked and distributed computing systems. Following a discussion by the Program Committee, eight regular papers and three short papers were selected based on their originality and quality for publication in this volume. In addition to the presentations of these contributed papers, the conference program included keynotes by the following renowned researchers:

- Gilles Barthe (MPI for Security and Privacy)
- Nicolaj Bjorner (Microsoft Research)
- Karima Echihabi (M6PU)
- Nate Foster (Cornell University)
- Iordanis Kerenidis (Université Paris Diderot)
- Peter Müller (ETH Zurich)
- Ruzica Piskac (Yale University)
- Adnane Saoud (M6PU)

As program chairs of NETYS 2023, our deepest gratitude goes to everyone who contributed to the success of the conference. Foremost, we sincerely thank the authors for their high-quality contributions and the keynote speakers for their engaging and insightful presentations. We warmly thank the members of the Program Committee and the external reviewers for their constructive reviews and their active participation in the discussions. Our special gratitude goes to all who contributed to the organization of NETSYS 2023, in particular, the members of the Organizing Committee and especially Yahya Benkaouz (UM5, Morocco). Finally, we thank the general chairs Ahmed Bouajjani (Université de Paris, France), Mohammed Erradi (ENSIAS, Morocco), and Rachid Guerraoui (EPFL Lausanne, Switzerland) for their helpful guidance and invaluable feedback.

May 2023

David Mohaisen
Thomas Wies

Organization

Program Committee

Parosh Aziz Abdulla	Uppsala University, Sweden
Afsah Anwar	Florida A&M University, USA
Mohamed Faouzi Atig	Uppsala University, Sweden
Slimane Bah	Ecole Mohammadia d'Ingénieurs - Mohammed V University, Morocco
Yahya Benkaouz	Mohammed V University in Rabat, Morocco
Nathalie Bertrand	INRIA, France
Erik-Oliver Blass	Airbus Group Innovations, Germany
Abdellah Boulouz	Université Ibn Zohr, Morocco
Eric Chan-Tin	Loyola University Chicago, USA
Songqing Chen	George Mason University, USA
Karima Echihabi	Mohammed VI Polytechnic University, Morocco
Amr El Abbadi	University of California, Santa Barbara, USA
Constantin Enea	Ecole Polytechnique, France
Bernd Freisleben	University of Marburg, Germany
Hossein Hojjat	Tehran Institute for Advanced Studies, Iran
Youssef Iraqi	Khalifa University, UAE
Rhongho Jang	Wayne State University, USA
Zahi Jarir	Cadi Ayyad University, Morocco
Mohamed Jmaiel	University of Sfax, Tunisia
Eric Koskinen	Stevens Institute of Technology, USA
Mohammed-Amine Koulali	Université Mohammed V Souissi, Morocco
Ori Lahav	Tel Aviv University, Israel
David Mohaisen	University of Central Florida, USA
Ouzzif Mohammed	Hassan II University, Morocco
Madhavan Mukund	Chennai Mathematical Institute, India
K. Narayan Kumar	Chennai Mathematical Institute, India
Guevara Noubir	Northeastern University, USA
Jeman Park	Georgia Institute of Technology, USA
Shaz Qadeer	Facebook, USA
Arnaud Sangnier	Université Paris Diderot, CNRS, France
Pierre Sutra	Télécom SudParis, France
Francois Taïani	Université de Rennes, CNRS, Inria, IRISA, France
Daniel Takabi	Georgia State University, USA

Klaus V. Gleissenthall	Vrije Universiteit Amsterdam, The Netherlands
An Wang	Case Western Reserve University, USA
Thomas Wies	New York University, USA
Guanhua Yan	State University of New York at Binghamton, USA

Additional Reviewers

Ahmad, Ishtiyaque
Fathololumi, Parisa
Fersi, Ghofrane
Lahami, Mariam
Lim, Lawrence
Ruppert, Eric
Subrahmanyam, K. V.
Zhao, Fuheng

Contents

Distributed Systems

Machine Learning

Detection of Fake News Through Heterogeneous Graph Interactions

Raed Alharbi, Tre' R. Jeter, and My T. Thai[✉]

University of Florida, Gainesville, FL 32603, USA
{r.alharbi,t.jeter,mythai}@ufl.edu

Abstract. Fake news is one of the most prominent forms of disinformation. Unfortunately, today's advanced social media platforms allow for the rapid transmission of fake news, which may negatively impact several aspects of human society. Despite the significant progress in detecting fake news, the focus of most current work lies in the detection based on content-based or user context-based methods. We believe that such methods suffer from two limitations: the lack of characterizing the news variation (fake news can appear in different forms via tweets, such as writing different tweets about the same news article) and news repetition (fake news is shared repeatedly via retweets); and the absence of the temporal engagement among different social interactions. Thus, we propose a novel detection framework, namely the Temporal graph Fake News Detection Framework (T-FND), that is effectively able to capture heterogeneous and repetitive characteristics of fake news behavior, resulting in better prediction performance. We empirically evaluate the effectiveness of our model on two real-world datasets, showing that our solution outperforms the state-of-the-art baseline methods

Keywords: Fake news detection · Disinformation · GNN

1 Introduction

The popularity and widespread usage of social media platforms have significantly changed the way individuals communicate and engage online, producing an ideal environment for disseminating fake news [6]. The massive transmission of fake news has started a data war in recent years, raising disinformation and fake news concerns, reducing the legitimacy of news outlets in ecosystems, and perhaps affecting readers' views on serious matters for our community [11].

Despite the remarkable improvement achieved in exploring propagation patterns of information and how they might be used in fake news detection models [10,11], we believe it is still essential to understand news propagation structures and how the news interact with each other in a social media environment to develop an effective fake news detection model. For example, on Twitter, fake news is often spread by a number of tweets about a news article [11], followed by a series of retweets, along with their temporal engagement and users' information, as represented in Fig. 1.

© The Author(s), under exclusive license to Springer Nature Switzerland AG 2023
D. Mohaisen and T. Wies (Eds.): NETYS 2023, LNCS 14067, pp. 3–16, 2023.
https://doi.org/10.1007/978-3-031-37765-5_1

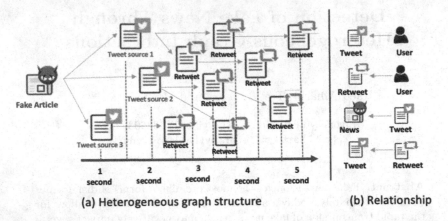

(a) Heterogeneous graph structure   (b) Relationship

Fig. 1. Heterogeneous graph structure on Twitter. (a) A propagation example of one fake news article. (b) Different connections in the heterogeneous network between nodes.

Modeling such propagation structure is crucial to fake news detection for varied purposes. Variation and repetition are two key characteristics that can distinguish patterns of fake news patterns from those of real news. (i) *Variation*: Fake news is carried out continuously in various forms (different tweets provide different descriptions of a news article), and (ii) *Repetition*: Fake news is repeatedly shared in the form of retweets by one or more users. In the real world, news propagation networks often involve multi-levels (variation and repetition). Exploiting such news entities' interactions by analyzing the content of tweets/retweets implies that the propagation network of news on social networks might be utilized effectively to predict fake news [10]. Another key feature that might be exploited in detecting fake news is a relatively short period of time between sequential article-tweets/tweet-retweets to limit the fast spread of fake news.

However, modeling the heterogeneous propagation structure on Twitter presents a number of challenges. (i) **Sparsity.** The dynamic structure of entities' interactions, where most retweets are directed toward tweet users, results in a "hub" where the owner's degree is significantly higher than the retweets' degrees [7]. As a result, the interaction graph might be sparse. (ii) **Repetition.** Characterizing the repetition of fake news activity is challenging because we must satisfy at least two requirements concurrently: the fake news context behaviors (in different forms) and temporal engagement characteristics among different interactions.

To address these concerns, this paper proposes a **Temporal-graph Fake News Detection** framework (T-FND) that consists of three components: (1) Social context representation; (2) Temporal graph learning; and (3) A heterogeneous social network. The first part of the model aims to extract tweets and retweets representations of texts along with user information characteristics and then approximate those values features. The temporal graph in the second part is to construct a relationship interactions graph (e.g., tweet-article and retweet-tweet) by encoding those interactions' content and temporal engagement behavior. The last part selects the interaction graph with informative meta path (relationship interactions), aggregates its information representations, and then performs the fake news detection. Extensive experiments on two benchmarks demonstrate our approach's efficacy.

Organization. The remainder of the paper is structured as follows. Section 2 presents the related works. Our proposed T-FND model is introduced in Sect. 3 while the experimental evaluations are discussed in Sect. 4. Finally, Sects. 5 and 6 present the paper's limitations and conclusion, respectively.

2 Related Work

Graph-Based Fake News Detection. Graph neural networks (GNNs) have gained popularity as a reliable technique for modeling real world applications, like fake news detection [11]. The graph-based fake news detection exploits not only content and context of texts but also the interactions among various nodes in the graph, such as user-user interactions or content-content interactions [4]. Understanding the interaction patterns of fake news dissemination is critical since it provides valuable information for identifying fake news.

Many efforts have been presented to learn graph representations efficiently. The Graph Attention Network (GAT) learns feature representation of nodes by using an attention approach to distribute multiple weights for the properties of surrounding nodes [12]. The Hierarchical Attention Network (HAN) in [13] learns multiple sorts of relationships and interactions between nodes via a hierarchical attention mechanism on a heterogeneous graph, whereas the Heterogeneous Graph Neural Network (HetGNN) model aggregates and learns heterogeneous structural information on a graph to handle a variety of graph tasks [15].

Recent efforts have developed graph embeddings to transform detailed network information into organized multi-dimensional characteristics to leverage the most informative features from graph interactions. Dong *et al.* in [3] proposes Metapath2vec, a heterogeneous network representation that uses the meta path-based random walk to perform node embeddings utilizing skip-gram models. In contrast, Yun *et all* propose Graph Transformer Network (GTN), a method to learn node representation on a heterogeneous graph in which no predefined meta-paths are required [14].

Our work is related to exploring GTN for fake news detection. Characterizing interactions between tweets, retweets, or users is central to the modeling process. Yet, no attempt has been made previously to explore graph transformer network for fake news detection. Therefore, to maximize the utility of GTN, we incorporate two critical aspects: temporal features into the edge weight calculation and a fake news classifier.

Context-Based Methods. Context-based approaches are primarily concerned with features generated from user-based, post-based, and network-based data [9]. Previous efforts have relied on a wide range of contextual features with the aim of detecting fake content, such as using posts and comments [6]. Such features can help in describing the details of user behavior and the process of news propagation across time [11], providing crucial supplementary information for determining the authenticity of news articles.

Unlike conventional methods that focus exclusively on news content or one of the context-based features, we believe that effective collaboration of heterogeneous social media information, such as the content and context of tweets, retweets, user information, social media engagement with users, and temporal features, are informative to improve the detection of fake news.

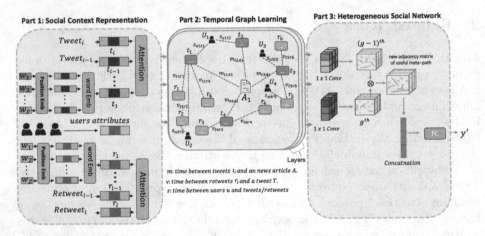

Fig. 2. Overview of T-FND. **Left.** The social context representation component hierarchically establishes the tweet sequences t_i (blue), retweet sequences r_l (green), and user attributes. **Middle.** The temporal graph learning component establishes a heterogeneous interaction graph with their temporal engagement interactions, where nodes represent tweets, retweets, users, and edges reflect the time duration between various relationships. **Right.** The heterogeneous social network component aggregates the information representation learned from graph interactions and leverages the idea of GTN to learn the new graph with a proper meta path and then perform the final classification (fake or real news). (Color figure online)

3   The Proposed Framework - T-FND

We develop a **T**emporal-graph **F**ake **N**ews **D**etection framework (T-FND) to detect fake news by incorporating heterogeneous data from various categories, including tweets, retweets, and user characteristics along with their temporal engagement features. The architecture of the framework is depicted in Fig. 2.

T-FND consists of three parts: (1) A social context component to encode (i) tweets and retweets based on their textual contents and (ii) users by considering the information reflected in their profiles. (2) A temporal graph learning component that constructs an interactions graph of different entities and models their temporal properties. The proposed graph jointly captures the diverse features, including tweets and retweets content information, user characteristics, and temporal engagement features between different interactions; and (3) A heterogeneous social network component that aggregates the information representation learned from graph interactions and leverages the idea of GTN to learn the news graph with a useful meta path to then perform the final classification (fake or real news).

3.1 Social Context Representation Component

Representing the properties of tweets, retweets and a user's historical information is essential for determining (i) user intent, which appears in the context of their utterances, and (ii) user traits such as personalities and linguistic patterns. Thus, the goal of the social context representation component in (part 1 in Fig. 2) is to extract the tweets and retweets features of texts and approximate those informative features. We begin with a description of tweets and retweets' characteristics.

Context Encoding. The variation of a news article in the form of tweets and the repeated sharing of retweets can impact large users to distribute fake news, such as making people post fake news more often. Thus, the content of tweets is the first sign of fake news detection, whereas understanding retweets characteristics is also crucial to the detection process as the sharing mechanism is commonly used in the transmission of fake news, which often includes one or more users.

To capture those representations, we divide the social context representation into three levels. The first level is segment embedding, which is used to separate sentences within a sentence pair and is subsequently used to assess whether a certain embedding belongs to a specific sentence pair. The second level employs position embedding in a sentence to define a word's position inside a sentence, such that each location has its own distinct representation (word context for a sentence). The last level is the word embedding, which converts the tweet $t_i = \{W_1, ..., W_M\}$, where M is the word size of the tweet, and the retweet $r_l = \{W_1, ..., W_Z\}$, where Z is the retweet size word, to a series of vectors with high dimensions (hidden state) $t_i = \{h_1, ..., h_M\}$ and $r_l = \{h_1, ..., h_Z\}$, respectively.

Nevertheless, the words in a tweet or retweet are not equally important in the context of fake news. Therefore, we use word-level attention to identify informative words from a tweet or retweet automatically. Hence, the tweet vector representation t of M words, and the retweet vector representation r of Z words are computed as follow:

$$t_i = \sum_{\tau=1}^{M} \alpha_{i\tau} h_{i\tau} \qquad (1) \qquad\qquad r_l = \sum_{\omega=1}^{Z} e_{l\omega} h_{l\omega} \qquad (2)$$

where $\alpha_{i\tau}$ represents the attention weights of the τth word in the tweet i and $e_{l\omega}$ represents the attention weights of the ωth word in the retweet l. $h_{i\tau}$ and $h_{l\omega}$ refer to tweet and retweet words vector representations, which is obtained utilizing the (**UNI**fied pre-trained **L**anguage **M**odel) [2] to learn the universal language representations. The $\alpha_{i\tau}$ of the tweet is computed as:

$$h'_{i\tau} = \tanh(h_{i\tau}) \qquad (3)$$

$$\alpha_{i\tau} = \frac{\exp\left(h'_{i\tau} h'^{T}_{W}\right)}{\sum_{m=1}^{M} \exp\left(h'_{im} h'^{T}_{W}\right)} \qquad (4)$$

where $h'_{i\tau}$, h'^{T}_{W} are tweet words new hidden state and the learnable parameters, respectively. Similarly, the $e_{l\omega}$ of the retweet is computed as:

$$h'_{l\omega} = \tanh(h_{l\omega}) \qquad (5)$$

$$e_{l\omega} = \frac{\exp\left(h'_{l\omega} h'^{T}_{W}\right)}{\sum_{z=1}^{Z} \exp\left(h'_{lz} h'^{T}_{W}\right)} \qquad (6)$$

where $h'_{l\omega}$, h'^{T}_{W} are retweet words new hidden state and learnable parameters, respectively. $\alpha_{i\tau}$ and $e_{l\omega}$ are used to create semantic vectors that reflect the input of tweets and retweets by computing a weighted sum of hidden representations.

User Encoding. As the content of tweets and retweets posted by a user is rather reflected by the user's behavior, the purpose of user encoding is to improve the capturing of users' behavior and personality characteristics as reflected in their profiles.

Recent efforts have revealed that fake news behavior has a strong connection with user popularity [8]. Consequently, we crawl the user characteristics associated with tweets and retweets, including the user's number of followers, friends, and tweets, then model user history using the previously mentioned context modeling technique.

3.2   Temporal Graph Learning Component

Learning a heterogeneous temporal graph can help address two fundamental network interaction representation issues. The first challenge is that the temporal graph based on a tweet and retweet might be sparse since most tweets are directed at the owner of the news article, and retweets are directed at the tweets associated with it. The second challenge is related to the distinct characteristics of fake news - content is repeatedly shared by different entities within a relatively short time. Such challenges may be effectively addressed by simultaneously modeling networks' heterogeneous content and temporal characteristics.

Therefore, the temporal network interaction learning module in Fig. 2 aims to learn the temporal characteristics of interactions between entities and capture the repeating patterns of fake news behavior (Fig. 1). The module achieves this goal by first constructing a temporal interaction graph (Next section). We, then, presents the details of extracting temporal characteristics of various interactions.

Temporal Graph Construction. As shown in temporal graph learning in Fig. 2, we design a temporal network where nodes are news articles, users, tweets, and retweets, and edges are time intervals between the nodes. In particular, each news article has several tweets, and a tweet consists of multiple retweets posted by different users. Such flow is essential for identifying informative connections between nodes in the graph and capturing their temporal characteristics. Thus, we assume the release time of a tweet occurs after the publication date of the news article, and the release time of a retweet occurs after writing date of the tweet.

Table 1. Characteristics of fake and real news

From	To	Edge Weight
Tweets	News articles	Time since article publication
Tweet reply	Original tweet	Time since the original tweet
Retweets	Original tweet	Time since the original tweet
Users	Tweets or retweets	Constant (1)

Since the paper's primary goal is to use the influence of such information flow for fake news detection, we have eliminated tweets and retweets with invalid time and dates to prevent noise information created during feature extraction. Table 1 shows the relationship pairings for the tweet, retweet, and user nodes in the heterogeneous network we construct.

Temporal Engagement Behaviour. The temporal proximity of prescribed interactions in Table 1 is a critical aspect in capturing recurrence. The propagation of fake news via tweets and a fast rupture of retweets can be identified by capturing the time duration among each part of article-tweet and tweet-retweet interactions.

We define a simple but effective weight function (embedded in an adjacency matrix as described in the next section) on the graph's edges to overcome the challenges. Let m denote the time that has been converted to Unix time. (00 : 00 : 00 UTC on 1 $January 1970$). Given a graph $G = (V, E)$, where V, and

E donate the number of nodes and edges. if the two nodes are connected, the weight q on the edge between them is computed as follows:

$$q_s = m_v - m_{v+1} \tag{7}$$

where s is the encoded edge by the time difference of nanoseconds of both nodes v and $v + 1$, where $v \in V$

3.3   Heterogeneous Social Network (HSN)

The ultimate objective of this paper is to enhance fake news detection using heterogeneous interaction models and their temporal engagement interaction. In this section, we detail how to aggregate the tweets, retweets, user, and temporal characteristics of heterogeneous interaction in a coherent framework called the heterogeneous social network. The HSN learns the graph with the proper meta path and then optimizes the fake detection performance.

Inspired by GTN, heterogeneous social network is defined as $G = (V, E)$, where V, and E are the number of nodes and edges, along with node type mapping function $\phi : V \rightarrow Q$ and the edge type mapping function $\psi : E \rightarrow J$, where Q and J denote the node and relation types, $|Q| + |J| > 2$. Specifically, $Q = a, t, r, u$, where a, t, r, u donate the type of article, tweet, retweet and user, respectively. $J = \{t$ write about a, t is shared by r, u is related to t, u isrelated to $r\}$. The input to our social network architecture is a set of multiple heterogeneous graph structures, where each graph represents a single news article a along with its associated tweets, retweets, and users. The summary input of one graph structure is as follows:

- **Node features.** We construct our feature matrix $X \in \mathbb{D} \times N$, where N is the concatenated representation of nodes' features, including tweets t_i, retweets r_l, and users characteristics u for each news article. $\mathbb{D}$ represents the combined length of node features. The length of the node feature vector is $\mathbb{D} = l + 3$, where l represents the hidden state dimension of the social context encoder and the additional three dimensions are reserved for user features.
- **Adjacency matrices.** A set of adjacency matrices $\{A\}_{b=1}^{B}$ can represent the heterogeneous graph , where $B = |J|$. $A_b \in N \times N$ is an adjacency matrix where $A_b[m_v, m_{v+1}]$ is non-zero when there is a bth type edge from v to $v+1$. The edge weight represents the temporal features among interactions in the heterogeneous graph as presented in Sect. 3.2.

The main idea of the HSN is to learn a new adjacency matrix A of proper and informative meta-path p linked by specific relation types. This provides an opportunity to identify graph structures with more relevant meta-paths, which can subsequently be utilized to do the classification task.

Based on the above observations, each gth layer in HSN starts to choose adjacency matrices (relation types) by performing 1×1 convolution with the softmax weights function as (part 3 in Fig. 2):

$$F(A; \theta^g) = con_{1 \times 1}(A; softmax(\theta^g)) \tag{8}$$

The meta-path adjacency matrix is then produced by multiplying the output matrix with the output matrix of the previous $(g-1)^{th}$ GT Layer.

$$A^{(g)} = (D^{(g)})^{-1} A^{(g-1)} F(A; \theta^{(g)}) \tag{9}$$

where $D^{(g)}$ is a degree matrix that represents the result of multiplying the two matrices $A^{(g-1)} F(A; \theta^{(g)})$. GNNs are deployed for each channel of the output tensor $A^{(g)}$ after the stack of gth layer and then node representation C is updated following the same procedures in [14]. Finally, the label of the fake news y' is computed via several fully connected layers and a softmax layer:

$$y' = Softmax(\mathbf{W}(C) + b) \tag{10}$$

where $\mathbf{W}$ is the learnable parameter and b is the bias value. $y' = [0, 1]$, where 1 is for fake news and 0 for real news.

4   Experiments

This section begins with an overview of the used datasets for detecting false news as described in 4.1. The experimental setup, including baselines, evaluation metrics, and implementations, is then detailed in Sect. 4.2. The predictive performance of T-FND in comparison to existing fake news detection models is detailed in Sect. 4.3, where Sect. 4.4 evaluates the effectiveness of the architecture components on the overall performance.

Table 2. The statistics of PolotiFact and GossipCop dataset

Platform	PolitiFact	GossipCop
# Users	31,524	94,647
# Fake news	346	4,592
# Real news	308	13,925
# Tweets	328,954	106,640,5
# Retweets	707,98	228,360

4.1   Dataset

We use FakeNewsNet [10], a well-known fake news dataset. Obtaining the dataset demands a crawl using these references described by the Kai script [10]. However, we can not crawl the dataset directly due to API changes by Twitter.

Thus, we adjust the script by (i) Updating the old libraries and performing the needed changes and (ii) modifying the code to match Twitter policy. Also, as Twitter limits the number of requests that users are allowed to use the API in an arbitrary time, the total download of the dataset takes about three months. Furthermore, we eliminate the missing news articles and tweets (not available any more). We also find sources of noise. For example, some of the referenced tweets are part of multiple news articles of both classes (real/fake). In this case, we drop these tweets from our dataset. The detailed statistics of the dataset are shown in Table 2

4.2 Experimental Setup

For each dataset, we randomly select 75% of the dataset for training and 25% for testing. The sentence length is 280 characters, while the word length is set to 20 characters. The embedding dimension is set to 200 for textual input, and the dropout rate is 0.2. Each experiment is conducted five times, and the average performance is reported.

Evaluation Metrics. We utilize four well-known evaluation metrics in binary classification tasks: accuracy, precision, recall, and F1 score. These measures have been demonstrated to perform well on imbalanced datasets [9].

Baselines. We compare our proposed model with state-of-the-art models, including the following categories: graph neural network methods (GAT [12], HetGNN [15], and GSAGE [4]), Text classification methods (HAN [13], text-CNN [5]), and fake news detection models (TGNF [11], GCAL [6], and BiGCN [1])

Table 3. Performance Comparison

Method	PolitiFact				GossipCop			
	Accuracy%	Precision%	Recall%	F1%	Accuracy%	Precision%	Recall%	F1%
GAT	80.2	82.3	79.9	80	78.8	77.4	75.4	74
HetGNN	82.7	77.1	73.2	74.5	80.1	75.5	71.3	72.5
GSAGE	72.5	68.2	70.3	70	71.3	67.3	70.2	69.8
HAN	73.3	74.3	65	68.4	70.4	72.4	62.7	65
Text-CNN	77.8	72.2	74	75.5	69.6	69.1	68.5	67.2
TGNF	90.4	88.2	**91.4**	88	82.6	81.4	80.1	79.9
GCAL	89.35	88.8	86.3	87	81.7	80.7	80.4	81.4
BiGCN	89.1	87.6	86.3	84	80.9	80.1	79.9	80.2
T-FND	**92.5**	**91.2**	91.3	**90**	**84.6**	**83.5**	**82**	**83.1**

4.3   Performance Evaluation

This section describes the overall performance of our proposed T-FND model for detecting fake news. All findings are determined by the average value, which is obtained by repeating the same procedure five times. The detailed evaluation measure values for all techniques are shown in Table 3, along with their respective findings.

Comparing T-FND with other fake news baselines that also consider various kinds of features, such as temporal features, we observe that T-FND outperforms other methods in most circumstances with both datasets. Such predictive success may be driven by the fact that our technique efficiently represents diverse interactions in a graph neural network with an emphasis on the temporal characteristics of different nodes. The generalized representation of our proposed model that can capture temporal characteristics also improve the identification of the repetitive characteristics of fake news behavior. The enhancement further comes from modeling user personality features while learning user interaction.

By evaluating different approaches' performances, we also observe that: (1) GNNs approaches, such as HetGNN, provide considerably better performances than text classification approaches, such as Text-CNN and Text-RNN. (2) Another key is that models that are designed particularly for fake news detection, such as GCAL and BiGCN can further improve the performance. (3) Introducing temporal features improves feature-based models. For instance, TGNF introduces a temporal feature that captures dynamic evolution patterns of news propagation. As a result, the TGNF outperforms GCAL.

Table 4. Ablation study results on Politifact and Gossipcop datasets.

Method	PolitiFact				GossipCop			
	Accuracy%	Precision%	Recall%	F1%	Accuracy%	Precision%	Recall%	F1%
T-FND w/o TemF	89	88.1	88.2	88.2	82.1	81.2	81	82
T-FND w/o RetF	88.3	87.6	88.4	87.5	82.3	81.7	82.2	82
T-FND w/o UserF	90.2	90.1	90	89.9	83.7	83.4	83.5	82.5
T-FND	92.5	91.8	91.4	90.2	84.6	83.5	82.5	82.2

4.4   Ablation Study

In this section, we conduct experiments to determine the influence of the major components on T-FND. In particular, we compare T-FND to the following variations by deleting specific components from the T-FND model during the model training step: (i) *T-FND w/o TemF*: The temporal dynamic features are removed, (ii) *T-FND w/o RetF*: The retweet context features are removed, and (iii) *T-FND w/o UserF*: We eliminated user features, such as number of followers. The leave-one-out technique is used to examine the influence of each of the three components - retweet content, temporal characteristics, and user information - on T-FND performance, as summarized in Table 4.

Table 4 show that all three aspects are significant for detecting fake news in both datasets. When retweets' content characteristics are eliminated from the learning process, T-FND's performance deteriorates the most. As a result, modeling the interplay between tweets and retweets is critical. T-FND enforces correlations between semantically relevant tweets and retweets by explicitly connecting the tweet content's edge weights to the retweet content's modeling, hence decreasing context-induced noise. For example, introducing the temporal dynamic features improve the performance from 89% to 92.5%. Capturing and representing temporal characteristics (Table 1) in the temporal graph further enhances performance substantially. Moreover, the consideration of user information enhances the performance of T-FND, indicating the effectiveness of modeling users' personalities' behavior. By integrating these three aspects, T-FND can reach the best overall performance.

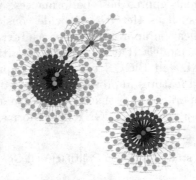

Fig. 3. An example of a propagation graph for two news articles: One for fake news (red node) and the other one for real news (green node). The blue and yellow nodes represent the tweets and retweets, respectively. We can observe the number of retweets for the fake news article is larger than the number of retweets for the real news article. (Color figure online)

5   Discussion

Graphs are usually represented by adjacent matrices. As these adjacent matrices have a shape of N × N (N representing the count of nodes), they become significantly larger when there are many nodes. Detecting the spread of fake news on social media can mean that there are tens of thousands of participants for a single news article. Even if one would only utilize the tweets, the FakeNews-Net dataset has data points with more than 20,000 tweets, resulting in an input shape for the model of more than 20,000 * 20,000. With a footprint of 32 bits, the adjacent matrix itself would have a memory footprint of 1.49 GB. As most

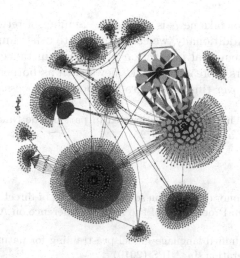

Fig. 4. An example of a propagation graph for random news articles. Red and blue nodes represent the fake and real news articles, respectively. The blue and yellow nodes represent the tweets and retweets, respectively, where the gray nodes refer to the users. We can observe the number of retweets for the fake news article is larger than the number of retweets for the real news article. (Color figure online)

values in the adjacent matrix are zero, one possible solution is to use advanced sparse data structures to ameliorate the situation.

Similar issues with model memory are given when using a large language model to encode the contents of the tweets, as they also have high embedding dimensions per token. With 40 tokens per tweet, 20,000 tweets, 768 embedding dimensions per tweet, and a float 32-bit encoding, the input data of this single example datapoint becomes 2.29 GB. The size of the input data only delivers additional challenges, as model size and gradients have to fit into the memory of GPUs as well. This makes research for small labs only utilizing consumer graphics cards impossible. No optimization technique allowed us to train this model on hardware with 16GB memory. Instead, the training required us to use GPUs with bigger memory.

6 Conclusion

In this paper, we show that modeling tweets, retweets, and temporal interaction is crucial for capturing fake news behavior's repetitive and variation characteristics, resulting in better prediction performance. This paper proposes T-FND, fake news detection framework with a focus on heterogeneous interactions. We empirically evaluate the effectiveness of our model and its components on real-world datasets which outperform state-of-the-art methods for fake news detection.

Our paper opens several key avenues for future work. One such direction is investigating the district sharing pattern by social media platforms, as the

number of retweets for fake news is double the number of retweets for real news
(Fig. 3 and Fig. 4). Additionally, we can incorporate other important aspects of
fake news into the temporal interaction graph. For instance, we can consider
different roles of users (spreaders of fake news such as botnets) and study how
a user's role evolves over time in the graph modeling process.

Acknowledgment. This work was supported in part by the National Science Foundation Program under award No. 1939725.

References

1. Bian, T., et al.: Rumor detection on social media with bi-directional graph convolutional networks. In: Proceedings of the AAAI Conference on Artificial Intelligence (2020)
2. Dong, L., et al.: Unified language model pre-training for natural language understanding and generation. In: NIPS (2019)
3. Dong, Y., Chawla, N.V., Swami, A.: metapath2vec: scalable representation learning for heterogeneous networks. In: Proceedings of the 23rd ACM SIGKDD International Conference on Knowledge Discovery and Data Mining (2017)
4. Hamilton, W., Ying, Z., Leskovec, J.: Inductive representation learning on large graphs. In: Advances in Neural Information Processing Systems (2017)
5. Kim, Y.: Convolutional neural networks for sentence classification. In: EMNLP, pp. 1746–1751 (2014)
6. Liao, H., Liu, Q., Shu, K., et al.: Fake news detection through graph comment advanced learning. arXiv preprint arXiv:2011.01579 (2020)
7. Ravazzi, C., Tempo, R., Dabbene, F.: Learning influence structure in sparse social networks. IEEE Transactions on Control of Network Systems (2017)
8. Sharma, K., Qian, F., Jiang, H., Ruchansky, N., Zhang, M., Liu, Y.: Combating fake news: A survey on identification and mitigation techniques. ACM Transactions on Intelligent Systems and Technology (TIST) (2019)
9. Shu, K., Cui, L., Wang, S., Lee, D., Liu, H.: dEFEND: explainable fake news detection. In: Proceedings of the 25th ACM SIGKDD International Conference on Knowledge Discovery & Data Mining (2019)
10. Shu, K., Mahudeswaran, D., Wang, S., Lee, D., Liu, H.: FakeNewsNet: a data repository with news content, social context, and spatiotemporal information for studying fake news on social media. Big data (2020)
11. Song, C., Shu, K., Wu, B.: Temporally evolving graph neural network for fake news detection. Inf. Process. Manag. **58**, 102712 (2021)
12. Veličković, P., Cucurull, G., Casanova, A., Romero, A., Liò, P., Bengio, Y.: Graph attention networks. In: International Conference on Learning Representations (2018)
13. Yang, Z., Yang, D., Dyer, C., He, X., Smola, A., Hovy, E.: Hierarchical attention networks for document classification. In: Proceedings of the 2016 Conference of the North American Chapter of the Association for Computational Linguistics: Human Language Technologies (2016)
14. Yun, S., Jeong, M., Kim, R., Kang, J., Kim, H.J.: Graph transformer networks. In: NIPS (2019)
15. Zhang, C., Song, D., Huang, C., Swami, A., Chawla, N.V.: Heterogeneous graph neural network. In: Proceedings of the 25th ACM SIGKDD International Conference on Knowledge Discovery & Data Mining (2019)

Edge-Based Bird Species Recognition
via Active Learning

Hicham Bellafkir(✉) ⓘ, Markus Vogelbacher ⓘ, Daniel Schneider ⓘ,
Markus Mühling ⓘ, Nikolaus Korfhage ⓘ, and Bernd Freisleben ⓘ

Department of Mathematics and Computer Science, University of Marburg,
Marburg, Germany
{bellafkir,vogelbacher,schneider,muehling,korfhage,
freisleb}@informatik.uni-marburg.de

Abstract. Monitoring and mitigating the ongoing decline of biodiversity
is one of the most important global challenges that we face today. In this
context, birds are important for many ecosystems, since they link habitats,
resources, and biological processes and thus serve as important early warn-
ing indicators for the health of an ecosystem. State-of-the-art bird species
recognition approaches typically rely on a closed-world assumption, i.e.,
deep learning models are trained once on an acquired dataset. However,
changing environmental conditions may decrease the recognition quality.
In this paper, we present a distributed system for bird species recognition based on active learning with human feedback to improve a deployed
deep neural network model during operation. The system consists of three
components: an embedded edge device for real-time bird species recognition and detection of misclassifications, a client-server web application for
gathering human feedback and a backend component for training, evaluation, and deployment. Misclassifications during operation are detected
based on a novel combination of reliability scores and an ensemble consisting of a bird detection and a bird species recognition model. Wrongly
classified examples are sent to the human feedback component. Once sufficient feedback examples are labeled by a human expert, a new training
process is triggered in the backend, and the trained deep learning model is
optimized and deployed on the edge device. We performed several experiments to evaluate the quality of the bird species recognition model, the
detection of misclassifications, and the overall system to demonstrate the
feasibility of the proposed approach.

Keywords: Active Learning · Bird Species Recognition · Edge
Computing · Passive Acoustic Monitoring · Biodiversity

1   Introduction

The continuous loss of biodiversity is a global phenomenon that has significant ecological and socio-economic implications. Bird monitoring has emerged
as a crucial approach in assessing and mitigating the impacts of this loss. Birds
are considered to be reliable indicators of environmental health, and changes

© The Author(s), under exclusive license to Springer Nature Switzerland AG 2023
D. Mohaisen and T. Wies (Eds.): NETYS 2023, LNCS 14067, pp. 17–34, 2023.
https://doi.org/10.1007/978-3-031-37765-5_2

in avian populations can provide valuable insights into broader trends in biodiversity, making them a vital component of biodiversity monitoring efforts. For many decades, biodiversity monitoring has been conducted manually by human experts. However, there is a strong need to provide automated monitoring methods to scale up biodiversity monitoring efforts in a resource-efficient manner.

Recent years have brought great advances in the automated recognition of bird species based on audio recordings. Most current approaches adopt convolutional neural networks (CNNs) to identify the corresponding bird species in audio spectrograms. Annotating such audio recordings for training a CNN is a tedious and time-consuming task. To enable efficient, continuous spectrogram evaluations, some monitoring approaches make use of embedded edge devices. Typically, embedded CNN models for bird species recognition are trained based on a closed-world assumption that limits their effectiveness, especially in dynamic and complex environments. The disadvantages are, among others, discrepancies in the distribution of the source and target domain, such as missing information in the training data, and inflexibility due to the difficulty of incorporating new knowledge into the CNN model and adapting the CNN model to changing environments. The model must be trained to handle all potentially possible situations, and at the same time the model may become out-dated over time when facing changing environmental conditions.

In this paper, we present a distributed system for bird species recognition based on active learning with human feedback to improve a deployed deep neural network model during operation. To reduce the annotation effort and to improve the deep neural network model, we select new training data samples using a combination of reliability scores and ensemble predictions. Our method is integrated into a distributed system consisting of three components. An embedded edge device performs real-time bird species recognition and detects misclassifications using our proposed querying approach for selecting new training samples. The chosen samples are sent to a client-server web application to be labeled by human experts. When a certain amount of newly annotated data is reached, a backend component initiates a new training process. Finally, the newly trained deep neural network model is deployed on the embedded edge device, and the next iteration of active learning begins. In particular, our contributions are:

- We present a novel deep learning approach for bird species recognition on edge devices based on active learning with human feedback.
- We present a novel approach for automatically detecting misclassification on edge devices based on a combination of reliability scores and ensemble predictions, consisting a bird detection and bird species recognition model.
- We present several experiments to evaluate the quality of the bird species recognition model, the detection of misclassifications, and the overall system to demonstrate the feasibility of the proposed approach.

The paper is organized as follows. Section 2 discusses related work. In Sect. 3, we describe our proposed system for bird species recognition using active learning with human feedback. Experimental results are presented and discussed in Sect. 4. Section 5 concludes the paper and outlines areas of future work.

2 Related Work

Our related work is divided into three relevant areas. We present the state-of-the-art in bird species recognition in Sect. 2.1, we discuss edge artificial intelligence (AI) approaches for biodiversity monitoring in Sect. 2.2, and we discuss current methods for active and continual learning in Sect. 2.3.

2.1 Bird Species Recognition

Ornithologists manually monitored bird populations for years by identifying birds visually and acoustically in their habitats. However, the introduction of autonomous recording units (ARUs) has provided new possibilities. Machine learning methods, particularly CNNs, are on the rise for automated bird species recognition based on soundscapes. The most well known approach is BirdNET, which is a CNN model trained on a large audio data set using extensive data pre-processing, augmentation, and mixup to achieve state-of-the-art performance [12]. The audio spectrograms are generated using a Fast Fourier Transform (FFT) with a high temporal resolution. BirdNET is based on a ResNet [5] deep neural network architecture and is capable of identifying 984 North American and European bird species. More recently, BirdNET-Lite[1] has been released. This neural network is optimized for mobile and edge devices and can recognize more than 6,000 bird species. It takes raw audio as its input and generates spectrograms on-the-fly. Mühling et al. [21] proposed a task-specific neural network created by neural architecture search, [39] which won the BirdCLEF 2020 challenge [11]. It also operates on raw audio data and contains multiple auxiliary heads and recurrent layers.

The winning approach at BirdCLEF 2021 employs Mel spectrograms, network architectures based on ResNet-50 [5], and gradient boosting to refine the results using metadata. Meanwhile, the runners-up, Henkel et al. [7], presented an ensemble of nine CNNs. During training, they utilized 30-second Mel spectrograms to mitigate the effect of weakly labeled training data and applied a novel mixup scheme within and across training samples for extensive data augmentation. Furthermore, a binary bird call/no bird call classifier contributed to the final result.

In the latest edition of BirdCLEF, several participants used Henkel et al.'s approach as a foundation for their work. They extended it with several new post-processing steps, like class-wise thresholds [2,17] or a penalization that reduces output probabilities proportional to the amount of training data [2]. Sampathkumar et al. [30] conducted extensive data augmentation experiments on their single model approach. They found that Gaussian noise, loudness normalization, and tanh distortion have the biggest impact on training an EfficientNet-B0 [34]. Due to great data imbalances, Miyaguchi et al. [20] developed an unsupervised feature extraction method based on Motif mining [32].

---

[1] https://github.com/kahst/BirdNET-Lite.

2.2   Edge AI for Biodiversity Monitoring

Executing machine learning models on edge devices has clear advantages for automated biodiversity monitoring. A fine-grained audio observation in time and space produces significant amounts of data. Up to very recently, high-performance GPU servers in the cloud have been used to analyze the audio recordings. However, neither collecting SD cards by humans in the field and uploading the data manually, nor transmitting the raw audio files from an edge device to a cloud server is a feasible solution for real-time biodiversity monitoring. Embedded edge devices offer a solution to these problems by processing the data on site and transmitting only the results to the cloud, which significantly reduces data traffic and hence energy consumption. Furthermore, edge AI systems enable real-time observation of biodiversity even in remote places.

Several studies demonstrate the feasibility of executing deep learning models on the edge and hence enable the fine-grained monitoring of biodiversity in time and space [3,4,9,40]. Disabato et al. [3] deployed a bird species recognition model at the edge. Their deep learning model provides high accuracy while reducing computational and memory requirements. The edge AI system Bird@Edge [9] is based on an Nvidia Jetson Nano board in combination with several microphones, which in turn are based on ESP32 microcontroller units. The proposed system supports the automatic recognition of bird species in the field and the transmission of the results to a server to support real-time biodiversity monitoring.

2.3   Active Learning

Active learning is a form of semi-supervised learning. It focuses on identifying the most relevant data samples from a pool of unlabeled data for minimizing the target loss function in future training iterations [23,28]. In active learning, data samples that challenge a trained machine learning algorithm during operation are collected and labeled by human observers. Then, the algorithm is re-trained with the original training data plus these labeled data samples, and the process is repeated. This iterative approach can continuously improve the algorithm's performance, maintain its effectiveness over time, and ensure its reliability in real-world scenarios.

By filtering data instances that are expected to yield large quality gains to limit computational resource consumption or labeling costs, active learning can be highly beneficial to support extended definitions of continual learning [23] that include active data queries, capture the importance of data choice and curricula learning, and are aware of the open world assumption. While continual learning has been of great interest in recent years, the adjacent field of active learning is often overlooked in the deep learning era [23].

In the context of supervised continual learning, the process of detecting misclassification of a trained deep neural network model allows us to identify instances where the algorithm may be struggling. Hendrycks et al. [6] presented a simple yet effective method for detecting misclassified and out-of-distribution (OOD) samples in neural network classifiers. The proposed method is based on the idea of measuring the confidence of the neural network's predictions using the maximum softmax output probability. Qiu et al. [27] extended this work by developing an error detector on top of the base classifier to estimate uncertainty of the detection scores using Gaussian processes. Mukhoti et al. [22] used focal loss training to calibrate the model score, which can detect OOD samples more accurately. The authors argue that cross-entropy models tend to produce overconfident and poorly calibrated predictions.

The paradigm of active learning has been applied to several sound classification tasks [35]. Up to now, little attention has been paid to active learning regarding bird sound and bird species recognition. Qian et al. [26] proposed two methods for choosing samples from unlabeled data. Sparse-instance-based active learning takes samples expected to be from sparse classes as the most informative samples to counter class imbalances. The second method, namely least-confidence-score-based active learning, simply assumes the samples with the lowest confidence score to be the most interesting samples for training. Instead of training on certain bird species, Kholgi et al. [14] considered a greater variety of environmental sounds and presented results for six different query strategies. However, these methods mostly focus on confidence scores and entropy values, but do not take characteristics of bird sounds into account. Thus, we present an active learning approach tailored to bird species recognition.

3 Bird Species Recognition via Active Learning

In this section, we describe our proposed system for bird species recognition using active learning with human feedback to improve a deep neural network for bird species recognition during operation. The system is designed as an edge AI system based on distributed embedded edge devices (called edge stations) that analyze bird vocalizations in soundscapes in real-time. A microphone that continuously records audio data is connected to each edge station. It analyzes the audio signal by recognizing bird species and by detecting misclassifications during operation. The recognition results from different edge stations are transmitted to a backend server for further analysis. The results are stored in a time-series database. The overall system is shown in Fig. 1. To create a list of bird species at an edge station, parts of the incoming audio signal are passed to the deployed neural networks to predict a certainty value for each of the target bird species. The prediction is analyzed in a post-processing step to determine whether the prediction has been correctly classified. Otherwise, the audio is sent to a web-based annotation application where the data sample and the corresponding prediction are presented to a human expert for correcting the annotation (see Fig. 3). Once enough samples are available, the model is fine-tuned. After the training has been completed and the performance of the model has been verified, the newly trained model is deployed on the edge stations.

In the following, the used hardware, the embedded deep neural network models, the approach for detecting misclassification, as well as the component for human feedback are described in more detail.

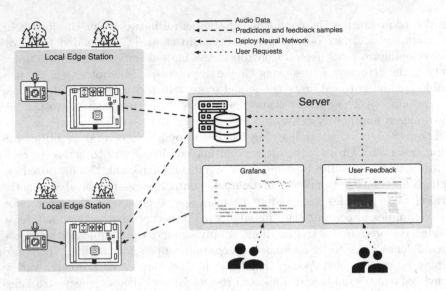

Fig. 1. Overview of the system

3.1   Hardware

Our system consists of (a) microphones that record audio data at the point of use, and (b) edge stations that receive audio data from their corresponding microphones and run the processing pipeline. Figure 2 gives an overview of the hardware components used in our system.

Our microphones are AudioMoths [8], low-cost, open-source acoustic monitoring devices based on Silicon Labs'[2] Gecko processor series. It is a small, robust, and energy-efficient device that can continuously record sounds and store them on a microSD card for several weeks. Furthermore, the device may also be converted into a full-spectrum USB microphone connected to a computing station. The device can capture a wide range of sounds of up to 384 kHz, including bird calls and insect sounds as well as the high-frequency vocalizations of bats and other nocturnal animals. AudioMoths are widely used in research and conservation projects around the world [19,31].

The heart of our edge stations is a Raspberry Pi 4B 2 GB. It allows the efficient execution of machine learning models in a low power environment. In addition, a Huawei E3372H LTE modem is installed to connect to the Internet in rural areas. The station is powered by a 12 V solar battery system connected to the Raspberry Board via a 12 V/5 V step down converter. The hardware of an edge station costs about 632€, with 150€ for the Raspberry Pi, 40€ for the LTE modem, 120€ for the Audiomoth, and 322€ for battery and solar panel (prices currently fluctuate strongly).

---

[2] https://www.silabs.com.

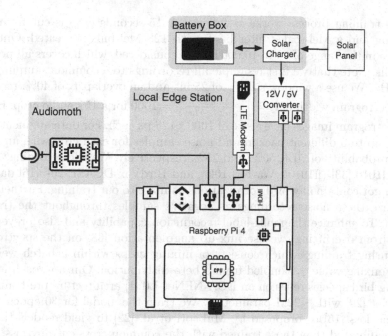

Fig. 2. Hardware components

3.2 Bird Detection and Bird Species Recognition

In this section, we provide an overview of the methodology used to train the neural networks for the purposes of bird detection and bird species recognition.

Recognizing bird species in audio recordings can be reformulated as an image classification task by using spectrograms. Classifying spectrograms is often more efficient than classifying raw audio data, since they provide a visual representation of the audio signal, breaking it down into its constituent frequencies over time. This representation enables a deep learning algorithm to identify patterns in the audio signal more easily, since it can focus on specific frequency bands and changes in those bands over time. In contrast, raw audio data is typically much larger in size and contains a large amount of noise and irrelevant information that can make it difficult for a deep learning algorithm to identify meaningful patterns. Processing raw audio data also requires a large amount of computational power and storage capacity, making it less efficient than processing spectrograms, in particular on edge devices.

Initially, we train a bird species recognition model for all 214 species that are known to occur in our observation area. To train a model for recognizing bird species based on their unique acoustic signatures, we use the publicly available Xeno-Canto [36] dataset. This dataset contains a large and diverse collection of bird vocalizations, including songs and calls. Using training examples for each of the 214 different bird species from Xeno-Canto, we can build an initial model for our system that can distinguish between the different bird species.

The training process works as follows. A 15-seconds crop is cut from each recording and a Mel-scaled filter bank with 128 Mel-bins is created. Only frequencies in the range of 50 to 16,000 Hz are considered, which covers all possible bird calls. Note that we first resample all recordings to a common sampling rate of 32 kHz. We use a window size f_w of 25 ms and an overlap f_o of 40%, resulting in a spectrogram width of $l_s = \left\lfloor \frac{15,000}{f_w - (f_w * f_o)} \right\rfloor = 1000$ for a 15 s audio crop. Hence, the spectrogram images have a size of 1000×128 px each. For data augmentation, we add up to 3 different background noise samples for each crop with an application probability of 70%, 50%, and 25%, respectively. We add recordings of the freefield1010 [33] (ff1010), Warblrb10k[3], and BirdVox-DCASE-20k [16] datasets that do not contain any bird vocalizations as noise to our training. Furthermore, we utilize these noise recordings as negative samples throughout the training process. To enhance the multi-label recognition capability and also prevent the model from overfitting, we use mix-up augmentation [38] on the spectrogram level during training, which consists of mixing crops within a batch weighted with a mixing value γ, sampled from a beta distribution. Our approach for recognizing bird species relies on an ECA-NFNet-L0 [1] architecture pre-trained on ImageNet [29] with ~22M parameters. We train the model for 30 epochs using the focal loss [15] as proposed by Mukhoti et al. [22] to yield models that are better calibrated than those trained with the common cross-entropy loss.

In addition, we train a bird detector that predicts the presence of bird vocalizations for a given audio recording. Our approach for bird sound detection is based on a ResNest-26d [37] architecture pre-trained on ImageNet with ~17M parameters. We train the model with the same settings as the species recognition model. As our training and evaluation datasets, we use the ff1010bird [33], Warblrb10k, and BirdVox-DCASE-20k [16] datasets, as well as recordings from the Xeno-Canto and iNaturalist [10] to increase the number of positive samples. From Xeno-Canto, we use only recordings with durations less than 15 s to ensure that there are bird vocalizations within our crops.

3.3 Detecting Misclassifications

Selecting misclassified samples is crucial for adapting the model to the target domain and iteratively improving the accuracy of the recognition model. In our approach, we utilize a combination of techniques, including analyzing the uncertainty of our model as well as including our bird detector predictions to identify misclassifications. Once the misclassified samples have been identified, they are sent to the backend server for annotation, where a team of experts thoroughly reviews each data sample. The labeled data samples are then used to fine-tune our recognition model, which results in a significant performance improvement.

The following section outlines our method for identifying misclassifications in a multi-label task. Through an examination of our model outputs on the validation set, we observed that true-positive samples typically receive highly confident predictions with scores close to 1. It is worth noting that a sample

---

[3] https://www.warblr.co.uk.

is only considered as correctly classified if all of the predicted species match the given annotations exactly while using a predefined threshold of t over the score. In contrast, false-positive samples often receive less certain predictions, as previously noted by Hendrycks et al. [6]. However, it is important to note that this assumption only applies when bird vocalizations are present, since our model is trained to generate scores near 0 for all species in the absence of bird vocalizations. The presence of bird vocalizations is then predicted by our bird detector, which enables us to differentiate between a negative sample and a possible misclassification. We leverage this observation to identify instances where misclassifications may have occurred. However, recognizing bird species poses a challenge, since it involves a multi-label task. Consequently, simply relying on the maximum score for identifying misclassifications [6] may not be effective. In some cases, the model may accurately identify certain bird species while incorrectly labeling others for a given sample. To tackle this issue, we use a predefined threshold t_{c_i} for each class, where $i \in \{0, .., N\}$ and N is the number of classes. These thresholds are determined as the values that yield the maximum F1-scores on the validation set. Using this approach, we can infer the number of bird species present by identifying all species with scores greater than the corresponding threshold t_{c_i}:

$$f_{count}(S) := \sum_{s \in S} (s > t_{c_i})_1, \qquad (1)$$

where S is the output score vector. Next, we select the top k predictions, where $k = f_{count}(S)$ is the number of species predicted. We then calculate the mean value of the top k scores m_{S_k} and use a threshold t_m that is determined on the validation data set to identify any misclassifications. We consider a prediction as misclassified if $m_{S_k} < t_m$, but only if bird vocalizations are present, as determined by the bird detector prediction. Furthermore, we utilize the binary bird detector to identify more misclassifications by recognizing samples with inconsistent predictions between the detector and the species classifier. These annotated samples can be beneficial for improving the performance of the models when used for training. This approach is summarized in Algorithm 1.

3.4 Human Feedback

Our human feedback component consists of a web-based tool that enables human experts to provide feedback on detected misclassifications (see Fig. 3). The potential misclassifications are presented to the human experts as audio elements, so they can listen to them and identify the species. Additionally, the corresponding spectrograms are visualized. To further aid human experts in the identification process, we present the species predictions made by an edge station and the corresponding reliability scores. Human experts can then assess the accuracy of the system's predictions and make informed decisions about the correct bird species. Once the groundtruth labels are identified by the human expert, a dropdown menu can be used to select the correct bird species. This feature ensures

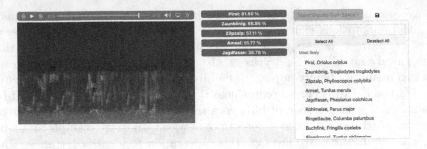

Fig. 3. Annotation view: an audio sample and its spectrogram (left), the model predictions (middle), and the human feedback component (right).

Algorithm 1. Misclassification Detection

1: **Input:** x - Audio crop, f_d - Detector, f_c - Classifier
2: **Output:** d - Misclassification detection decision   ▷ true if x is misclassified
3: $S_d \leftarrow f_d(x)$
4: $S_c \leftarrow f_c(x)$
5: $hasBird \leftarrow S_{d1} > t_d$ ▷ t_d: detection threshold
6: $birdCount \leftarrow f_{cnt}(x)$
7: **if** $hasBird$ **and** $birdCount = 0$ **then**   ▷ f_d, f_c contradict
8:     $d \leftarrow$ true
9: **else if** $\neg hasBird$ **and** $birdCount > 0$ **then**   ▷ f_d, f_c contradict
10:    $d \leftarrow$ true
11: **else if** $hasBird$ **and** $birdCount > 0$ **then**
12:    $S_k \leftarrow$ top-k$(S_c, birdCount)$
13:    $d \leftarrow$ mean$(S_k) < t_m$
14: **else**
15:    $d \leftarrow$ false
16: **end if**

---

that the human feedback is accurately recorded and can be used to improve the recognition accuracy of the system in future iterations. The application is implemented using the Python web framework Flask[4].

4   Experimental Evaluation

In this section, we evaluate different aspects of our proposed system. Section 4.1 describes the used quality metrics. In Sect. 4.2, we present experimental results of the initial bird detection and bird species recognition models including runtimes on the local edge station. In Sect. 4.3, we evaluate the component for misclassification detection. Finally, we analyze one iteration of our active learning cycle in Sect. 4.4.

---

[4] https://flask.palletsprojects.com.

4.1 Quality Metrics

To evaluate the performance of our bird species recognition approach, we use average precision (AP) and the F1-score as our quality metrics.

The F1-score is a commonly used metric for evaluating the performance of a binary classification model. It combines precision and recall into a single metric that provides a measure of the model's overall performance. Precision is the proportion of true positive predictions out of all positive predictions made by the model. Recall is the proportion of true positive predictions out of all actual positive instances in the dataset. The F1-score is the harmonic mean of precision and recall, and it ranges from 0 to 1, with higher values indicating better model performance. It is defined as follows:

$$F1 = 2 * \frac{precision * recall}{precision + recall}$$

The Macro F1-score is calculated by first computing the F1-score for each class individually. Once the F1-scores are computed, the Macro F1-score is obtained by taking the mean of these values. On the other hand, the Micro F1-score takes into account the total number of true positives, false positives, and false negatives across all classes and calculates the F1-score based on these values.

The AP score is the most commonly used quality metric for retrieval results and approximates the area under the precision-recall curve. The task of bird call recognition can be considered as a retrieval problem for each species where the annotated audio samples represent the relevant documents. Then, the AP score is calculated from the list of ranked documents as follows:

$$AP(\rho) = \frac{1}{|R \cap \rho^N|} \sum_{k=1}^{N} \frac{|R \cap \rho^k|}{k} \psi(i_k),$$

$$\text{with} \quad \psi(i_k) = \begin{cases} 1 & \text{if } i_k \in R \\ 0 & \text{otherwise} \end{cases}$$

where N is the length of the ranked document list (total number of analyzed audio samples), $\rho^k = \{i_1, i_2, \ldots, i_k\}$ is the ranked document list up to rank k, R is the set of relevant documents (audio samples containing a bird call), $|R \cap \rho^k|$ is the number of relevant documents in the top-k of ρ and $\psi(i_k)$ is the relevance function. Generally speaking, AP is the average of the precision values at each relevant document. To evaluate the overall performance, the Macro AP is calculated by taking the mean value of the AP of each species, while the Micro AP is calculated globally over all species by flattening the label and score vectors. The scikit-learn [24] library is used to calculate the quality metrics.

4.2 Bird Detection and Bird Species Recognition

We used different datasets for the evaluation of the bird detection and species recognition models. For bird species recognition, we conducted our experiments

Table 1. Overview of the Xeno-Canto dataset splits

Split	Recordings	Duration (h)
Train	147,993	2,793
Validation	18,501	77
Test	18,502	77

Table 2. Overview of datasets for bird detection

Dataset	ff1010bird	Warblrb10k	BirdVox	iNaturalist	Xeno-Canto
Recordings	7,690	8,000	20,000	6,447	10,475
Duration (h)	21	22	55	8	12

on bird sound recordings from the publicly accessible Xeno-Canto [36] database, which contains an extensive collection of bird vocalizations. Specifically, our work focuses on the bird species that are native to our region of interest, totaling 214 species. Altogether, we collected a comprehensive set of 184,996 recordings, resulting in 3480 h hours of audio material.

To ensure reliable and accurate results, we split the dataset into three disjoint sets. For each species, we use 80% of the recordings for training purposes, while the remaining 20% are equally split between the validation and test set (see Table 1). During the training process, we apply a random cropping technique to extract 15-seconds samples. However, while evaluating or testing, we limit the analysis to the first 15 s, since this portion is more likely to contain the annotated birds. The performance of our neural network is measured by both the AP and F1-score metrics, and the outcomes of the preliminary training are demonstrated in Table 3. We used a threshold of 50% when computing the F1-score. Our model achieves 75.3% in terms of Macro AP and 71.7% in terms of F1-score on the test set.

The bird detection model has been trained and evaluated using the datasets outlined in Table 2. During this procedure, we utilized the ff1010bird dataset to conduct performance testing while using the remaining datasets for training. The ff1010bird dataset consists of 5,755 negative samples indicating the absence of bird vocalizations and 1,935 positive samples. To balance our test set, we randomly selected 2,000 negative samples and used all the positive samples to compute the accuracy of our model, which is 81.7%.

Moreover, Table 4 contains the runtime measurements of the bird detection and species recognition models on the Raspberry PI 4B. The detection model can be executed within 0.738 s and the bird species recognition model within 1.84 s for a 15-seconds chunk of audio stream. This allows the entire pipeline to be executed under 3 s for a 15-seconds input chunk, enabling the system to run in real-time using a step size of 5 s.

Table 3. Results of the initial model for species recognition

Dataset	Macro F1-Score	Micro F1-Score	Macro AP	Micro AP
Validation	0.734	0.690	0.770	0.766
Test	0.717	0.685	0.753	0.764

Table 4. Runtime results

Model	Parameters	Detection	Recognition	Inference Time (s)
ECA-NFNet-L0	22M		✓	1.840
ResNest-26d	17M	✓		0.738

4.3   Misclassification Detection

In the following, we describe our experiments to identify misclassifications on the Xeno-Canto validation and test set. Details of our approach are described in Sect. 3.3, which involves analyzing the scores of our models. After computing the threshold vector t_c on the validation set to determine the optimal values for maximizing the F1-score of every class c, we proceed to present the distribution of m_{S_k} on the test set in Fig. 4 a). Notably, this distribution allows us to differentiate between accurate and incorrect classifications, which is not the case using the maximum score per sample [6], as demonstrated in Fig. 4 b). This behavior is expected, since bird species recognition is a multi-label task. To assess the approach more thoroughly, we measure several metrics on both the validation and test set, including the area under the receiver operating characteristic (AUROC), the area under the precision recall curve (AUPR), and the detection error. The score $1 - m_{S_k}$ is used to calculate these metrics, where a high score indicates a possible misclassification. The approach demonstrates its effectiveness by attaining an AUROC of 80.1% and an AUPR of 79.1% on the test set. We investigated the possible reasons for misclassification. We found that samples containing bird songs in the background are one of the most common sources of error, since they pose a major challenge for accurate prediction. This observation is supported by the fact that only 33% of the training data includes more than one bird species. Consequently, our approach can identify suitable samples to improve the model's performance in this specific area.

4.4   Active Learning

We now evaluate our active learning approach. For this purpose, we apply our misclassification detection (MD) strategy for data sample selection described in Sect. 3.3 to the validation set, add the selected data samples to the training set, retrain the bird species recognition model, and evaluate it on the test set.

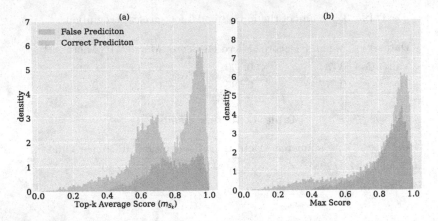

Fig. 4. Distribution of m_{S_k} on the test set

Table 5. Misclassification detection results

Dataset	AUROC ↑	AUPR ↑	Detection Error ↓
Validation	0.792	0.771	0.398
Test	0.801	0.791	0.406

In addition, we conduct a comparison between two data sample selection strategies: (a) the MD strategy and (b) a strategy inspired from the ideas of Qian et al. [25] who utilize the least-confident-max-score samples (called Least-Score below) for selecting data samples. While Qian et al. rank the unlabeled data according to the prediction scores and randomly select 100 data samples from a 20% portion of the least score data samples, we modified the method to be applied on-the-fly and use a fixed threshold to dynamically select data samples from the input stream. We adapted the threshold to yield a similar number of selected samples as in the MD strategy. Thus, both selection strategies selected about 8,000 additional training samples from the validation set.

During fine-tuning, we also use the training data from the initial model to prevent catastrophic forgetting [13,18]. This approach allows the model to retain its previously learned representations while also incorporating new data.

We then evaluated the performance on the test set. The results are presented in Table 6. Note that we set t_m of MD to 77%, since it is the value that yields the maximum F1-score for misclassification detection. The MD strategy improves the base model by 3.5% in terms of the macro F1 score. This is a significant improvement, since by comparison such a gain results in a jump from the 14th place to 1st place in the BirdCLEF 2021 challenge, in terms of Macro AP by 1.8%, and outperforms the Least-Score strategy in terms of Macro F1-Score by 0.5%. The latter performance difference would be probably larger if the dataset contained background data samples without bird vocalizations, since they do not improve the performance of the bird species recognition model. The MD

Table 6. Fine-tuning results on the test set

Strategy	Macro F1-Score	Macro F1-Score	Macro AP	Micro AP
Least-Score	0.738	0.701	0.764	0.764
MD	**0.742**	**0.707**	**0.767**	**0.767**

strategy rejects these data samples, while the Least-Score strategy considers them. Furthermore, it should be taken into account that the baseline model has already been trained with a large number of data samples, and with about 8,000 data samples we added only about 5% training data samples in the active learning iteration.

5 Conclusion

We presented a edge-based approach for bird species recognition based on active learning with human feedback to adapt a deployed deep neural network model during operation. Our approach consists of embedded edge devices, such as the Audiomoth and Raspberry Pis, that operate in a distributed system to provide real-time monitoring and collect the most informative data samples in an active learning scheme to iteratively improve our deep learning models and adapt them to the environment in which the system is deployed.

Misclassifications are detected based on a novel combination of reliability scores and an ensemble consisting of a bird detection and a bird species recognition model. Wrongly classified examples are sent to a human expert who annotates them with the correct classes. Then, a new training process is triggered in the backend server, and the trained deep learning model is optimized and deployed to the edge devices. We performed several experiments to evaluate the quality of the bird species recognition model, the detection of misclassifications, and the overall system to demonstrate the feasibility of the proposed approach.

There are several areas for future work. First, it would be interesting to fuse information from adjacent microphones for detecting misclassifications. Second, federated learning of the bird species recognition models at the edge is an interesting future research topic. Finally, the system should be tested over multiple periods in a real-world scenario with a larger number of edge devices and multiple human annotators.

Acknowledgments. This work is funded by the Hessian State Ministry for Higher Education, Research and the Arts (HMWK) (LOEWE Natur 4.0, LOEWE emergenCITY, and hessian.AI Connectom AI4Birds, AI4BirdsDemo), and the German Research Foundation (DFG, Project 210487104 - SFB 1053 MAKI).

References

1. Brock, A., De, S., Smith, S.L., Simonyan, K.: High-performance large-scale image recognition without normalization. In: 38th International Conference on Machine Learning (ICML), Virtual Event. Proceedings of Machine Learning Research, vol. 139, pp. 1059–1071. PMLR (2021). http://proceedings.mlr.press/v139/brock21a.html

2. Conde, M.V., Choi, U.: Few-shot long-tailed bird audio recognition. In: Proceedings of the Working Notes of CLEF 2022 - Conference and Labs of the Evaluation Forum, Bologna, Italy. CEUR Workshop Proceedings, vol. 3180, pp. 2036–2046. CEUR-WS.org (2022). http://ceur-ws.org/Vol-3180/paper-161.pdf

3. Disabato, S., Canonaco, G., Flikkema, P.G., Roveri, M., Alippi, C.: Birdsong detection at the edge with deep learning. In: IEEE International Conference on Smart Computing (SMARTCOMP), Irvine, CA, USA. pp. 9–16. IEEE (2021). https://doi.org/10.1109/SMARTCOMP52413.2021.00022

4. Gallacher, S., Wilson, D., Fairbrass, A., Turmukhambetov, D., Firman, M., Kreitmayer, S., Mac Aodha, O., Brostow, G., Jones, K.: Shazam for bats: Internet of things for continuous real-time biodiversity monitoring. IET Smart Cities 3(3), 171–183 (2021). https://doi.org/10.1049/smc2.12016

5. He, K., Zhang, X., Ren, S., Sun, J.: Deep residual learning for image recognition. In: IEEE Conference on Computer Vision and Pattern Recognition (CVPR) (2016). https://doi.org/10.1109/CVPR.2016.90

6. Hendrycks, D., Gimpel, K.: A baseline for detecting misclassified and out-of-distribution examples in neural networks. In: 5th International Conference on Learning Representations (ICLR), Toulon, France, Conference Track Proceedings. OpenReview.net (2017). https://openreview.net/forum?id=Hkg4TI9xl

7. Henkel, C., Pfeiffer, P., Singer, P.: Recognizing bird species in diverse soundscapes under weak supervision. In: Working Notes of CLEF 2021 - Conference and Labs of the Evaluation Forum, Bucharest, Romania. CEUR Workshop Proceedings, vol. 2936, pp. 1579–1586. CEUR-WS.org (2021). http://ceur-ws.org/Vol-2936/paper-134.pdf

8. Hill, A.P., Prince, P., Snaddon, J.L., Doncaster, C.P., Rogers, A.: Audiomoth: A low-cost acoustic device for monitoring biodiversity and the environment. HardwareX 6, e00073 (2019). https://doi.org/10.1016/j.ohx.2019.e00073

9. Höchst, J., et al.: Bird@edge: Bird species recognition at the edge. In: Networked Systems - 10th International Conference (NETYS), Virtual Event, Proceedings. Lecture Notes in Computer Science, vol. 13464, pp. 69–86. Springer (2022). https://doi.org/10.1007/978-3-031-17436-0_6

10. iNaturalist: A community for naturalists, https://www.inaturalist.org/

11. Kahl, S., et al.: Overview of BirdCLEF 2020: Bird sound recognition in complex acoustic environments. In: Working Notes of CLEF 2020 - Conference and Labs of the Evaluation Forum, Thessaloniki, Greece. CEUR Workshop Proceedings, vol. 2696. CEUR-WS.org (2020). http://ceur-ws.org/Vol-2696/paper_262.pdf

12. Kahl, S., Wood, C.M., Eibl, M., Klinck, H.: BirdNET: a deep learning solution for avian diversity monitoring. Ecol. Inf. 61, 101236 (2021). https://doi.org/10.1016/j.ecoinf.2021.101236

13. Kemker, R., McClure, M., Abitino, A., Hayes, T., Kanan, C.: Measuring catastrophic forgetting in neural networks. In: Proceedings of the AAAI conference on artificial intelligence. vol. 32 (2018). https://doi.org/10.1609/aaai.v32i1.11651

14. Kholghi, M., Phillips, Y., Towsey, M., Sitbon, L., Roe, P.: Active learning for classifying long-duration audio recordings of the environment. Meth. Ecol. Evol. **9**(9), 1948–1958 (2018). https://doi.org/10.1111/2041-210X.13042

15. Lin, T., Goyal, P., Girshick, R.B., He, K., Dollár, P.: Focal loss for dense object detection. In: IEEE International Conference on Computer Vision (ICCV), Venice, Italy. pp. 2999–3007. IEEE Computer Society (2017). https://doi.org/10.1109/ICCV.2017.324

16. Lostanlen, V., Salamon, J., Farnsworth, A., Kelling, S., Bello, J.P.: Birdvox-full-night: A dataset and benchmark for avian flight call detection. In: IEEE International Conference on Acoustics, Speech and Signal Processing (ICASSP), Calgary, AB, Canada. pp. 266–270. IEEE (2018). https://doi.org/10.1109/ICASSP.2018.8461410

17. Martynov, E., Uematsu, Y.: Dealing with class imbalance in bird sound classification. In: Proceedings of the Working Notes of CLEF 2022 - Conference and Labs of the Evaluation Forum, Bologna, Italy. CEUR Workshop Proceedings, vol. 3180, pp. 2151–2158. CEUR-WS.org (2022), http://ceur-ws.org/Vol-3180/paper-170.pdf

18. McCloskey, M., Cohen, N.J.: Catastrophic interference in connectionist networks: The sequential learning problem. In: Psychology of learning and motivation, vol. 24, pp. 109–165. Elsevier (1989)

19. Michez, A., Broset, S., Lejeune, P.: Ears in the sky: potential of drones for the bioacoustic monitoring of birds and bats. Drones **5**(1), 9 (2021). https://doi.org/10.3390/drones5010009

20. Miyaguchi, A., Yu, J., Cheungvivatpant, B., Dudley, D., Swain, A.: Motif mining and unsupervised representation learning for birdCLEF 2022. In: Proceedings of the Working Notes of CLEF 2022 - Conference and Labs of the Evaluation Forum, Bologna, Italy. CEUR Workshop Proceedings, vol. 3180, pp. 2159–2167. CEUR-WS.org (2022), http://ceur-ws.org/Vol-3180/paper-171.pdf

21. Mühling, M., Franz, J., Korfhage, N., Freisleben, B.: Bird species recognition via neural architecture search. In: Working Notes of CLEF 2020 - Conference and Labs of the Evaluation Forum, Thessaloniki, Greece. CEUR Workshop Proceedings, vol. 2696. CEUR-WS.org (2020). http://ceur-ws.org/Vol-2696/paper_188.pdf

22. Mukhoti, J., Kulharia, V., Sanyal, A., Golodetz, S., Torr, P.H.S., Dokania, P.K.: Calibrating deep neural networks using focal loss. In: Advances in Neural Information Processing Systems 33: Annual Conference on Neural Information Processing Systems (NeurIPS), Virtual Event (2020), https://proceedings.neurips.cc/paper/2020/hash/aeb7b30ef1d024a76f21a1d40e30c302-Abstract.html

23. Mundt, M., Hong, Y., Pliushch, I., Ramesh, V.: A wholistic view of continual learning with deep neural networks: forgotten lessons and the bridge to active and open world learning. Neural Netw. **160**, 306–336 (2023). https://doi.org/10.1016/j.neunet.2023.01.014

24. Pedregosa, F., et al.: Scikit-learn: machine learning in Python. J. Mach. Learn. Res. **12**, 2825–2830 (2011)

25. Qian, K., Zhang, Z., Baird, A., Schuller, B.: Active learning for bird sound classification via a kernel-based extreme learning machine. J. Acoust. Soc. Am. **142**(4), 1796–1804 (2017). https://doi.org/10.1121/1.5004570

26. Qian, K., Zhang, Z., Baird, A., Schuller, B.: Active learning for bird sounds classification. Acta Acustica united with Acustica **103**, 361–341 (04 2017). https://doi.org/10.3813/AAA.919064

27. Qiu, X., Miikkulainen, R.: Detecting misclassification errors in neural networks with a gaussian process model. In: Proceedings of the AAAI Conference on Artificial Intelligence. pp. 8017–8027. AAAI Press (2022). https://ojs.aaai.org/index.php/AAAI/article/view/20773

28. Ren, P., et al.: A survey of deep active learning. ACM Comput. Surv. **54**(9), 1–40 (2021). https://doi.org/10.1145/3472291

29. Russakovsky, O., et al.: Imagenet large scale visual recognition challenge. Int. J. Comput. Vis. **115**(3), 211–252 (2015). https://doi.org/10.1007/s11263-015-0816-y

30. Sampathkumar, A., Kowerko, D.: TUC media computing at birdclef 2022: Strategies in identifying bird sounds in a complex acoustic environments. In: Proceedings of the Working Notes of CLEF 2022 - Conference and Labs of the Evaluation Forum, Bologna, Italy. CEUR Workshop Proceedings, vol. 3180, pp. 2189–2198. CEUR-WS.org (2022). http://ceur-ws.org/Vol-3180/paper-174.pdf

31. Shamon, H., et al.: Using ecoacoustics metrices to track grassland bird richness across landscape gradients. Ecol. Indic. **120**, 106928 (2021). https://doi.org/10.1016/j.ecolind.2020.106928

32. Silva, D.F., Yeh, C.M., Zhu, Y., Batista, G.E., Keogh, E.J.: Fast similarity matrix profile for music analysis and exploration. IEEE Trans. Multim. **21**(1), 29–38 (2019). https://doi.org/10.1109/TMM.2018.2849563

33. Stowell, D., Plumbley, M.: An open dataset for research on audio field recording archives: freefield1010. In: Audio Engineering Society Conference: 53rd International Conference: Semantic Audio (2014). http://www.aes.org/e-lib/browse.cfm?elib=17095

34. Tan, M., Le, Q.V.: Efficientnet: Rethinking model scaling for convolutional neural networks. In: Proceedings of the 36th International Conference on Machine Learning (ICML), Long Beach, California, USA. Proceedings of Machine Learning Research, vol. 97, pp. 6105–6114. PMLR (2019). arxiv:1905.11946

35. Wang, Y., Mendez Mendez, A.E., Cartwright, M., Bello, J.P.: Active learning for efficient audio annotation and classification with a large amount of unlabeled data. In: IEEE International Conference on Acoustics, Speech and Signal Processing (ICASSP). pp. 880–884 (2019). https://doi.org/10.1109/ICASSP.2019.8683063

36. Xeno-canto: Sharing bird sounds from around the world, https://www.xeno-canto.org/

37. Zhang, H., et al.: ResNeSt: Split-attention networks. In: IEEE/CVF Conference on Computer Vision and Pattern Recognition Workshops, CVPR Workshops 2022, New Orleans, LA, USA. pp. 2735–2745. IEEE (2022). https://doi.org/10.1109/CVPRW56347.2022.00309

38. Zhang, H., Cissé, M., Dauphin, Y.N., Lopez-Paz, D.: mixup: Beyond empirical risk minimization. In: 6th International Conference on Learning Representations, ICLR 2018, Vancouver, BC, Canada. OpenReview.net (2018). https://openreview.net/forum?id=r1Ddp1-Rb

39. Zoph, B., Le, Q.V.: Neural architecture search with reinforcement learning. In: 5th International Conference on Learning Representations, (ICLR), Toulon, France, Conference Track Proceedings (2017). https://openreview.net/forum?id=r1Ue8Hcxg

40. Zualkernan, I., Judas, J., Mahbub, T., Bhagwagar, A., Chand, P.: An AIoT system for bat species classification. In: IEEE International Conference on Internet of Things and Intelligence System (IoTaIS). pp. 155–160 (2021). https://doi.org/10.1109/IoTaIS50849.2021.9359704

A Peer to Peer Federated Graph Neural Network for Threat Intelligence

Mouad Bouharoun[1]([✉]), Bilal Taghdouti[1], and Mohammed Erradi[2]

[1] Henceforth, Rabat, Morocco
b.taghdouti@henceforth.ma
[2] ENSIAS, Mohammed V University of Rabat, Rabat, Morocco

Abstract. Threat intelligence is the process of collecting and analyzing information about potential cyber threats. Several approaches have been conducted for cyber threat detection based on the federated learning method. These approaches aim to establish a collaborative threat intelligence sharing between the participants, in order to reinforce their security defense systems. However, these approaches face scalability limitations and raise security and privacy issues: availability, inference attacks, poisoning attacks. To address these issues, we propose a peer-to-peer federated graph neural network (FGNN) approach for threat intelligence. The approach incorporates techniques to ensure data security and privacy. It includes secure aggregation methods and a decentralized sampling technique to reduce the number of exchanged messages. This approach includes also a reputation scoring technique to detect and prevent poisoning attacks, which makes it resilient in the presence of malicious participants.

Keywords: Threat intelligence · Federated learning · Peer-to-Peer · Graph Neural Network

1 Introduction and Related Works

Threat intelligence helps organisations to develop proactive defense strategies, and serves at improving incident response by understanding attackers' tactics [5]. In this context, federated learning (FL) has been successfully applied. It is a distributed approach that enables sharing threat intelligence knowledge while preserving data privacy. Several approaches have been proposed in this area for enhancing cyber security, including network intrusion detection [10], HTTP Malware detection [6], cloud ecosystems, [8] Internet of Things [9].

The FL algorithms perform several rounds until convergence. In each round, the participating nodes train a local model in parallel. Then, the nodes share their updated models with a central aggregator which averages incoming models into a unique model. The resulted model is then used for the next round. However, these approaches present several security issues. First, they have a limited capability to handle increased traffic. Second, the failure of the central aggregator will compromise training progress. Third, they are targeted with inference attacks [4].

© The Author(s), under exclusive license to Springer Nature Switzerland AG 2023
D. Mohaisen and T. Wies (Eds.): NETYS 2023, LNCS 14067, pp. 35–40, 2023.
https://doi.org/10.1007/978-3-031-37765-5_3

The objective of the suggested approach is to present a peer-to-peer federated graph neural network (FGNN) approach for threat intelligence. It allows for knowledge sharing between multiple parties in a scalable and secure manner. To ensure privacy, FGNN employs a secure aggregation technique through secure multi-party computation (SMPC), which allows for a collaborative computation while keeping data confidential. However, the use of SMPC leads to a high number of communications, which can impact the performance. To overcome this, FGNN employs a decentralized sampling technique where a subset of nodes is selected for training in each round, resulting in a faster and more efficient training process.

In addition, the system performance is greatly impacted by the presence of malicious nodes in the network. Several studies have looked at these poisoning attacks [1,2,11]. Others propose defense strategies to mitigate these attacks [6, 7,12]. To tackle this problem, we propose a reputation-based algorithm that evaluates the behavior of each node and assigns it a reputation score. It measures the trustworthiness of the participants in the system.

In the rest of this paper, we provide a detailed description of the adversary scenarios that we address, as well as the various components of the proposed FGNN approach.

2 Threat Model

2.1 Scenario 1: Inference Attack

We have n participants, and the victim is the client whose private data the attacker wants to reconstruct. We denote the victim client by v. and w_{vt} the update from the victim v at the round t. The attacker utilizes a Generative Adversarial Network (GAN) model with a discriminator to obtain information on the victim. [3] This method allows the discriminator to distinguish the victim's identity, using the same architecture as the shared model. The discriminator is updated through a combination of the received updates from the victim and the samples generated by the GAN, which are used to approximate the victim's data (see Fig. 1).

2.2 Scenario 2: Poisoning Attack

We discuss the model poisoning attack in which a malicious participating node tries to compromise the global model performance [1,2,11]. It's important to mitigate this attack vector when designing a peer-to-peer federated learning algorithm. To perform this attack a participant could modify the model updates that he sends to bias the global model during training. Similarly, a compromised client might be used to inject a backdoor into the training process, allowing the attacker to control the training model (see Fig. 2).

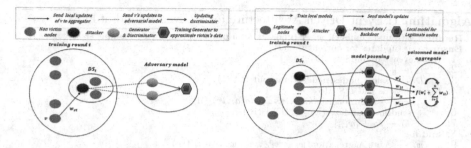

Fig. 1. Threat model scenario 1   **Fig. 2.** Threat model scenario 2

3   System Model

3.1   Design of FGNN

FGNN works by performing several federated learning rounds until convergence. The figure (Fig. 3) highlights two rounds of federated training. In the round t FGNN selects a sample DS_t of nodes to participate. The selected nodes should have a reputation score greater than a fixed threshold (see Algoritm 1). We denote $n_t = card(DS_t)$ the number of nodes selected at the round t.

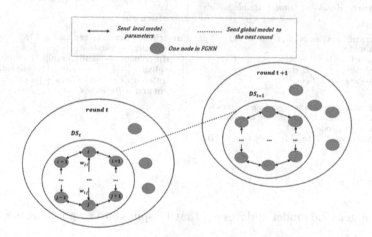

Fig. 3. Training progress on FGNN

Each node $i \in [1, n_t]$ train the graph neural network (GNN) model on it's data locally in an iterative way (see Eq. 1)

$$
\begin{cases}
h_v^{(0)} = x_v \\
\\
h_v^{(l)} = \sigma\left(\frac{1}{|\mathcal{N}(v)|} \sum_{u \in \mathcal{N}(v)} w^{(l)} h_u^{(l-1)} + h_v^{(l-1)}\right) \quad \text{for } l \geq 1
\end{cases}
\tag{1}
$$

Algorithm 1: Event Driven Architecture for a Given Round of FGNN

Require: t (round number), w_{t-1} (updates from previous round), S_t (sample size)
Ensure: w_t (updates for current round)
 1: Upon event ⟨RoundStart | t⟩
 2:     $L_t \leftarrow []$
 3:     $DS_t \leftarrow$ select_nodes($nodes$, threshold, S_t) **(i)**
 4: **for** each node i in DS_t **do**
 5:         $w_{t,i} \leftarrow$ train_local_model($i, w_{t-1}, data_i, lr$) **(ii)**
 6:         send_local_updates($w_{t,i}, i, DS_t$) **(iii)**
 7:         $L_t \leftarrow L_t + [w_{t,i}]$
 8: **end for**
 9:     $w_t \leftarrow$ secure_aggregation($w_{t,1}, w_{t,2}, \ldots, w_{t,|DS_t|}$) **(iv)**
10: Trigger ⟨RoundEnd | t, w_t⟩
11: Upon event ⟨RoundEnd | $t, nodes, w_t$⟩
12:     save_global_model(w_t)
13:     update_reputation_scores($nodes$) (see Algorithm 2)
14: Trigger ⟨RoundStart | $t + 1$⟩

The main functions used in the algorithm are defined here:

Function select_nodes($nodes, threshold, k$):
  eligible_nodes $\leftarrow$ [node in nodes :
  node.reputation_score $\leq$ threshold]   **(i)**
  if $eligible\_nodes.size \leq k$ **then**
    return $eligible\_nodes$
  else
    return $RandomSample(eligible\_nodes, k)$

Function train_local_model($i, w, data, lr$):
  Run on node i
  Split $data$ into batches B **(ii)**
  for each batch b in B **do**
    $w \leftarrow w - lr \nabla L(w, b)$
  return w

Function send_local_updates($w, node, nodes$):
  split_data $\leftarrow$ split_into_random($w, |nodes|$)
  for i in 1 to $|nodes|$ **do**
    return $split\_data[i]$ to node i ;   **(iii)**

Function secure_aggregation($W, eligible\_nodes$):
  $K \leftarrow |eligible\_nodes|$
  for each w in W **do**
    $sum \leftarrow 0$ **(iv)**
    for k in 0 to K **do**
      $sum \leftarrow sum + mk * w/m$
  return sum

Function split_into_random(w, k):
  split_list $\leftarrow$ random($\{-\infty, w\}, k$)   **(v)**
  differences $\leftarrow$ [split_list[0]] + [split_list[i] -
  split_list[i-1] for i in range(1, $len(split\_list)$)]
  differences $\leftarrow$ differences + [w - split_list[-1]]
  return $differences$

Then it gets the model updates w_i, that he splits into n_t portions (see Eq. 2).

$$
\begin{cases}
w_1 = w_{11} + \ldots + w_{1j} + \ldots + w_{1n_t} \\
\ldots \\
w_i = w_{i1} + \ldots + w_{ij} + \ldots + w_{in_t} \\
\ldots \\
w_{n_t} = w_{n_t 1} + \ldots + w_{n_t j} + \ldots + w_{n_t n_t}
\end{cases}
\tag{2}
$$

Each participant $i \in [1, n_t]$ doesn't share w_{ii}, he shares the w_{ij} with the participant j, such as $i \neq j$. This makes inference attacks difficult to perform since each participant has access to a portion of the model update. Then the participants calculate the aggregation function in a peer to peer manner using secure multi party computation (see Eq. 3). The result of the calculation is used in the round $t+1$.

$$w_t = AGG(w_1, w_2, ..., w_{n_t}) = \sum_{i=1}^{n_t} \frac{m_i \times w_i}{m} \tag{3}$$

where $\{m_i\}_{i=1}^{n}$ are some coefficients of proportionality and

$$m = \sum_{i=1}^{n} m_i \tag{4}$$

3.2 Reputation Scoring Technique:

We have introduced a reputation scoring technique to deal with the model poisoning problem (see Algorithm 2). This algorithm aims to detect and prevent malicious behavior in FGNN by using reputation scores to identify trustworthy and untrustworthy participants. When an event occurs, the algorithm updates the reputation score of the relevant participant. This will be performed using the rules for positive or negative events in R. Positive events indicate a positive contribution of a participant in the round and they increase the reputation score, while negative events decrease it. By continually updating these scores, the algorithm helps us to ensure the overall integrity and security of the system.

Algorithm 2: Reputation Scoring technique for the Nodes in FGNN

Input : N a set of nodes, M a set of metrics for measuring node performance, S a scoring system, E set of events, E^+ positive events, E^- negative events
Output: R_s a reputation score for each node in N
1 **for** *each node n in N* **do**
2   **for** *each metric m in M* **do**
3         $p_{n,m}$ ← measure the performance of node n for metric m;
4   R_s ← calculate the reputation score of node n using the scoring system S;
5 **for** *each event e in E* **do**
6   **if** *e is in E^+* **then**
7         $R_s \leftarrow R_s + 1$
8   **else if** *e is in E^-* **then**
9         $R_s \leftarrow R_s - 1$

---

4 Conclusion

In this paper, we presented FGNN, a peer to peer federated graph neural network for threat intelligence. FGNN leverages a distributed machine learning architecture in which multiple participating nodes train a global model. The contribution of this work is to incorporate several security and privacy preserving capabilities(e.g., secure aggregation, reputation scoring technique, etc.) to address several issues(e.g., inference attacks, poisoning attacks, etc.). While progress has been made in the development of FGNN, there are still other challenges that need to be addressed(e.g., data modeling, data and model heterogeneity, fault tolerance, etc.). We plan to apply FGNN in various security domains like network intrusion detection, malware detection, IoT attack detection, etc.

References

1. Bagdasaryan, E., Veit, A., Hua, Y., Estrin, D., Shmatikov, V.: How to backdoor federated learning. In: International Conference on Artificial Intelligence and Statistics. pp. 2938–2948. PMLR (2020)
2. Cao, X., Gong, N.Z.: MPAF: model poisoning attacks to federated learning based on fake clients. In: Proceedings of the IEEE/CVF Conference on Computer Vision and Pattern Recognition, pp. 3396–3404 (2022)
3. Hitaj, B., Ateniese, G., Perez-Cruz, F.: Deep models under the GAN: information leakage from collaborative deep learning. In: Proceedings of the 2017 ACM SIGSAC conference on computer and communications security, pp. 603–618 (2017)
4. Hu, H., Salcic, Z., Sun, L., Dobbie, G., Zhang, X.: Source inference attacks in federated learning. pp. 1102–1107 (2021)
5. Leong, Y.: The implementation of strategic threat intelligence for business organization. J. IT Asia, **9**, 41–48 (2021)
6. Ongun, T., Boboila, S., Oprea, A., Eliassi-Rad, T., Hiser, J., Davidson, J.: Celest: federated learning for globally coordinated threat detection. arXiv preprint arXiv:2205.11459 (2022)
7. Ashwinee Panda, Saeed Mahloujifar, Arjun Nitin Bhagoji, Supriyo Chakraborty, and Prateek Mittal. Sparsefed: Mitigating model poisoning attacks in federated learning with sparsification. In: Gustau Camps-Valls, Francisco J. R. Ruiz, and Isabel Valera, editors, Proceedings of The 25th International Conference on Artificial Intelligence and Statistics of Proceedings of Machine Learning Research. vol. 151, pp. 7587–7624. PMLR, 28–30 (2022)
8. Payne, J., Kundu, A.: Towards deep federated defenses against malware in cloud ecosystems. In: 2019 First IEEE International Conference on Trust, Privacy and Security in Intelligent Systems and Applications (TPS-ISA), pp. 92–100 (2019)
9. Rey, V., Sánchez, P.M.S., Celdrán, A.H., Bovet, G.: Federated learning for malware detection in IoT devices. Comput. Netw. **204**, 108693 (2022)
10. Sarhan, M., Layeghy, S., Moustafa, N., Portmann, M.: A cyber threat intelligence sharing scheme based on federated learning for network intrusion detection (2021)
11. Zhang, J., Chen, J., Wu, D., Chen, B., Yu, S.: Poisoning attack in federated learning using generative adversarial nets. In: 2019 18th IEEE International Conference On Trust, Security And Privacy In Computing And Communications/13th IEEE International Conference On Big Data Science And Engineering (TrustCom/BigDataSE). pp. 374–380 (2019)
12. Zhang, Z., Cao, X., Jia, J., Neil Zhenqiang Gong, N.Z.: Fldetector: defending federated learning against model poisoning attacks via detecting malicious clients. In: Proceedings of the 28th ACM SIGKDD Conference on Knowledge Discovery and Data Mining. pp. 2545–2555 (2022)

Formal Methods

A Formal Analysis of Karn's Algorithm

Max von Hippel[1(✉)], Kenneth L. McMillan[2], Cristina Nita-Rotaru[1],
and Lenore D. Zuck[3]

[1] Northeastern University, Boston, MA, USA
{vonhippel.m,c.nitarotaru}@northeastern.edu
[2] University of Texas at Austin, Austin, TX, USA
zuck@uic.edu
[3] University of Illinois Chicago, Chicago, IL, USA
kenmcm@cs.utexas.edu

Abstract. The stability of the Internet relies on timeouts. The timeout value, known as the Retransmission TimeOut (RTO), is constantly updated, based on sampling the Round Trip Time (RTT) of each packet as measured by its sender – that is, the time between when the sender transmits a packet and receives a corresponding acknowledgement. Many of the Internet protocols compute those samples via the same sampling mechanism, known as Karn's Algorithm.

We present a formal description of the algorithm, and study its properties. We prove the computed samples reflect the RTT of some packets, but it is not always possible to determine which. We then study some of the properties of RTO computations as described in the commonly used RFC6298. All properties are mechanically verified.

Keywords: Internet protocols · RTT sampling · Karn's Algorithm

1 Introduction

This paper examines Karn's algorithm [33], a mechanism that is widely used across the Internet to estimate the round trip time (RTT) of transmissions. Many of the Internet's protocols use Karn's algorithm to measure RTT for the specific purpose of computing the *Retransmission TimeOut* (RTO), which is used to detect congestion and trigger retransmissions of lost data. We examine the RTO computation based on the RTT computations of Karn's algorithm, formally verify properties of the RTT and RTO computations, and discuss their interactions. To the best of our knowledge, this is the first formal and automated study of these algorithms.

Protocols leverage RTT information for many purposes, such as one-way delay estimation [1] or network topology optimization [52,59]. The most common use of RTT is for RTO computation. Internet protocols are described in *Request for Comments* documents (RFCs), and the RTO computation is defined in RFC6298 [49], which states:

> The Internet, to a considerable degree, relies on the correct implementation of the RTO algorithm [. . .] in order to preserve network stability and avoid congestion collapse.

© The Author(s), under exclusive license to Springer Nature Switzerland AG 2023
D. Mohaisen and T. Wies (Eds.): NETYS 2023, LNCS 14067, pp. 43–61, 2023.
https://doi.org/10.1007/978-3-031-37765-5_4

On one hand, an RTO that is too low may cause false timeouts by hastily triggering a timeout mechanism that delays the proper functioning of the protocol, and also exposes it to denial-of-service attacks. On the other hand, an RTO that is too high causes overuse of resources [51] by unnecessarily delaying the invocation of timeout mechanisms when congestion occurs. A poorly chosen RTO can have disastrous consequences, including *congestion collapse*, wherein the demands put on the network far exceed its capacity, leading to excessive message dropping and thus excessive retransmission. Congestion collapse was first observed in October 1986, during which time total Internet traffic dropped by over 1000x [30]. At the time this kind of network failure was an engineering curiosity, but today it would spell global economic disaster, loss of life, infrastructural damage, etc.

Both Karn's algorithm and the RTO computation are widely used across the Internet, as we detail in Subsect. 1.1. Hence, the correctness of these two mechanisms is fundamental for the correctness of the Internet as a whole. It is interesting to note that some theoretical papers analyzing congestion control, the original motivation for computing RTO, explicitly ignore the topic of timeouts, and hence implicitly ignore how RTO is computed (e.g., [7,45,64]).

Computing a "good" RTO requires a "good" estimate of the RTT. The RTO computation depends solely on the estimated RTT and some parameters that are fixed. Thus, understanding the mechanism which estimates RTT is fundamental to understanding any quantitative property of the Internet. The RTT of a packet (or message, datagram, frame, segment, etc.) is the time that elapsed between its transmission and some confirmation of its delivery. Both events (transmission and receipt of confirmation of delivery) occur at the same endpoint, namely, the one that transmits the packet, which we call the *sender*. In essence, if the sender transmits a packet at its local time t, and first learns of its delivery at time $t + \delta$, it estimates the RTT for this packet as δ.

TCP uses a *cumulative* acknowledgement mechanism where every packet received generates an acknowledgment (ACK) with the sequence number of the first unreceived packet.[1] Thus, if all packets $p_1, \ldots, p_x$ are received and packet p_{x+1} is not, the receiver will ACK with $x + 1$, which is the sequence number of the first unreceived packet in the sequence, even if packets whose sequence number is greater than $x + 1$ were received.

If the Internet's delivery mechanism were perfect, then packets would be received in order, acknowledged in order, and the sender would always be able to compute the RTT of each packet. In reality, of course, the Internet is not perfect. TCP operates on top of IP, whose only guarantee is that every message received was sent. Thus, messages are neither invented nor corrupted, but at least theoretically, may be duplicated, reordered, or lost. In practice duplication is sufficiently rare that it is ignored, and reordering is sometimes ignored and sometimes restricted. But losses are never ignored, and are the main focus of all congestion control algorithms. When a loss is suspected, a packet is retransmitted (often, the retransmission is at a lower rate than the original transmissions). If it is later acknowledged, one cannot determine whether the ACK is for the initial transmission or for the retransmission. Karn's algorithm [33] addresses this ambiguity by assuming that packets may have been retransmitted and providing an RTT estimate that ignores the retransmitted packets. RFC6298 [49] then computes

---

[1] Some implementations of TCP use additional types of acknowledgements, yet, the cumulative ones are common to TCP implementations.

an estimated RTT as a weighted (decaying) average of the samples output by Karn's algorithm, and computes an RTO based on this estimate and a measure of the RTT variance. The RTO is then used to gauge whether a packet is lost, and then, usually, to transition to a state where transmission rate is reduced. Thus, the RTT sampling in Karn's algorithm is what ultimately informs the transmission rate of protocols. And while RF6298 pertains to TCP, numerous non-TCP protocols also refer to RFC6298 for the RTO computation, as we outline in Subsect. 1.1.

Here, we first formalize (our understanding of) Karn's algorithm [49], and prove some high-level properties about the relationship between acknowledgments and packets. In particular, we show that Karn's algorithm computes the "real" RTT of some packet, but the identity of this packet may be impossible to determine, unless one assumes (as many do) that acknowledgements are delivered in a FIFO ordering, and the identity of this packet can be determined. Next, we examine the RTO computation defined in RFC6298 [49] and its relationship to Karn's algorithm. For example, we show that when the samples fluctuate within a known interval, the estimated RTT eventually converges to the same interval. This confirms and generalizes prior results.

All our results are automatically checked. For the first part, where we study Karn's algorithm, we use Ivy [60]. Ivy is an interactive prover for inductive invariants, and provides convenient, built-in facilities for specifying and proving properties about protocols, which makes it ideal for this part of the work. For the second part, we study the RTO computation (and other computations it relies on), defined in RFC6298. These are purely numerical computations and, in isolation, do not involve reasoning about the interleaving of processes or their communication. Each computation has rational inputs and outputs, and the theorems we prove bound these computations using exponents and rational multiplication. We also prove the asymptotic limits of these bounds in steady-state conditions, which we define. Since Ivy lacks a theory of rational numbers or exponentiation, we turn to the automated theorem prover ACL2s [16,19] for the remainder of the work. All of our code is open-source and available at github.com/rto-karn. We believe this is the first paper that formalizes properties of the RTT sampling via Karn's algorithm, as well as properties of the quantities RFC6298 computes, including the RTO. Additionally, our work provides a useful example of how multiple formal methods approaches can be used to study different angles of a single system.

1.1 Usage of Karn's Algorithm and RFC6298

Many protocols use Karn's Algorithm to sample RTT, e.g., [2,9,20,27,42,49]. Unfortunately, the samples output by Karn's Algorithm could be noisy or outdated. RFC6298 addresses this problem by using a rolling average called the *smoothed RTT*, or srtt. Protocols that use the srtt in conjunction with Karn's Algorithm (at least optionally) include [14,20,26,34,50,52,53,57,58,61]. RFC6298 then proposes an RTO computation based on the srtt and another value called the rttvar, which is intended to capture the variance in the samples. Note, when referring specifically to the RTO output by RFC6298, we use the convention rto. This is a subtle distinction as the RTO can be implemented in other ways as well (see e.g., [10,35]). These three computations (srtt, rttvar, and rto) are used in TCP and in many other protocols, e.g. [31,50,53,58,61], although some such protocols omit explicit mention of RFC6298 (see [51]).

Not all protocols use retransmission. For example, in QUIC [29] every packet has a unique identifier, hence retransmitting a packet assigns it a new unique identifier and the matching ACK indicates whether it is for the old or new transmission. Consequently, Karn's algorithm is only used when a real retransmission occurs, which covers most of the protocols designed when one had to be mindful of the length of the transmitted packets and could not afford unique identifiers. On the other hand, even protocols that do not use Karn's algorithm nevertheless utilize a retransmission timeout that is at least adapted from RFC6298 – and in fact, QUIC is one such protocol.

2   The Formal Setup

We partition messages, or datagrams, into *packets* P and *acknowledgments* A. Each packet $p \in P$ is uniquely identified by its id $p.id \in \mathbb{N}$. Each acknowledgment $a \in A$ is also uniquely identified by its $a.id$. In the sequel we identify packets and acknowledgments by their ids.

Messages (packets and acknowledgments) typically include additional information such as destination port or sequence number, however, we abstract away such information in our model. Also, some protocols distinguish between packets and *segments*, where a segment is a message containing multiple packets, but we abstract away this distinction as well.

2.1   The Model

The model consists of two endpoints (*sender* and *receiver*) connected over a bi-directional *channel*, as shown in Fig. 1. The sender sends packets through the channel to the receiver, and the receiver sends acknowledgements through the channel to the sender.

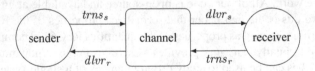

Fig. 1. The sender, channel, and receiver. The sender sends messages by $trns_s$ actions which are received by $dlvr_s$ actions at the receiver's endpoint, and similarly, the receiver sends messages by $trns_r$ actions which are received by $dlvr_r$ actions at the receiver's endpoint.

Actions. The set of actions, Act, is partitioned into four action types:

1. $trns_s$ that consists of the set of the sender's transmit actions. That is, $trns_s = \cup_{p \in P}\{trns_s(id) : id = p.id\}$.
2. $dlvr_s$ that consists of the set of the receiver's delivery actions. That is, $dlvr_s = \cup_{p \in P}\{dlvr_s(id) : id = p.id\}$.
3. $trns_r$ that consists of the set of the receiver's transmit actions. That is, $trns_r = \cup_{a \in A}\{trns_r(id) : id = a.id\}$.

4. $dlvr_r$ that consists of the set of the sender's delivery actions. That is, $dlvr_r = \cup_{a \in A} \{dlvr_r(id) : id = a.id\}$.

For a finite sequence σ over Act, we denote the length of σ by $|\sigma|$ and refer to an occurrence of an action in σ as an *event*. That is, an event in σ consists of an action and its position in σ.

The sender's input actions are $dlvr_r$, and its output actions are $trns_s$. The receiver's input actions are $dlvr_s$ and its output actions are $trns_r$. The channel's input actions are $trns_s \cup trns_r$ and its output actions are $dlvr_s \cup dlvr_r$.

We assume that the channel is CSP-like synchronously composed with its two endpoints, the sender and the receiver. That is, for every $q \in \{s, r\}$, a $trns_q$ action occurs simultaneously at both q and the channel, and similarly for $dlvr_q$ actions. The sender and the receiver can be asynchronous. Modules are input-enabled in the I/O-automata sense, i.e., modules can always receive inputs (messages). In real implementations, modules' inputs are restricted by buffers, but since the channel is allowed to drop messages (as we see later), restrictions on the input buffer sizes can be modeled using loss. Hence the assumption of input-enabledness does not restrict the model.

2.2   Executions

Let σ be a sequence of actions. We say that σ is an *execution* if every delivery event in σ is preceded by a matching transmission event, that is, both events carry the same message. (This does not rule out duplication, reordering, or loss – more on that below.) Formally, for every $q \in \{s, r\}$ and $x \in \mathbb{N}$, if $e_i = dlvr_q(x) \in \sigma$, then for some $j < i$, $e_j = trns_q(x) \in \sigma$. This requirement rules out corruption and insertion of messages. In addition, for TCP-like executions, we may impose additional requirements on the ordering of $trns$-events of the endpoints. An example execution is illustrated in the rightmost column of Fig. 2.

The Sender. We adopt the convention that it only transmits a packet after it had transmitted all the preceding ones. Formally, for every $x \in \mathbb{N}$, if $e_i = trns_s(x + 1) \in \sigma$, then for some $j < i, e_j = trns_s(x) \in \sigma$.

The Receiver. We assume here the model of *cumulative acks*. That is, the receiver executes a $trns_r(id)$ action only if it has been delivered all packets p such that $p.id < id$ and it had not been delivered packet p such that $p.id = id$. Thus, for example, the receiver can execute $trns_r(17)$ only after it had been delivered all packets whose id is < 17 and had not been delivered the packet whose id is 17. In particular, it may have been delivered packets whose id is > 17, just not the packet whose id is 17.

Many TCP models mandate the receiver transmits exactly one acknowledgement in response to each packet delivered (e.g., [6,7,13,17,21,22]). The assumption is common in congestion control algorithms where the sender uses the number of copies of the same acknowledgement it is delivered to estimate how many packets were delivered after a packet was dropped, and thus the number of lost packets. There are however some TCP variants, such as Data Center TCP and TCP Westwood, that allow a *delayed* ACK option wherein the receiver transmits an ACK after every n^{th} packet delivery [11,44], or Compound TCP that allows *proactive acknowledgments* where the receiver transmits before having receiving all the acknowledged packets, albeit at a pace that is proportional to the pace of packet deliveries [55]. Another mechanism that is sometimes allowed is *NACK* (for Negative ACK) where the receiver sends, in addition to the cumulative acknowledgement, a list of gaps of missing packets [3]. Since TCP datagrams are restricted in size, the NACKs are partial. Newer protocols (such as QUIC) allow for full (unrestricted) NACKs [29].

Our Ivy model assumes the receiver transmits one acknowledgement per packet delivered. That is, we assume that in the projection of σ onto the receiver's actions, $trns_r$ and $dlvr_s$ events are alternating. In fact, the results listed in this paper would still hold even under the slightly weaker assumption that the receiver transmits an acknowledgment whenever it is delivered a packet that it had not previously been delivered, but for which it had previously been delivered all lesser ones. However, the stronger assumption is easier to reason about, and is more commonly used in the literature (for example it is the default assumption for congestion control algorithms where the pace of delivered acknowledgments is used to infer the pace of delivered packets). Consequently, our results apply to traditional congestion control algorithms like TCP Vegas and TCP New Reno where the receiver transmits one acknowledgement per packet delivered, however, our results might not apply to atypical protocols like Data Center TCP, and TCP Westwood, or Compound TCP that use alternative acknowledgment schemes.

The Channel. So far, we only required that the channel never deliver messages to one endpoint that were not previously transmitted by the other. This does not rule out loss, reordering, nor duplication of messages. In the literature, message duplication is assumed to be so uncommon that it can be disregarded. The traditional congestion control protocols [5,22,28,39,55] assume bounded reordering, namely, that once a message is delivered, an older one can be delivered only if transmitted no more than k transmissions ago (usually, $k = 4$). Packet losses are always assumed to occur, but the possibility of losing acknowledgements is often ignored.

It is possible to formalize further constraints on the channel, for example, by restricting the receiver-to-sender path to be loss- and reordering-free. For instance, the work in [4] formalizes a constrained channel by assuming a mapping from delivery to transmission events, and using properties of this mapping to express restrictions. Reordering is ruled out by having this mapping be monotonic, duplication is ruled out by having it be one-to-one, and loss is ruled out by having it be onto.

Most prior works assume no loss or reordering of acknowledgments [6–8,25,64], or did not model loss or reordering at all [18,24,40]. Some prior works assume both loss and reordering but do not study the computation of RTO or other aspects of congestion control [4,54].

Since, as we describe in Sect. 5, some works on RTO assume the channel delivers acknowledgements in perfect order, and since this assumption has implications on the RTT computation (see Observation 4), we define executions where the receiver's messages are delivered, without losses, in the order they are transmitted as follows. An execution σ is a *FIFO-acknowledgement execution* if $\sigma|_{dlvr_r} \preceq \sigma|_{trns_r}$ is an invariant of sigma, where $\sigma|_a$ is the projection of σ onto the a actions, and $\preceq$ is the prefix relation. That is, in a FIFO-acknowledgement execution, the sequences of ACK's delivered to the sender is always a prefix of the sequence of ACK's transmitted by the receiver.

The following observation establishes that the sequence of acknowledgements the receiver transmits is monotonically increasing. Its proof follows directly from the fact that the receiver is generating cumulative acks. (Recall that all Observations in this section and the next are established in Ivy.)

Observation 1. *Let* σ *be an execution, and assume* i *and* j, $i < j$, *such that* $e_i = trns_r(a_i), e_j = trns_r(a_j)$ *are in* σ. *Then* $a_i \leq a_j$.

2.3 Sender's Computations

So far, we abstracted away from the internals of the sender, receiver, and channel, and focused on the executions their composition allows. As we pointed out at the beginning of this section, real datagrams can contain information far beyond ids, and there are many mechanisms for their generation, depending on the protocol being implemented and the implementation choices made. Such real implementations have *states*. All we care about here, however, is the set of observable behaviors they allow, in terms of packet and acknowledgement ids. We thus choose to ignore implementation details, including states, and focus on executions, namely abstract observable behaviors.

In the next section we study a particular mechanism that is imposed over executions. In particular, we describe a pseudo code for an algorithm for sampling the RTT of packets. This pseudo code, say P, is (synchronously) composed with the sender's algorithm (on which we only make a single assumption, that is, that a packet is transmitted only after all prior ones were transmitted). We can view the algorithm as a *non-interfering monitor*, that is, P "observes" the sender's actions ($trns_s$ and $dlvr_r$) and performs some bookkeeping when each occurs. In fact, after initialization of variables, it consists of two parts, one that describes the update to its variables upon a $trns_s$ action, and one that describes the updates to its variables after a $dlvr_r$ action.

Let V be the set of variables P uses. To be non-interfering, V has to be disjoint from the set of variables that the sender uses to determine when to generate $trns_s$'s and process $dlvr_r$'s. We ignore this latter set of variables since it is of no relevance to our purposes. Let a *sender's state* be a type-consistent assignment of values V. For a sender's state s and a variable $v \in V$, let $s[v]$ be the value of v at state s. For simplicity's sake (and consistent with the pseudo code we present in the next section) assume that P is deterministic, that is, given a state s and a sender's action α, there is a unique sender state s' such that s' is the successor of s given α.

Let σ be an execution. Let $\sigma|_s$ be the projection of σ onto the sender's events (the $trns_s$ and $dlvr_r$ events). Since P is deterministic, the sequence $\sigma|_s$ uniquely defines a sequence of sender's states $\kappa_\sigma : s_0, \ldots$ such that s_0 is the initial state, and every s_{i+1} is a successor of s_i under P according to $\sigma|_s$. We refer to κ_σ as the *sender's computation under* P *and* σ.

3 Karn's Algorithm and Its Analysis

As discussed in Sect. 1, having a good estimate of RTT, the round-trip time of a packet, is essential for determining the value of RTO, which is crucial for many of the Internet's protocols (see Subsect. 1.1 for a listing thereof). The value of RTT varies over the lifetime of a protocol, and is therefore often sampled. Since the sender knows the time it transmits a packet, and is also the recipient of acknowledgements, it is the sender whose role it is to sample the RTT. If the channel over which packets and acknowledgements are communicated were a perfect FIFO channel, then RTT would be easy to compute, since then each packet would generate a single acknowledgement, and the time between the transmission of the packets and the delivery of its acknowledgement would be the RTT. However, channels are not perfect. Senders retransmit packets they believe to be lost, and when those are acknowledged the sender cannot disambiguate which of the transmissions to associate with the acknowledgements. Moreover, transmitted acknowledgments can be lost, or delivered out of order. In [33], an idea, referred to as "Karn's Algorithm," was introduced to address the first issue. There, sampling of RTT is only performed when the sender receives a new acknowledgement, say h, greater than the previously highest received acknowledgement, say ℓ, where all the packets whose id is in the range $[\ell, h)$ were transmitted only once. It then outputs a new sample whose value is the time that elapsed between the transmission of the packet whose id is ℓ and delivery of the acknowledgement h. The reason ℓ (as opposed to h) is used for the base of calculations is the possibility that the id of the packet whose delivery triggers the new acknowledgement is ℓ, and the RTT computation has to be cautious in the sense of over-approximating RTT.

The real RTT of a packet may be tricky to define. The only case where it is clear is when packet i is transmitted once, and an ACK $i + 1$ is delivered before any other ACK $\geq i + 1$ is delivered. We can then define the RTT of packet i, rtt(i), to be the time, on the sender's clock, that elapses between the (first and only) $trns_s(i)$ action and the $dlvr_r(i + 1)$ action. Since the channel is not FIFO, it's possible that $h > \ell + 1$, and then the sample, that is, the time that elapses between $trns_s[\ell]$ and $dlvr_r(h)$ is the RTT for some packet $j \in [\ell, h)$, denoted by, rtt(j), but we may not be able to identify j. Moreover, the sample over-approximates the RTT of all packets in the range. Note that rtt is a partial function. We show that when the channel delivers the receiver's messages in FIFO ordering, then the computed sample is exactly rtt(ℓ).

We model the sender's sampling of RTT according to Karn's Algorithm, see pseudocode in Algorithm 1. The sampling is a non-interfering monitor of the sender. Its inputs are the sender's actions, the $trns_s(i)$'s and $dlvr_r(j)$'s. Its output is a (possibly empty) sequence of samples denoted by S. To model time, we use an integer counter (τ) that is initialized to 1 (we reserve 0 for "undefined") and is incremented with each step. Upon a $trns_s(i)$ input, the algorithm stores, in $numT[i]$, the number of times packet i is transmitted, and in $time[i]$ the time of the first time it is transmitted. The second step is for $dlvr_r$ events, where the sender determines whether a new sample can be computed, and if so, computes it. An example execution, concluding with the computation of a sample via Karn's Algorithm, is given in Fig. 2.

In Algorithm 1, $numT[i]$ stores the number of times a packet whose id is i is transmitted, $time[i]$ stores the sender's time where packet whose id is i is first transmitted, $high$ records the highest delivered acknowledgement, and when a new sample is computed (in S) it is outputted. The condition ok-to-$sample(numT, high)$ in Line 13 checks whether sampling should occur. When $high > 0$, that is, when this is not the

---

Algorithm 1: RTT Sampling

input : $trns_s(i), dlvr_r(j), i, j \in \mathbb{N}^+$
output: $S \in \mathbb{N}^+$
1 $numT, time\colon \mathbb{N}^+ \to \mathbb{N}$ **init** all 0
2 $high\colon \mathbb{N}$ **init** 0
3 $\tau\colon \mathbb{N}$ **init** 1
4 **if** $trns_s(i)$ *is received* **then**
5 $\quad$ $numT[i] := numT[i] + 1$
6 $\quad$ **if** $time[i] = 0$ **then**
7 $\quad\quad$ $time[i] := \tau$
8 $\quad$ **end**
9 $\quad$ $\tau := \tau + 1$
10 **end**
11 **if** $dlvr_r(j)$ *is received* **then**
12 $\quad$ **if** $j > high$ **then**
13 $\quad\quad$ **if** *ok-to-sample(numT, high)* **then**
14 $\quad\quad\quad$ $S := \tau - time[high]$
15 $\quad\quad\quad$ **Ouput** S
16 $\quad\quad$ **end**
17 $\quad\quad$ $high := j$
18 $\quad$ **end**
19 $\quad$ $\tau := \tau + 1$
20 **end**

---

first acknowledgement received, then the condition is that all the packets in the range $[high, j)$ were transmitted once. If, however, $high = 0$, since ids are positive, the condition is that all the packets in the range $[1, j)$ were transmitted once. Hence, *ok-to-sample(numT, high)* is:

$$(\forall k.high < k < j \to numT[k] = 1) \; \land \; (high > 0 \to numT[high] = 1)$$

If *ok-to-sample(numT, high)*, Line 14 computes a new sample S as the time that elapsed since packet *high* was transmitted until acknowledgement j is delivered, and outputs is in the next line. Thus, a new sample is *not computed* when a new ACK, that is greater than *high*, is delivered but some packets whose id is less than the new ACK, yet $\geq high$ were retransmitted. Whether or not a new sample is computed, when such an ACK is delivered, *high* is updated to its value to reflect the currently highest delivered ACK.

3.1 Properties of Karn's Algorithm

We show, through a sequence of observations, that Algorithm 1 computes the true RTT of *some* packet, whose identity cannot also be uniquely determined. While much was written about the algorithm, we failed to find a clear statement of what exactly it computes, but then, unitl now, it is stated informally and the main focus is on its implications to RTO estimates. In [33], it is shown that if a small number of consecutive samples are equal then the computed RTT (which is a weighted average of the sampled RTTs) is

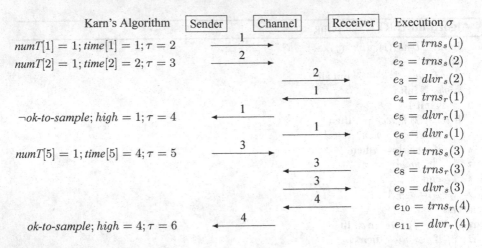

Fig. 2. Message sequence chart illustrating an example execution. Time progresses from top down. Instructions executed by Algorithm 1 are shown on the left, and the sender's execution is on the right. $trns_s$ events are indicated with arrows from sender to channel, $dlvr_s$ events with arrows from channel to receiver, etc. After the final $dlvr_r$ event, sender executes Line 14 and outputs the computation $S = 6 - 2 = 4$.

close to the value of those samples. See the next section for further discussion on this issue. Our focus in this section is what exactly is computed by the algorithm.

The set of variables in Algorithm 1 is $V = \{\tau, numT, time, high, S\}$. Let σ be an execution, and let κ_σ be the sender's computation under Algorithm 1 and σ. The following observation establishes two invariants over κ_σ. Both follow from the assumption we made on the sender's execution, namely that the sender does not transmit p without first transmitting $1, \ldots, p - 1$. The first establishes that if a packet is transmitted (as viewed by $numT$), all preceding ones were transmitted, and the second that the first time a packet is transmitted must be later than the first time every preceding packet was transmitted.

Observation 2. *The following are invariants over sender's computations:*

$$0 < i < j \;\wedge\; numT[j] > 0 \longrightarrow numT[i] > 0 \qquad (I1)$$
$$0 < i < j \;\wedge\; numT[j] > 0 \longrightarrow time[i] < time[j] \quad (I2)$$

Assume $\kappa_\sigma : s_0, s_1, \ldots$. We say that a state $s_i \in \kappa_\sigma$ is a *fresh sample* state if the transition leading into it contains an execution of Lines 13–16 of Algorithm 1. The following observation establishes that in a fresh sample state, the new sample is an upper bound for the RTT of a particular range of packets (whose ids range from the previous $high$ up to, but excluding, the new $high$), and is the real RTT of one of them.

Observation 3. *Let σ and κ_σ be as above and assume that $s_i \in \kappa_\sigma$ is a fresh sample state. Then the following all hold:*

1. *For every packet with id ℓ, $s_{i-1}\lfloor high \rfloor \leq \ell < s_i \lfloor high \rfloor$ implies that $\mathrm{rtt}(\ell) \leq s_i \lfloor S \rfloor$. That is, the fresh sample is an upper bound of the RTT for all packets between the old and the new high.*

2. *There exists a packet with id ℓ, $s_{i-1}\lfloor high \rfloor \leq \ell < s_i\lfloor high \rfloor$ such that $\text{rtt}(\ell) = s_i\lfloor S \rfloor$.* *That is, the fresh sample is the RTT of some packet between the old and new high.*

We next show under the (somewhat unrealistic, yet often made) assumption of FIFO-acknowledgement executions, the packet whose RTT is computed in the second clause of Observation 3 is exactly the packet whose id equals to the prior *high*. In particular, that if s_i is a fresh sample state, then the packet whose RTT is computed is p such that $p.id$ equals to the value of *high* just before the new fresh state is reached.

Observation 4. *Let σ be a FIFO-acknowledgement execution σ, and assume κ_σ contains a fresh sample state s_ℓ. Then $s_\ell\lfloor S \rfloor = \text{rtt}(s_{\ell-1}\lfloor high \rfloor)$.*

Let σ be a (not necessarily FIFO) execution and let κ_σ be the sender's computation under Algorithm 1 and σ that outputs some samples. We denote by $S_1, \ldots$ the sequence of samples that is the output of κ_σ. That is, S_k is the kth sample obtained by Algorithm 1 given the execution σ.

4 Analyzing RFC6298 Calculation of RTO

We next analyze the computation of RTOs as described in RFC6298. Each new sample triggers a new RTO computation, that depends on sequences of two other variables (srtt and rttvar) and three constants (α, β, and G). In this Section, we consider the scenario in which the samples produced by Karn's algorithm are consecutively bounded. We show that in this context, we can compute corresponding bounds on srtt, as well as an upper bound on rttvar; and that these bounds converge to the bounds on the samples and the distance between those bounds, respectively, as the number of bounded samples grows. These observations allow us to characterize the asymptotic conditions under which the RTO will generally exceed the RTT values, and by how much. In other words, these observations allow us to reason about whether timeouts will occur in the long run.

Let $\{\text{srtt}, \text{rttvar}, \text{rto}, \alpha, \beta, G\} \in \mathbb{Q}^+$ be fresh variables. As mentioned before, $\alpha < 1$, $\beta < 1$, and G are constants. Let σ be an execution and κ_σ be the sender's computation under Algorithm 1 and σ. Assume that κ_σ outputs some samples $S_1, \ldots, S_N$.

RFC6298 defines the RTO and the computations it depends upon as follows:

$$\text{rto}_i = \text{srtt}_i + \max(G, 4 \cdot \text{rttvar}_i)$$

$$\text{srtt}_i = \begin{cases} S_i & \text{if } i = 1 \\ (1 - \alpha)\text{srtt}_{i-1} + \alpha S_i & \text{if } i > 1 \end{cases}$$

$$\text{rttvar}_i = \begin{cases} S_i/2 & \text{if } i - 1 \\ (1 - \beta)\text{rttvar}_{i-1} + \beta|\text{srtt}_{i-1} - S_i| & \text{if } i > 1 \end{cases}$$

where G is the clock granularity (of τ), srtt is referred to in RFC6298 as the *smoothed RTT*, and rttvar as the *RTT variance*. The srtt is a rolling weighted average of the sample values and is meant to give an RTT estimate that is resilient to noisy samples. The rttvar is described as a measure of variance in the sample values, although as we show below, it is not the usual statistical variance. The rto is computed from srtt and rttvar and is the amount of time the sender will wait without receiving an ACK before it determines that congestion has occurred and takes some action such as decreasing its output and retransmitting unacknowledged messages. We manually compute, and mechanically verify the computations, of these variables using ACL2s. The choice of ACL2s stems from Ivy's lack of support of the theory of the Rationals, which is necessary for this analysis.

Intuitively, the srtt is meant to give an estimate of the (recent) samples, while the rttvar is meant to provide a measure of the degree to which these samples vary. However, the rttvar is not actually a variance in the statistical sense. For example, if $S_1 = 1$, $S_2 = 44$, $S_3 = 13$, $\alpha = 1/8$, and $\beta = 1/4$, then the statistical variance of the samples is $1477/3$ but $\text{rttvar}_3 = 4977361/65536 \neq 1477/3$.

If the rttvar does not compute the statistical variance, then what does it compute? And what does the srtt compute? We answer these questions under the (realistic) restriction that the samples fall within some bounds, which we formalize as follows. Let c and r be positive rationals and let i and n be positive naturals. Suppose that $S_i, \ldots, S_{i+n}$ all fall within the bounded interval $[c - r, c + r]$ with center c and radius r. Then we refer to $S_i, \ldots, S_{i+n}$ as c/r *steady-state samples*. In the remainder of this section, we study c/r steady-state samples and prove both instantaneous and asymptotic bounds on the rttvar and srtt values they produce. Figure 3 illustrates two scenarios with c/r steady-state samples – one in which the samples are randomly drawn from a uniform distribution, and another where they are pathologically crafted to cause infinitely many timeouts – and shows for each scenario, the lower and upper bounds on the srtt which we report below in Observation 5, as well as the upper bound on the rttvar which we report below in Observation 6. The asymptotic behavior of the reported bounds is also clearly visible.

In [33], Karn and Partridge argue that, given $\alpha = 1/8$ and $\beta = 1/4$, after six consecutive identical samples S, assuming the initial srtt $\geq \beta S$, the final srtt approximates S within some tolerable ϵ. We generalize this result in the following observation.

Observation 5. *Suppose α, c, and r are reals, c is positive, r is non-negative, and $\alpha \in (0, 1]$. Further suppose i and n are positive naturals, and $S_i, \ldots, S_{i+n}$ are c/r steady-state samples. Define L and H as follows.*

$$L = (1 - \alpha)^{n+1}\text{srtt}_{i-1} + (1 - (1 - \alpha)^{n+1})(c - r)$$
$$H = (1 - \alpha)^{n+1}\text{srtt}_{i-1} + (1 - (1 - \alpha)^{n+1})(c + r)$$

Then $L \leq \text{srtt}_{i+n} \leq H$. Moreover, $\lim_{n \to \infty} L = c - r$, and $\lim_{n \to \infty} H = c + r$.

As an example, suppose that $n = 5$, $\alpha = 1/8$, $\beta = 1/4$, $r = 0$, and $\text{srtt}_{i-1} = 3\beta c$. Then $L = H \approx 0.89c$, hence srtt_{i+4} differs from $S_i, \ldots, S_{i+4} = c$ by about 10% or less. Observation 5 also generalizes in the sense that as n grows to infinity, $[L, H]$ converges to $[c - r, c + r]$, meaning the bounds on the srtt converge to the bounds on the samples – or if $r = 0$, to just the (repeated) sample value $S_i = c$.

Next, we turn our attention to bounding the rttvar. The following observation establishes that when the difference between each sample and the previous srtt is bounded above by some constant Δ, then each rttvar is bounded above by a function of this Δ. Moreover, as the number of consecutive samples grows for which this bound holds, the upper bound on the rttvar converges to precisely Δ. Note, in this observation we use the convention $f^{(m)}$ to denote m-repeated compositions of f, for any function f, e.g., $f^{(3)}(x) = f(f(f(x)))$.

Observation 6. *Suppose $1 < i$, and $0 < \Delta \in \mathbb{Q}$ is such that $|S_j - \text{srtt}_{j-1}| \leq \Delta$ for all $j \in [i, i+n]$. Define $B_\Delta(x) = (1 - \beta)x + \beta\Delta$. Then all the following hold.*

- *Each rttvar$_j$ is bounded above by the function $B_\Delta(\text{rttvar}_{j-1})$.*
- *We can rewrite the (recursive) upper bound on rttvar$_{i+n}$ as follows:*

$$B_\Delta^{(n+1)}(\text{rttvar}_{i-1}) = (1 - \beta)^{n+1}\text{rttvar}_{i-1} + (1 - (1 - \beta)^{n+1})\Delta$$

- *Moreover, this bound converges to Δ, i.e., $\lim_{n \to \infty} B_\Delta^{(n+1)}(\text{rttvar}_{i-1}) = \Delta$.*

Note that if $S_i, \ldots, S_{i+n}$ are c/r steady-state samples then by Observation 5:

$$|S_n - \text{srtt}_{n-1}| \leq \Delta = (1 - \alpha)^{n+1}\text{srtt}_{i-1} + 2r - (1 - \alpha)^{n+1}(c + r)$$

Since $\lim_{n \to \infty} \Delta = 2r$, in c/r steady-state conditions, it follows that the rttvar asymptotically measures the diameter $2r$ of the sample interval $[c - r, c + r]$.

Implications for the rto *Computation.* Assume n are c/r consecutive steady-state samples. As $n \to \infty$, the bounds on srtt$_n$ approach $[c - r, c + r]$, and the upper bound Δ on rttvar$_n$ approaches $2r$. Thus, as n increases, assuming $G < 4\text{rttvar}_n$, $c - r + 4\text{rttvar}_n \leq \text{rto}_n \leq c + 3r$. With these bounds, if rttvar$_n$ is always bounded from below by r, then the rto exceeds the (steady) RTT, hence no timeout will occur. On the other hand, we can construct a pathological case where the samples are c/r steady-state but the rttvar dips below r, allowing the rto to drop below the RTT. One such case is illustrated in the bottom of Fig. 3. In that case, every 100th sample is equal to $c + r = 75$, and the rest are equal to $c - r = 60$. At the spikes (where $S_i = 75$) the sampled RTT exceeds the rto, and so a timeout would occur. This suffices to show that steady-state conditions alone do not guarantee a "steady-state" in terms of avoiding timeouts. Characterizing the minimal, sufficient conditions for avoiding timeouts during a c/r steady-state is a problem left for future work.

5 Related Work

To the best of our knowledge, ours is the first work to formally verify properties of Karn's algorithm or the RTO defined in RFC6298. However, formal methods have previously been applied to proving protocol correctness [18,40,47,54], and lightweight formal methods have been used for protocol testing [12,46]. One such lightweight approach, called PACKETDRILL, was used to test a new implementation of the RTO computation from RFC6298 [15]. The PACKETDRILL authors performed fourteen successful tests on the new RTO implementation. After publication, their tool was used externally to find a bug in the tested RTO implementation [62]. In contrast to such lightweight FM, in which an implementation is strategically tested, we took a proof-based approach to the verification of fundamental properties of the protocol design.

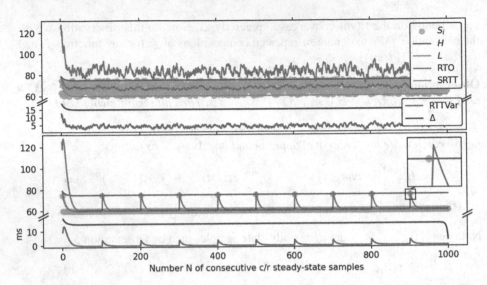

Fig. 3. Top: Uniformly random c/r steady-state scenario. Bottom: Pathological scenario.
X-axis is index in the fresh subsequence; Y-axis is time in ms. On top, samples are uniformly distributed over $[60, 75]$, whereas on bottom, every 100th sample equals $c + r = 75$, and the rest equal $c - r = 60$. On top, timeouts rarely occur, but on bottom, a timeout occurs every 100 samples (see zoomed inset). In both, $\alpha = 1/8$, $\beta = 1/4$, $\text{srtt}_{i-1} = 80$, and $\text{rttvar}_{i-1} = 11.25$.

Some prior works applied formal methods to congestion control algorithms [6,7,23, 37,41,43]. A common theme of these works is that they make strong assumptions about the network model, e.g., assuming the channel never duplicates messages or reorders or loses acknowledgments. In this vein, we study case in which acknowledgments are communicated FIFO in Observation 4. Congestion control algorithms were also classically studied using manual mathematics (as opposed to formal methods) [45,56,64]. One such approach is called *network calculus* [38] and has been used to simulate congestion control algorithms [36]. Network calculus has the advantage that it can be used to study realistic network dynamics, in contrast to our Ivy-based approach, which is catered to logical properties of the system. For example, Kim and Hou [36] are able to determine the minimum and maximum throughput of traditional TCP congestion control, but do not prove any properties about what precisely Karn's algorithm measures, or about bounds on the variables used to compute the RTO.

Another line of inquiry aims to integrate formal methods directly into the RFC drafting process, either by analyzing RFC documents using natural language processing [48,63], or by manually drafting a formal specification for one or more RFCs, and then using the specification to interrogate real-world implementations [32]. The Internet Engineering Task Force is exploring such techniques with its recently introduced Usable Formal Methods Research Group, of which we are members.

6   Conclusion

In this work we applied formal methods to Karn's algorithm, as well as the rto computation described by RFC6298 and used in many of the Internet's protocols. These two algorithms were previously only studied with manual mathematics or experimentation. We presented open-source formal models of each, with which we formally verified the following important properties.

Obs. 1: Acknowledgements are transmitted in nondecreasing order.

Obs. 2: Two inductive invariants regarding the internal variables of Karn's algorithm.

Obs. 3: Karn's algorithm samples a real RTT, but a pessimistic one.

Obs. 4: In the case where acknowledgments are neither dropped, duplicated, nor reordered, Karn's algorithm samples the highest ACK received by the sender before the sampled one.

Obs. 5: For the rto computation, when the samples are bounded, so is the srtt. As the number of bounded samples increases, the bounds on the srtt converge to the bounds on the samples.

Obs. 6: For the rto computation, when the samples are bounded, so is the rttvar. As the number of bounded samples increases, the upper bound on the rttvar converges to the difference between the lower and upper bounds on the samples.

We concluded by discussing the implications of these bounds for the rto.

In addition to rigorously examining some fundamental building blocks of the Internet, we also provide an example of how multiple provers can be used in harmony to prove more than either could handle alone. First, we used Ivy to model the underlying system and Karn's algorithm. Ivy offers an easy treatment for concurrency, which was vital for the behavior of the underspecified models we used for the sender, receiver, and channel. The underspecification renders our results their generality. We guided Ivy by providing supplemental invariants as hints, e.g., *if $dlvr_r(a)$ occurs in an execution, then for all $p < a$, $dlvr_s(p)$ occurred previously.* Then, since Ivy lacks a theory of rationals, we turned to ACL2s. We began by proving two lemmas.

- The α-summation "unfolds": $(1 - \alpha) \sum_{i=0}^{N} (1 - \alpha)^i \alpha + \alpha = \sum_{i=0}^{N+1} (1 - \alpha)^i \alpha$.
- The srtt is "linear": if $srtt_{i-1} \leq srtt'_{i-1}$ and, for all $i \leq j \leq i + n$, $S_j \leq S'_j$, then $srtt_{i+n} \leq srtt'_{i+n}$.

Then we steered ACL2s to prove Observation 5 and Observation 6 with these lemmas as hints.

Proving the limits of the bounds on srtt and rttvar was much trickier, and required manually writing ϵ/δ proofs directly in the ACL2s proof-builder. Nevertheless, they would have been impossible to do in Ivy. On the other hand, since ACL2s does not come with built-in facilities for reasoning about interleaved network semantics, we opted to leave the RTT computation proofs in Ivy. These choices were easier – and yielded cleaner proofs – compared to doing everything using just one of the two tools.

Acknowledgments. This material is based upon work supported by the National Science Foundation under Grant CCS-2140207, SHF-1918429, CNS-1801546, and GRFP-1938052, as well as by the Department of Defense under Grant W911NF2010310.

References

1. Abdou, A., Matrawy, A., van Oorschot, P.C.: Accurate one-way delay estimation with reduced client trustworthiness. IEEE Commun. Lett. **19**(5), 735–738 (2015)
2. Aboba, B., Wood, J.: Authentication, authorization and accounting (AAA) transport profile, June 2003. https://www.rfc-editor.org/rfc/rfc3539. Accessed 21 Mar 2023
3. Adamson, B., Bormann, C., Handley, M., Macker, J.: Negative-acknowledgment (NACK)-oriented reliable multicast (NORM) building blocks, November 2004. https://www.rfc-editor.org/rfc/rfc3941. Accessed 17 Mar 2023
4. Afek, Y., Attiya, H., Fekete, A., Fischer, M., Lynch, N., Mansour, Y., Wang, D.W., Zuck, L.: Reliable communication over unreliable channels. J. ACM (JACM) **41**(6), 1267–1297 (1994)
5. Allman, M., Paxson, V., Blanton, E.: TCP congestion control, September 2009. https://www.rfc-editor.org/rfc/rfc5681. Accessed 23 Feb 2023
6. Arun, V., Alizadeh, M., Balakrishnan, H.: Starvation in end-to-end congestion control. In: Proceedings of the ACM SIGCOMM 2022 Conference, pp. 177–192 (2022)
7. Arun, V., Arashloo, M.T., Saeed, A., Alizadeh, M., Balakrishnan, H.: Toward formally verifying congestion control behavior. In: SIGCOMM 2021 (2021)
8. Baccelli, F., Hong, D.: TCP is max-plus linear and what it tells us on its throughput. In: Proceedings of the Conference on Applications, Technologies, Architectures, and Protocols for Computer Communication, pp. 219–230 (2000)
9. Balakrishnan, H., Seshan, S.: The congestion manager, June 2001. https://www.rfc-editor.org/rfc/rfc3124. Accessed 21 Mar 2023
10. Balandina, E., Koucheryavy, Y., Gurtov, A.: Computing the retransmission timeout in coap. In: Internet of Things, Smart Spaces, and Next Generation Networking: 13th International Conference, NEW2AN 2013 and 6th Conference, ruSMART 2013, St. Petersburg, Russia, August 28–30, 2013. Proceedings. pp. 352–362. Springer (2013)
11. Bensley, S., Thaler, D., Balasubramanian, P., Eggert, L., Judd, G.: Data Center TCP (DCTCP): TCP congestion control for data centers, October 2017. https://www.rfc-editor.org/rfc/rfc8257. Accessed 15 Mar 2023
12. Bishop, S., Fairbairn, M., Norrish, M., Sewell, P., Smith, M., Wansbrough, K.: Rigorous specification and conformance testing techniques for network protocols, as applied to TCP, UDP, and sockets. In: Proceedings of the 2005 Conference on Applications, Technologies, Architectures, and Protocols for Computer Communications, pp. 265–276 (2005)
13. Brakmo, L.S., Peterson, L.L.: TCP vegas: end to end congestion avoidance on a global internet. IEEE J. Sel. Areas Commun. **13**(8), 1465–1480 (1995)
14. Camarillo, G., Drage, K., Kristensen, T., Ott, J., Eckel, C.: The Binary Floor Control Protocol (BFCP), January 2021. https://www.rfc-editor.org/rfc/rfc8855. Accessed 23 Feb 2023
15. Cardwell, N., et al.: packetdrill: scriptable network stack testing, from sockets to packets. In: 2013 USENIX Annual Technical Conference (USENIX ATC 13), pp. 213–218 (2013)
16. Chamarthi, H.R., Dillinger, P., Manolios, P., Vroon, D.: The ACL2 sedan theorem proving system. In: Abdulla, P.A., Leino, K.R.M. (eds.) TACAS 2011. LNCS, vol. 6605, pp. 291–295. Springer, Heidelberg (2011). https://doi.org/10.1007/978-3-642-19835-9_27
17. Cheng, Y., Cardwell, N., Dukkipati, N., Jha, P.: The RACK-TLP loss detection algorithm for TCP, February 2021. https://www.rfc-editor.org/rfc/rfc8985. Accessed 15 Mar 2023
18. Cluzel, G., Georgiou, K., Moy, Y., Zeller, C.: Layered formal verification of a TCP stack. In: 2021 IEEE Secure Development Conference (SecDev), pp. 86–93. IEEE (2021)
19. Dillinger, P.C., Manolios, P., Vroon, D., Moore, J.S.: Acl2s:"the ACL2 sedan". Electron. Notes Theoretical Comput. Sci. **174**(2), 3–18 (2007)

20. Eggert, L., Fairhurst, G., Shepherd, G.: UDP usage guidelines, March 2017. https://www. rfc-editor.org/rfc/rfc8085. Accessed 23 Feb 2023

21. Gerla, M., Sanadidi, M.Y., Wang, R., Zanella, A., Casetti, C., Mascolo, S.: TCP West-wood: congestion window control using bandwidth estimation. In: GLOBECOM'01. IEEE Global Telecommunications Conference (Cat. No. 01CH37270), vol. 3, pp. 1698–1702. IEEE (2001)

22. Henderson, T., Floyd, S., Gurtov, A., Nishida, Y.: The NewReno modification to TCP's fast recovery algorithm, April 2012. https://www.rfc-editor.org/rfc/rfc6582. Accessed 15 March 2023

23. Hespanha, J.P., Bohacek, S., Obraczka, K., Lee, J.: Hybrid modeling of TCP congestion control. In: Di Benedetto, M.D., Sangiovanni-Vincentelli, A. (eds.) HSCC 2001. LNCS, vol. 2034, pp. 291–304. Springer, Heidelberg (2001). https://doi.org/10.1007/3-540-45351-2_25

24. von Hippel, M., Vick, C., Tripakis, S., Nita-Rotaru, C.: Automated attacker synthesis for dis-tributed protocols. In: Casimiro, A., Ortmeier, F., Bitsch, F., Ferreira, P. (eds.) SAFECOMP 2020. LNCS, vol. 12234, pp. 133–149. Springer, Cham (2020). https://doi.org/10.1007/978-3-030-54549-9_9

25. Hu, K., Liu, C., Liu, K.: Modeling and verification of custom TCP using SDL. In: 2013 IEEE 4th International Conference on Software Engineering and Service Science, pp. 455–458. IEEE (2013)

26. Hurtig, P., Brunstrom, A., Petlund, A., Welzl, M.: TCP and Stream Control Transmis-sion Protocol (SCTP) RTO restart, February 2016. https://www.rfc-editor.org/rfc/rfc7765. Accessed 23 Feb 2023

27. Inamura, H., Montenegro, G., Ludwig, R., Gurtov, A., Khafizov, F.: TCP over second (2.5g) and third (3g) generation wireless networks, February 2007. https://www.rfc-editor.org/rfc/rfc3481. Accessed 21 Mar 2023

28. Iyengar, J., Swett, I.: QUIC loss detection and congestion control, May 2021. https://www.rfc-editor.org/rfc/rfc9002. Accessed 17 Mar 2023

29. Iyengar, J., Thomson, M.: QUIC: A UDP-Based Multiplexed and Secure Transport. RFC 9000, May 2021. https://doi.org/10.17487/RFC9000. https://www.rfc-editor.org/info/rfc9000

30. Jacobson, V.: Congestion avoidance and control. ACM SIGCOMM Comput. Commun. Rev. 18(4), 314–329 (1988)

31. Jennings, C., Lowekamp, B., Rescorla, E., Baset, S., Schulzrinne, H.: REsource LOcation And Discovery (RELOAD) Base Protocol (2014). https://www.rfc-editor.org/rfc/rfc6940. Accessed 23 Feb 2023

32. Kakarla, S.K.R., Beckett, R., Millstein, T., Varghese, G.: SCALE: automatically finding RFC compliance bugs in DNS nameservers. In: 19th USENIX Symposium on Networked Systems Design and Implementation (NSDI 22), pp. 307–323. USENIX Association, Renton, WA, April 2022. https://www.usenix.org/conference/nsdi22/presentation/kakarla

33. Karn, P., Partridge, C.: Improving round-trip time estimates in reliable transport protocols. ACM SIGCOMM Comput. Commun. Rev. 17(5), 2–7 (1987)

34. Keranen, A., Holmberg, C., Rosenberg, J.: Interactive Connectivity Establishment (ICE): A protocol for Network Address Translator (NAT) traversal, July 2018. https://www.rfc-editor.org/rfc/rfc8445. Accessed 23 February 2023

35. Kesselman, A., Mansour, Y.: Optimizing TCP retransmission timeout. In: Lorenz, P., Dini, P. (eds.) ICN 2005. LNCS, vol. 3421, pp. 133–140. Springer, Heidelberg (2005). https://doi.org/10.1007/978-3-540-31957-3_17

36. Kim, H., Hou, J.C.: Network calculus based simulation for TCP congestion control: the-orems, implementation and evaluation. In: IEEE INFOCOM 2004, vol. 4, pp. 2844–2855. IEEE (2004)

37. Konur, S., Fisher, M.: Formal analysis of a VANET congestion control protocol through probabilistic verification. In: 2011 IEEE 73rd Vehicular Technology Conference (VTC Spring), pp. 1–5. IEEE (2011)
38. Le Boudec, J.Y., Thiran, P.: Network calculus: a theory of deterministic queuing systems for the internet. Springer (2001)
39. Liu, S., Başar, T., Srikant, R.: TCP-Illinois: a loss and delay-based congestion control algorithm for high-speed networks. In: Proceedings of the 1st International Conference on Performance Evaluation Methodolgies and Tools, pp. 55-es (2006)
40. Lockefeer, L., Williams, D.M., Fokkink, W.: Formal specification and verification of tcp extended with the window scale option. Sci. Comput. Program. **118**, 3–23 (2016)
41. Lomuscio, A., Strulo, B., Walker, N.G., Wu, P.: Model checking optimisation based congestion control algorithms. Fund. Inform. **102**(1), 77–96 (2010)
42. Ludwig, R., Gurtov, A.: The Eifel response algorithm for TCP, February 2005. https://www.rfc-editor.org/rfc/rfc4015. Accessed 21 Mar 2023
43. Malik, M.H., Jamil, M., Khan, M.N., Malik, M.H.: Formal modelling of tcp congestion control mechanisms ecn/red and sap-law in the presence of udp traffic. EURASIP J. Wirel. Commun. Netw. **2016**, 1–12 (2016)
44. Mascolo, S., Casetti, C., Gerla, M., Sanadidi, M.Y., Wang, R.: Tcp westwood: bandwidth estimation for enhanced transport over wireless links. In: Proceedings of the 7th Annual International Conference on Mobile Computing and Networking, pp. 287–297 (2001)
45. Mathis, M., Semke, J., Mahdavi, J., Ott, T.: The macroscopic behavior of the tcp congestion avoidance algorithm. ACM SIGCOMM Comput. Commun. Rev. **27**(3), 67–82 (1997)
46. McMillan, K.L., Zuck, L.D.: Formal specification and testing of QUIC. In: Proceedings of the ACM Special Interest Group on Data Communication, pp. 227–240 (2019)
47. Okumura, N., Ogata, K., Shinoda, Y.: Formal analysis of RFC 8120 authentication protocol for http under different assumptions. J. Inf. Secur. Appl. **53**, 102529 (2020)
48. Pacheco, M.L., von Hippel, M., Weintraub, B., Goldwasser, D., Nita-Rotaru, C.: Automated attack synthesis by extracting finite state machines from protocol specification documents. In: 2022 IEEE Symposium on Security and Privacy (SP), pp. 51–68. IEEE (2022)
49. Paxson, V., Allman, M., Chu, J., Sargent, M.: Computing TCP's retransmission timer, June 2011. https://www.rfc-editor.org/rfc/rfc6298. Accessed 22 Feb 2023
50. Petit-Huguenin, M., Salgueiro, G., Rosenberg, J., Wing, D., Mahy, R., Matthews, P.: Session Traversal Utilities for NAT (STUN), February 2020. https://www.rfc-editor.org/rfc/rfc8489. Accessed 23 February 2023
51. Pothamsetty, V., Mateti, P.: A case for exploit-robust and attack-aware protocol RFCs. In: Proceedings 20th IEEE International Parallel and Distributed Processing Symposium (2006)
52. Schinazi, D., Pauly, T.: Happy eyeballs version 2: Better connectivity using concurrency, December 2017. https://www.rfc-editor.org/rfc/rfc8305. Accessed 23 Feb 2023
53. Shalunov, S., Hazel, G., Iyengar, J., Kuehlewind, M.: Low Extra Delay Background Transport (LEDBAT), December 2012. https://www.rfc-editor.org/rfc/rfc6817. Accessed 23 Feb 2023
54. Smith, M.A.S.: Formal verification of TCP and T/TCP. Ph.D. thesis, Massachusetts Institute of Technology (1997)
55. Sridharan, M., Tan, K., Bansal, D., Thaler, D.: Compound TCP: a new TCP congestion control for high-speed and long distance networks, November 2008. https://datatracker.ietf.org/doc/html/draft-sridharan-tcpm-ctcp-02. Accessed 15 Mar 2023
56. Srikant, R., Başar, T.: The mathematics of Internet congestion control. Springer (2004)
57. Stewart, R.: tream control transmission protocol, September 2007. https://www.rfc-editor.org/rfc/rfc4960. Accessed 23 Feb 2023
58. T. Henderson, A.G.: The Host Identity Protocol (HIP) Experiment Report, March 2012. https://www.rfc-editor.org/rfc/rfc6538. Accessed 23 Feb 2023

59. Tang, C., Chang, R.N., Ward, C.: Gocast: gossip-enhanced overlay multicast for fast and dependable group communication. In: 2005 International Conference on Dependable Systems and Networks (DSN 2005), pp. 140–149. IEEE (2005)

60. Taube, M., Losa, G., McMillan, K.L., Padon, O., Sagiv, M., Shoham, S., Wilcox, J.R., Woos, D.: Modularity for decidability of deductive verification with applications to distributed systems. In: Proceedings of the 39th ACM SIGPLAN Conference on Programming Language Design and Implementation, pp. 662–677 (2018)

61. Thubert, P.: IPv6 over Low-Power Wireless Personal Area Network (6LoWPAN) selective fragment recovery, November 2020. https://www.rfc-editor.org/rfc/rfc8931. Accessed 23 Feb 2023

62. Yang, P.: tcp: fix F-RTO may not work correctly when receiving DSACK. https://lore.kernel.org/netdev/165116761177.10854.18409623100154256898.git-patchwork-notify@kernel.org/t/. Accessed 24 Mar 2023

63. Yen, J., Lévai, T., Ye, Q., Ren, X., Govindan, R., Raghavan, B.: Semi-automated protocol disambiguation and code generation. In: Proceedings of the 2021 ACM SIGCOMM 2021 Conference, pp. 272–286 (2021)

64. Zarchy, D., Mittal, R., Schapira, M., Shenker, S.: Axiomatizing congestion control. In: Proceedings of the ACM on Measurement and Analysis of Computing Systems, July 2019

Comparing Causal Convergence
Consistency Models

Sidi Mohamed Beillahi[1]([✉]), Ahmed Bouajjani[2], and Constantin Enea[3]

[1] University of Toronto, Toronto, Canada
sm.beillahi@utoronto.ca
[2] Université Paris Cité, IRIF, CNRS, Paris, France
abou@irif.fr
[3] LIX, Ecole Polytechnique, CNRS and Institut Polytechnique de Paris, Paris, France
cenea@lix.polytechnique.fr

Abstract. In distributed databases, the CAP theorem establishes that a distributed storage system can only ensure two out of three properties: strong data consistency (i.e., reads returning the most recent writes), availability, or partition tolerance. Modern distributed storage systems prioritize performance and availability over strong consistency and thus offer weaker consistency models such as causal consistency.

This paper explores several variations of causal consistency (CC) that guarantee state convergence among replicas, meaning that all distributed replicas converge towards the same consistent state. We investigate a log-based CC model, a commutativity-based CC model, and a global sequence protocol-based CC model. To facilitate our study of the relationships between these models, we use a common formalism to define them. We then show that the log-based CC model is the weakest, while the commutativity-based CC and the global sequence protocol-based CC models are incomparable. We also provide sufficient conditions for a given application program to be robust against one CC model versus another, meaning that the program has the same behavior when executed over databases implementing the two CC models.

1 Introduction

In distributed databases, the CAP theorem establishes that a distributed storage system can only ensure two out of three properties: strong data consistency (i.e., reads returning the most recent writes), availability, or partition tolerance [14]. Modern distributed storage systems prioritize performance and availability over strong consistency and thus offer weaker consistency models such as causal consistency [20]. Causal consistency is a fundamental weak consistency model implemented in several production databases, e.g., CockroachDB and MongoDB, and extensively studied in the literature [6,8,9,18,24]. It guarantees the causal dependency relationship between transactions. Causal consistency requires that if a

---

This work is supported in part by the Agence National de Recherche project AdeCoDS (ANR-19-CE25-0007).

transaction t_1 affects another transaction t_2 (e.g., t_1 executes before t_2 in the same process or t_2 reads a value written by t_1) then the two transactions are observed by any other transaction in this order. Concurrent transactions, which are not causally related to each other, can be observed in different orders.

Modern distributed applications often use state replication to reduce latency when serving users from different parts of the world. Therefore, an essential property of these applications is ensuring that the different replicas (processes) eventually converge to the same state, ensuring consistent data across all processes. Recent works have proposed several weak consistency models that guarantee state convergence [11, 15–17, 21, 25].

In this paper, we focus on consistency models that guarantee both causal dependency and state convergence. In particular, we study three variations of causal consistency (CC) that guarantee state convergence across processes. We investigate a log-based CC model [17], a commutativity-based CC model [15], and a global sequence protocol-based CC model [11].

In the log-based CC model (LbCC), processes apply received updates immediately and each process keeps a log of all updates applied to the state. When a process receives a delayed update and more recent concurrent updates have already been applied to the state of the process, the process undoes the more recent updates. Then, the process applies the delayed update and uses the log to redo the more recent updates. Thus, concurrent updates are eventually applied by all processes in the same order (according to some total order mechanism like timestamps), ensuring that the processes converge towards the same state. In the commutativity-based CC model (CbCC), processes coordinate to apply conflicting updates that are concurrent in the same order. In particular, updates that are not commutative, i.e., the states reached when t_1 and t_2 are executed in this order and when t_2 and t_1 are executed in this order are different, are delivered to all process in the same order. Thus, the only updates that might be applied in different orders by different processes are commutative updates. This ensures that all processes converge toward the same state. In the global sequence protocol-based CC model (GSP), a process serving as the server coordinates all updates and propagates them as a single sequence to all processes. Specifically, processes transmit their updates to the server process, which adds them to the update sequence and then propagates the sequence to all processes. This ensures that all processes converge to the same state by applying the updates in the same order.

Indeed, all three models mentioned above ensure causal dependency and state convergence properties. However, an important question remains open regarding which model is the weakest or strongest. In particular, since a weaker consistency model provides better performance, it is important to identify the weakest level of consistency required by an application program to meet its specifications. In this paper, we aim to study the causal consistency variations mentioned above to characterize the relationships between them. To facilitate the study of the different causal consistency models, we use a common formalism to define them. Adopting a common formalism for different consistency models helps us to better understand these models and the differences between them. We then demonstrate that the LbCC model is the weakest, while the CbCC and the GSP models are incomparable.

We also present sufficient conditions for a given application program $\mathcal{P}$ designed under a CC model S to have different behaviors when run under a weaker CC model W. This property of the application program is generally known as *non-robustness* against substituting S with W. It implies that the specification of P may not be preserved when weakening the consistency model (from S to W).

The rest of the paper is organized as follows. We present a preliminary for program semantics that we use to formalize the paper's contribution in Sect. 2. We then provide the formal definitions for the three CC models we study in Sect. 3. In Sect. 4, we illustrate through simple programs the differences between the three CC models. We then present the characterizations of non robustness against substituting LbCC with CbCC and LbCC with GSP. Finally, we discuss related work in Sect. 6 and conclude the paper in Sect. 7.

2 Programs

To simplify the technical exposition, we assume a program $\mathcal{P}$ is a parallel composition of a bounded number of *processes* distinguished using a set of identifiers $\mathbb{P}$ and each process is a sequence of a bounded number of transactions. We use transactions to encapsulate accesses to the program state that is kept in a storage system. We assume a transaction is a function that takes a program state and returns a tuple of another program state and a return value.

Definition 1. *A transaction t is a function from a state (pre-state)* s *to a state (post-state)* s' *that returns a value* $ret \in V \cup \perp$*, i.e.,* $t(\mathsf{s}) = (\mathsf{s}', ret)$.

A transaction t is an update (write) if there exist a state s s.t. $t(\mathsf{s}) = (\mathsf{s}', \perp)$ where $\mathsf{s} \neq \mathsf{s}'$. A transaction t is a query (read) if for every state s, $t(\mathsf{s}) = (\mathsf{s}, ret)$ and $ret \neq \perp$.

Definition 2. *An execution ρ of a program $\mathcal{P}$ is the execution of all its transactions by all processes. We use* $\mathsf{s}_{\mathcal{P}}$ *to denote the program state and use* $\mathsf{s}_{\mathcal{P}}^{p}$ *to denote the state of a process p, i.e.,* $\rho : \mathsf{s}_{\mathcal{P}} = (\mathsf{s}_{\mathcal{P}}^{p0}, \mathsf{s}_{\mathcal{P}}^{p1}, \cdots, \mathsf{s}_{\mathcal{P}}^{pn}) \to \mathsf{s}'_{\mathcal{P}} = (\mathsf{s}'^{p0}_{\mathcal{P}}, \mathsf{s}'^{p1}_{\mathcal{P}}, \cdots, \mathsf{s}'^{pn}_{\mathcal{P}})$.

Next we define commutativity conditions between two update transactions and between an update and query transactions.

Definition 3. *Two update transactions t_1 and t_2 are commutative if for every state s, we have $t_1(s) = (s_1, \perp)$ and $t_2(s_1) = (s', \perp)$, and $t_2(s) = (s_2, \perp)$ and $t_1(s_2) = (s', \perp)$.*

Definition 4. *An update transaction t_1 and a query transaction t_2 are commutative if for every state s, we have $t_1(s) = (s', \perp)$, $t_2(s') = (s', val)$, and $t_2(s) = (s, val)$.*

The update transactions t_1 and t_2 in Fig. 1 are not commutative since executing t_1 after t_2 leads to $x = 1$ while executing t_2 after t_1 leads to $x = 2$. On the other hand, the two update transactions t_1 and t_3 are commutative since executing t_1 after t_3 leads to $x = 3$ which is the same state outcome when executing t_3 after t_1. The update transaction t_1 and the query transaction t_4 are not commutative since executing t_4 after t_1 results in $r = 1$. Note that also the update transaction t_2 and the query transaction t_4 are not commutative since executing t_4 followed by t_2 in the state $s : \{x = 1\}$ (after executing the update t_1) results in $r = 2$.

$$t_1\ [x := x + 1] \qquad t_2\ [x := 2 * x] \qquad t_3\ [x := x + 2] \qquad t_4\ [r := x] \qquad t_5 \begin{array}{l} [\text{if } x + 1 < 2 \\ \quad x := x + 1] \end{array}$$

Fig. 1. A program with five transactions. Initially $x = 0$.

To decide whether transactions reordering is observable we now define distinguishable criterion between update transactions. In particular, a query transaction can distinguish between the ordering of two update transactions t_2 and t_3, if its return value changes when the order of applying the updates changes.

Definition 5. *Given two update transactions t_2 and t_3, a query transaction t_1 distinguishes between t_2 and t_3 versus t_3 and t_2 iff for every state s we have $t_2(s) = (s_1, \bot)$, $t_3(s_1) = (s_2, \bot)$, $t_1(s_2) = (s_2, val)$, and $t_3(s) = (s'_1, \bot)$, $t_2(s'_1) = (s'_2, \bot)$, and $t_1(s'_2) = (s'_2, val')$ where $val \neq val'$.*

Next we extend the distinguishable criteria to a query transaction t_1 that returns different values if it occurred after an update transaction t_2 alone versus if it occurred after the update transactions t_2 followed by t_3 in this order.

Definition 6. *Given two update transactions t_2 and t_3, a query transaction t_1 distinguishes between t_2 versus t_2 and t_3 iff for every state s we have $t_2(s) = (s_1, \bot)$, $t_3(s_1) = (s_2, \bot)$, $t_1(s_1) = (s_1, val)$, and $t_1(s_2) = (s_2, val')$ where $val \neq val'$.*

In Fig. 1, the query transaction t_4 distinguishes between t_1 versus t_1 followed by t_3. On the other hand, it does not distinguish between t_1 versus t_1 followed by t_5.

2.1   Execution

We use $s^{\mathcal{P}} = (s^{p0}, s^{p1}, \cdots, s^{pn})$ to denote of the state of the program $\mathcal{P}$ constituted of n processes. We use $t^{s^p} : (s^{p0}, \cdots, s^p, \cdots, s^{pn}) \rightarrow (s^{p0}, \cdots, t(s^p), \cdots, s^{pn})$ to denote the transition of applying the transaction t to the state s^p of the process p. We use $\mathbb{T}$ to denote the set of transaction transition identifiers.

We say that an update transaction is initiated by a process, if the transaction was first executed by this process and the process propagated the transaction to other processes. A query transaction is executed by a single process that initiated the query. We use $\mathsf{pr}(t)$ to denote the process initiating the transaction t.

Definition 7. *An execution* $\rho = t^{s^p} \cdots t'^{s^{p'}} \subset \mathbb{T}$ *of a program* $\mathcal{P}$ *is a sequence of transitions the execution of transactions in the program* $\mathcal{P}$, *i.e.,* $\rho : s^{\mathcal{P}} = (s^{p0}, s^{p1}, \cdots, s^{pn}) \rightarrow s'^{\mathcal{P}} = (s'^{p0}, s'^{p1}, \cdots, s'^{pn})$.

A well-formed execution is an execution where the first occurrence of a transition t^{s^p} of a transaction t corresponds to the transition of applying t to the state s^p of the process p that initiated the transaction t, i.e., $\mathsf{pr}(t) = p$. For the rest of the paper, we assume that every execution is a well-formed execution.

We define a program order as a relation between transactions that are initiated by the process. In particular, given an execution ρ, such that the transition $t_1(s^p)$ occurs in ρ before the transition $t_2(s'^p)$ where $p = \mathsf{pr}(t_1) = \mathsf{pr}(t_2)$ then $(t_1, t_2) \in \mathsf{PO}$. Next, we define the causality relationship between transactions in an execution.

Definition 8. *Given an execution* ρ, *we say a transaction* t_1 *is causally related to another transaction* t_2 *if the transition* $t_2(s^p)$ *occurs in* ρ *before the transition* $t_1(s'^p)$ *where* p *is the process initiating the transaction* t_1 *and* s^p *and* s'^p *are states of* p, *denoted by* $(t_2^{s^p}, t_1^{s'^p}) \in \mathsf{CO}$.

We say an execution ρ satisfies causal delivery if for every transaction t_1 that is causally related to another transaction t_2 then $\forall\ t_2^{s^{p'}}\ t_1^{s'^{p'}} \in \rho.\ (t_2^{s^{p'}}, t_1^{s'^{p'}}) \in \mathsf{CO}$. For the rest of the paper, we assume all program executions satisfy causal delivery. Thus, for simplicity if t_1 is causally related to another transaction t_2, we use $(t_2, t_1) \in \mathsf{CO}$. Note that $\mathsf{PO} \subset \mathsf{CO}$.

Using the causal relation we define the conflict relation between transactions that are not commutative and are not related by the causal order.

Definition 9. *Given an execution* ρ, *we say a query transaction* t_1 *is conflicting with an update transaction* t_2, *if the two are not commutative and are not related by the causal order, i.e.,* $(t_2, t_1) \notin \mathsf{CO}$. *We use* $(t_1, t_2) \in \mathsf{CF}$ *to denote the conflict relation.*

Using the commutative information between transactions in a program we introduce the commutativity relation between them.

Definition 10. *Given an execution* ρ, *we say two update transactions* t_1 *and* t_2 *are related by commutativity relation, denoted by* $(t_2, t_1) \in \mathsf{CM}$, *if the two transactions do not commute and there exist a process* p *where the transition* $t_2(s^p)$ *occurs in* ρ *before the transition* $t_1(s'^p)$ *where* s^p *and* s'^p *are states of* p.

Next, we define the store order relation. Generally, the store order relation orders update transactions that write to a common variable. However, since we use an abstract model for transactions, thus it is not possible to statically know the variables that those transactions access. This is in contrast with traditional modeling of transactions as a sequence of simple register read and write operations. Therefore, to define the store order between update transactions we check whether they lead to observably distinguishable states. This allows to only order transactions that modify the state in an observable way. For instance, two transactions that write the same value will not be ordered by the store order.

Definition 11. *Given an execution ρ, we say two update transactions t_1 and t_2 are related by store order, denoted by $(t_2, t_1) \in$ ST, if there exist a process p where the transition $t_2(s^p)$ occurs in ρ before the transition $t_1(s'^p)$ where s^p and s'^p are states of p and one of the followings hold:*

- $(t_2, t_1) \in$ CM; *or*
- *there exist a query transaction t_3 in ρ s.t. one of the followings hold:*
  - t_3 *distinguishes between t_1 versus t_1 and t_2; or*
  - t_3 *distinguishes between t_2 versus t_2 and t_1.*

3 Consistency Models

In this section we present the three models of causal consistency using a set of constraints on the relations between transactions in a program execution.

3.1 Log-Based Causal Consistency (LbCC)

Kleppmann et al. [17] present a consistency model that allows concurrent move operations for replicated tree data structures, while guaranteeing that all replicas converge without compromising availability. The main idea of the model consists of keeping a log of operations by all replicas. Thus, replicas apply operations immediately when they are received. If a replica receives operations out-of-order, it can then undo and redo the operations to follow the correct order by fetching previously applied operations from its log to redo them.

Indeed, this operational model of using transactions logging is compatible with different data structures and protocols for message propagation between processes. In this paper, we focus on an instantiation of this operational model with the causal delivery protocol. This model guarantees both convergence and causal consistency. Thus, the store order relation between update transactions is acyclic, i.e., ST is acyclic. The definition of causal dependency and conflict relation imposes that their composition is acyclic, i.e., (CO; CF) is acyclic (; denotes the sequential composition of two relations). Also, note that the causal delivery ensures that ST are CO compatible, i.e., $\not\exists t_1, t_2. (t_1, t_2) \in$ CO *and* $(t_2, t_1) \in$ ST.

Definition 12. *We say an execution is allowed under the log-based causal consistency model (LbCC) iff (CO; CF) and ST are acyclics and $\not\exists t_1 t_2. (t_1, t_2) \in$ CO and $(t_2, t_1) \in$ ST.*

3.2 Commutativity-Based Causal Consistency (CbCC)

Houshmand and Lesani [15] propose a consistency model that synchronizes conflicting and dependent operations to ensure the integrity and convergence of the state in a replicated setting. They statically analyze state operations to infer conflicting and dependent operations and present distributed protocols that ensure coordination between them.

In this paper, we focus on an instantiation of this operational model with a causal delivery protocol. This consistency model guarantees causal consistency, ensuring that dependent operations are always delivered in order. Furthermore, for simplicity, we assume that conflicting operations correspond to update operations that are not commutative. Thus, the consistency model guarantees that update operations that are not commutative are received in the same order by all processes, thanks to the distributed protocol. Thus, CM is acyclic and implies causality relation, i.e., $CM \subset CO$.

Definition 13. *We say an execution is allowed under the commutativity-based causal consistency model (CbCC) iff $(CO; CF)$ and CM are acyclic, $CM \subset CO$, and $\nexists\ t_1\ t_2.\ (t_1, t_2) \in CO$ and $(t_2, t_1) \in ST$.*

3.3   Global Sequence Protocol (GSP)

Burckhardt et al. [11] present a consistency model that utilizes a server (a process that plays the role of a server for other processes[1]) to receive and arrange all exchanged operations, i.e., update transactions, into a totally ordered sequence and forward the sequence to other processes. Processes can delay transmitting their update transactions to the server and buffer those updates to be able to access them locally when they execute query transactions.

The GSP consistency model ensures that all processes agree on a global sequence of update transactions. Therefore, when a process receives an update operation, it must have received all update transactions that were ordered before it in the sequence, i.e., $ST; (CO \setminus PO) \subset CO$. The global sequencing of operations ensures that the store order relation between update transactions is acyclic, i.e., ST is acyclic.

Definition 14. *We say an execution is allowed under the global sequence protocol model (GSP) iff $ST; (CO \setminus PO) \subset CO$, $(CO; CF)$ and ST are acyclic, and $\nexists\ t_1,\ t_2.\ (t_1, t_2) \in CO$ and $(t_2, t_1) \in ST$.*

Note that from GSP and LbCC definitions, that GSP semantics is stronger than LbCC semantics.

Lemma 1. *GSP semantics model is stronger than LbCC semantics model.*

4   Relations Between Consistency Semantics

We will illustrate the differences between the various consistency models using the programs shown in Fig. 2. In all programs, transactions initiated by the same process are aligned vertically and ordered from top to bottom using the program order relation. Each query transaction is commented with the value it reads in the execution. Additionally, in all programs, the state consists of a single variable, x. We assume that initially $x = 2$.

---

[1] Note that the reliance on one server can create a single point of failure, however, processes can adopt a Byzantine fault tolerance consensus approach to elect new process to play the role of server.

Compared to CbCC and GSP semantics, LbCC allows processes to apply update transactions immediately when received. The program in Fig. 2a contains six transactions that are issued by four distinct processes. All transactions manipulate and query the state of the variable x. We emphasize an execution where t_3 reads 3, t_5 reads 4, and both t_4 and t_6 read 6. This execution is allowed under LbCC since the two update transactions t_1 and t_2 are not causally dependent and are received in different orders by the processes. Thus, one process first receives t_1 and applies it to its state, then performs the query t_3. It then receives t_2 and updates its state[2] and performs the second query t_3. The other process first receives t_2 and applies it to its state, then performs the query t_5. It then receives t_1, which results in undoing t_2 and applying t_1, then t_2 to the process's state. Finally, the last query t_6 is performed. However, this execution is not feasible under CbCC. In particular, the two transactions t_1 and t_2 are not commutative. Thus, they must be received in order by all processes. If we assume $(t_1, t_2) \in CO$, then it is not possible that the query t_5 reads only the update of t_2. Similarly, the above execution is not possible under GSP as well. In particular, the two transactions t_1 and t_2 will be arranged by the server before propagating them to other processes in a sequence. Thus, assuming that $(t_1, t_2) \in ST$ (note that $(t_1, t_2) \in CM$), then $(t_2, t_5) \in (CO \setminus PO)$ implies that $(t_1, t_5) \in CO$, which contradicts the fact that the query t_5 reads only the update of t_2.

t_1 $[x := x + 1]$ t_2 $[x := 2 * x]$ t_3 $[r1 := x]$ //3 t_5 $[r3 := x]$ //4
PO↓   PO↓
t_4 $[r2 := x]$ //6 t_6 $[r4 := x]$ //6

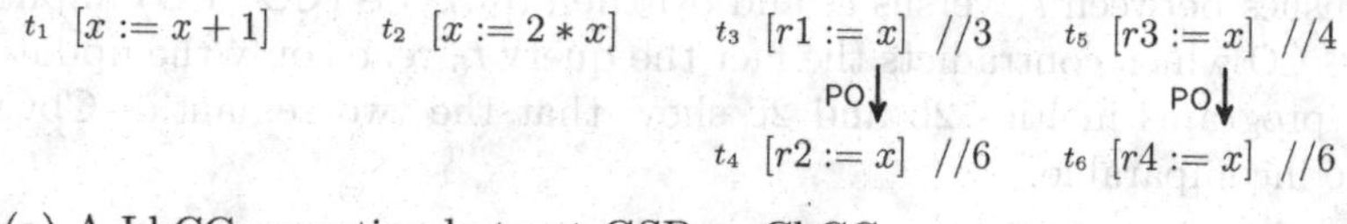

(a) A LbCC execution but not GSP or CbCC.

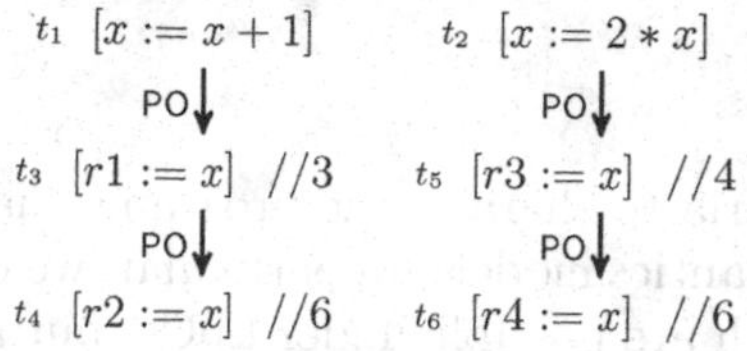

t_1 $[x := x + 1]$ t_2 $[x := 2 * x]$
PO↓   PO↓
t_3 $[r1 := x]$ //3 t_5 $[r3 := x]$ //4
PO↓   PO↓
t_4 $[r2 := x]$ //6 t_6 $[r4 := x]$ //6

(b) A LbCC and GSP execution but not CbCC.

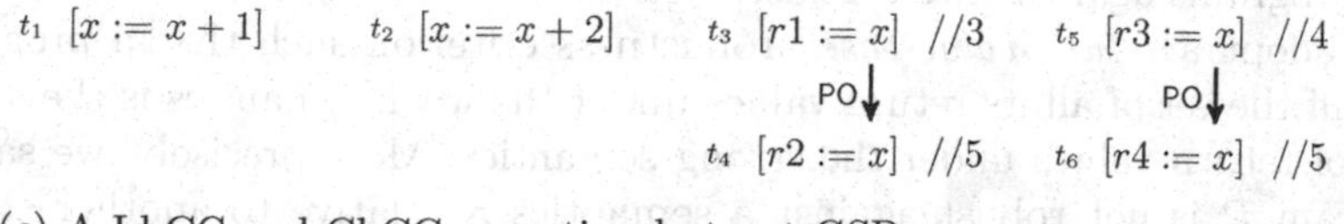

t_1 $[x := x + 1]$ t_2 $[x := x + 2]$ t_3 $[r1 := x]$ //3 t_5 $[r3 := x]$ //4
PO↓   PO↓
t_4 $[r2 := x]$ //5 t_6 $[r4 := x]$ //5

(c) A LbCC and CbCC execution but not GSP.

Fig. 2. Litmus programs. Initially $x = 2$.

In Fig. 2b, we show a program with six transactions initiated by two distinct processes. We highlight an execution where t_3 reads 3, t_5 reads 4, and both t_4 and

---

[2] We assume that t_1 is ordered before t_2 based on some mechanism like timestamps.

t_6 read 6 from x. This execution is allowed under GSP (and also under LbCC). In particular, the second process locally buffers transaction t_2 and delays the propagation of the update. It then performs the query t_5, obtaining its value by inspecting the updates stored in the buffer and its state. When t_1 is received, the process applies it to its state and then pops t_2 from the buffer and applies it to its state. Finally, it performs the last query t_6. On the other hand, the first process first applies the update t_1 to its state (without buffering) and then performs its first state query, t_3. Then it receives the second update t_1 and applies it to its state, performing the second state query, t_4. However, this execution is not feasible under CbCC. In particular, the two transactions t_1 and t_2 are not commutative. Thus, the two processes must coordinate and apply them to their states in the same order. In particular, if we assume $(t_1, t_2) \in \mathsf{CO}$, then it is not possible for query t_5 to read only the update of t_2.

In Fig. 2c, we show a program with six transactions that are initiated by four distinct processes. We highlight an execution where t_3 reads 3, t_5 reads 4 and both t_4 and t_6 read 5 from x. This execution is allowed under CbCC (and also under LbCC). In particular, the two transactions t_1 and t_2 are commutative. Thus, in CbCC processes will not coordinate and t_1 and t_2 can be applied in any order. However, this execution is not feasible under GSP. In particular, the two transactions t_1 and t_2 will be arranged by the server before propagating them to other processes in a sequence. Thus, if we assume $(t_1, t_2) \in \mathsf{ST}$ (note that t_3 distinguishes between t_1 versus t_1 and t_2) then $(t_2, t_5) \in (\mathsf{CO} \setminus \mathsf{PO})$ implies that $(t_1, t_5) \in \mathsf{CO}$ which contradicts the fact the query t_5 reads only the update of t_2.

The programs in Figs. 2b and 2c show that the two semantics CbCC and GSP are incomparable.

Lemma 2. *CbCC and GSP semantics models are incomparable.*

5   Robustness

In this section, we present sufficient criteria to characterize programs that have distinct behaviors under the different semantics models. In particular, we characterize programs that have behaviors which are possible under LbCC but are not possible under CbCC and GSP. We formulate those comparisons as robustness of the programs against LbCC relative CbCC and GSP.

We adopt a *return-value-based* robustness criterion such that a program is robust iff the set of all its return values under the weak semantics is the same as its set of return values under the strong semantics. More precisely, we say that a program $\mathcal{P}$ is not robust against a semantics X relative to another stronger semantics Y iff for every execution ρ of $\mathcal{P}$ under X we have a replica execution ρ' of $\mathcal{P}$ under Y where both executions contain the same executed transactions and the values returned by query transactions are the same.

Definition 15. *Given two consistency models X and Y, we say that a program $\mathcal{P}$ is robust against X relative to Y iff for every execution ρ of $\mathcal{P}$ under the semantics model X there must exist an execution ρ' of $\mathcal{P}$ under the semantics model Y s.t.*

– *for every state transition by a process p in ρ, i.e., $t(s_\rho^p) = (s_\rho'^p, val) \in \rho$, there exists a state transition by p in ρ', i.e., $t(s_{\rho'}^p) = (s_{\rho'}'^p, val) \in \rho'$, where the two transitions return the same value;*

– *for every update only state transition by a process p of a transaction t in ρ, i.e., $t(s_\rho^p) = (s_\rho'^p, \perp) \in \rho$, there exists a state transition by p of the transaction t in ρ', i.e., $t(s_{\rho'}^p) = (s_{\rho'}'^p, \perp) \in \rho'$.*

Note that in our definition of robustness, there are no programs that are not robust against CbCC relative to LbCC. Even though under CbCC update transactions that are commutative can be applied in different order by different processes which results in a cycle in the store order relation ST which is not allowed under LbCC semantics, this will not result in a query transaction returning a value under CbCC that is not possible to observe under LbCC. This is because the update transactions are commutative.

Lemma 3. *All programs are robust against CbCC relative to LbCC.*

In the following we give sufficient conditions based on a set of constraints of the transactions in a given program to characterize whether this program is robust or not against LbCC relative to CbCC or GSP.

5.1   LbCC Versus CbCC

The following robustness characterization theorem presents a sufficient conditions to characterize programs that are not robust against LbCC relative to CbCC as illustrated in Fig. 3. The theorem follows from the fact that CbCC enforces coordination between t_1 and t_2 since they are not commutative. Thus, in an execution where t_4 observes the updates of t_1 and t_2 in this order (or observes the update of t_1 without the update of t_2), this implies that any other process must observe these two updates in this order (or cannot observe the update of t_2 without observing the update of t_1). Therefore, it is not possible for t_3 to observe the update of t_2 without observing the update of t_1 under CbCC.

However, under LbCC, no coordination is enforced between t_1 and t_2, and t_3 can observe the update of t_2 without observing the update of t_1, while t_4 observes the updates of t_1 and t_2 in this order (or observes the update of t_1 without the update of t_2). When t_1 is received, the process will undo the update of t_2, apply the update of t_1, and then redo the update of t_2.

Theorem 1. *A program $\mathcal{P}$ is not robust against LbCC relative to CbCC if there exist four transactions t_1, t_2, t_3, and t_4 in $\mathcal{P}$ that satisfy the following:*

– *t_1 and t_2 are updates that are not commutative and are initiated by different processes.*

– *t_3 distinguishes between t_2 versus t_1 and t_2.*

– *One of the following holds:*
  - *t_4 distinguishes between t_1 and t_2 versus t_2 and t_1; or*
  - *t_4 distinguishes between t_1 versus t_2 and t_1.*

Proof. Let $\mathcal{P}$ with four transactions t_1, t_2, t_3, and t_4 that satisfy the conditions in the theorem statement. The following are possible executions of $\mathcal{P}$ under LbCC:

Notice that in both executions the two queries receive the updates in different orders. In the first execution, we have $(t_1, t_3) \in$ CO and $(t_3, t_2) \in$ CF which implies that $(t_2, t_1) \notin$ ST under CbCC, otherwise, we get contradiction if $(t_2, t_1) \in$ ST resulting in $(t_2, t_1) \in$ CO under CbCC since the two transactions are not commutative. Thus, $(t_1, t_2) \in$ ST which results in a contradiction as well since $(t_2, t_4) \in$ CO and $(t_4, t_1) \in$ CF. In the second execution, we have $(t_2, t_1) \in$ ST which implies that under CbCC $(t_2, t_1) \in$ CO which contradicts the fact that we have $(t_1, t_3) \in$ CO and $(t_3, t_2) \in$ CF in the execution.

In Fig. 2a, we have four query transactions in the program which is not robust against LbCC relative to CbCC. However, note that the two query transactions t_3 and t_5 (representing t_4 and t_3 in Theorem 1, respectively) are sufficient with the two update transactions t_1 and t_2 to show that this program is not robust against LbCC relative to CbCC. In Fig. 2b, we show another program that is not robust against LbCC relative to CbCC. Note that in this program t_1 and t_2 are initiated by the same processes initiating t_4 and t_3, respectively.

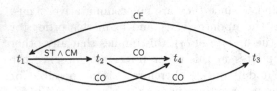 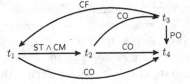

(a) T3 and T4 are initiated by different processes.

(b) T3 and T4 are initiated by the same process.

Fig. 3. Characterization of programs that are not robust against LbCC relative to CbCC.

5.2 LbCC Versus GSP

Next we present sufficient conditions to characterize programs that are not robust against LbCC relative to GSP as shown in Fig. 4. The theorem follows from the fact that GSP enforces a global sequencing between t_1 and t_2. If, in an execution, t_3 observes the update of t_2 but not the update of t_1, this implies that the server did not order t_1 before t_2 in the global sequencing of the operations.

Thus, it is not possible for t_4 to observe the update of t_1 without observing the update of t_2 under GSP semantics.

On the other hand, under LbCC semantics, since no global sequence is enforced between t_1 and t_2, t_4 can observe the update of t_1 without observing the update of t_2. When t_2 is received, the process will undo the update of t_1, apply the update of t_2, and then redo the update of t_1, assuming that t_2 is timestamped before t_1.

Theorem 2. *A program $\mathcal{P}$ is not robust against LbCC relative to GSP if there exist four transactions t_1, t_2, t_3, and t_4 in $\mathcal{P}$ that satisfy the following:*

- *t_1 and t_2 are updates related by ST and initiated by distinct processes.*
- *t_3 and t_4 are queries initiated by processes different from the processes of t_1 and t_2.*
- *t_3 distinguishes between t_2 versus t_1 and t_2.*
- *One of the following holds:*
  - *t_4 distinguishes between t_1 and t_2 versus t_2 and t_1; or*
  - *t_4 distinguishes between t_1 versus t_2 and t_1.*

Proof. Similar to before let $\mathcal{P}$ with four transactions t_1, t_2, t_3, and t_4 that satisfy the conditions in the theorem statement. The following are possible executions of $\mathcal{P}$ under LbCC:

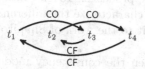

In both executions, the two queries receive the updates in different orders. In the first execution, we have $(t_1, t_3) \in$ CO and $(t_3, t_2) \in$ CF which implies that $(t_2, t_1) \notin$ ST under GSP, otherwise, we get contradiction if $(t_2, t_1) \in$ ST resulting in $(t_2, t_1) \in$ CO under GSP since the two transactions are not originating from the same processes as t_1. Thus, $(t_1, t_2) \in$ ST which results in a contradiction as well since $(t_2, t_4) \in$ CO and $(t_4, t_1) \in$ CF. Similarly, in the second execution, we have $(t_2, t_1) \in$ ST which implies that under GSP $(t_2, t_1) \in$ CO (store order relation between transactions originating from different processes implies visibility relation) which contradicts the fact that we have $(t_1, t_3) \in$ CO and $(t_3, t_2) \in$ CF in the execution.

Similar to CbCC in Fig. 2a, the two query transactions t_4 and t_5 (representing t_4 and t_3 in Theorem 2, respectively) are sufficient, along with the two update transactions t_1 and t_2, to show that this program is not robust against LbCC relative to GSP. In Fig. 2c, we present another program that is not robust against LbCC relative to GSP. It should be noted that in this program, t_1 and t_2 are commutative.

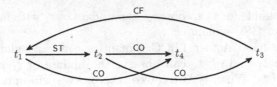

Fig. 4. Characterization of programs that are not robust against LbCC relative to GSP.

6   Related Work

There have been several studies investigating the problem of data consistency for applications that allow for concurrent modification of distributed replicas [9–11,15–17,25,26]. These works commonly examine consistency models that guarantee causal dependency and state convergence properties, as they offer a good balance between strong consistency and availability, and are suitable for various types of replicated applications. Different variations of causal consistency have been explored in the literature [6,9,10,24]. Additionally, several consistency models that ensure the state convergence property have been introduced recently [11,15–17,25].

In this paper we aimed to understand the relationships between three consistency protocols (LbCC, CbCC, and GSP) that ensure causal dependency and state convergence properties, using different approaches. To the best of our knowledge, this is the first work to classify and characterize the differences between these protocols. Our work is similar in spirit to the work of Shapiro et al. on consistency models classification [26].

In our characterization of the differences between the consistency models, we adopted a *return-value-based* robustness that is distinct from the standard *trace-based* and *state-based* robustness criterion. In state-based robustness, a program is robust iff the set of all its reachable states under the weak semantics is the same as its set of reachable states under the strong semantics. State-based robustness requires computing the set of reachable states under the weak semantics, which is in general a hard problem. Abdulla et al. [1] and Lahav and Boker [18] have investigated the decidability and the complexity computing the set of reachable states under release-acquire and causal consistency semantics, respectively, showing that it is either decidable but highly complex (non-primitive recursive), or undecidable. On the other hand, in trace-based robustness, a program is robust iff the set of all its execution traces under the weak semantics is the same as its set of execution traces under the strong semantics. Trace-based robustness has been investigated for several weak consistency models including causal consistency [2–5,7,8,13,19,22].

7   Conclusion

Towards comparing the three causal convergence consistency models, we have defined the three consistency models using a common formalism scheme allowing us to classify them. We showed that log-based causal consistency (LbCC) is the weakest while commutativity-based causal consistency (CbCC) and global sequence protocol (GSP) are incomparable. We then developed a robustness criterion based on return values to characterize programs that admit different behaviors under LbCC relative to CbCC and GSP.

In the future we plan to extend our work along a few dimensions to build on the work presented in this paper. First, we plan to investigate the relationship between the three causal consistency models and the stronger models such as prefix consistency [12] and serializability [23]. Second, we plan to develop a benchmark set of programs to compare the three causal consistency models using this benchmark set. Finally, we plan to investigate synchronization primitives to use to repair non-robust programs to become robust.

References

1. Abdulla, P.A., Arora, J., Atig, M.F., Krishna, S.N.: Verification of programs under the release-acquire semantics. In: McKinley, K.S., Fisher, K. (eds.) Proceedings of the 40th ACM SIGPLAN Conference on Programming Language Design and Implementation, PLDI 2019, Phoenix, AZ, USA, June 22–26, 2019, pp. 1117–1132. ACM (2019). https://doi.org/10.1145/3314221.3314649. https://doi.org/10.1145/3314221.3314649

2. Beillahi, S.M., Bouajjani, A., Enea, C.: Checking robustness against snapshot isolation. In: Dillig, I., Tasiran, S. (eds.) CAV 2019. LNCS, vol. 11562, pp. 286–304. Springer, Cham (2019). https://doi.org/10.1007/978-3-030-25543-5_17

3. Beillahi, S.M., Bouajjani, A., Enea, C.: Robustness against transactional causal consistency. In: Fokkink, W.J., van Glabbeek, R. (eds.) 30th International Conference on Concurrency Theory, CONCUR 2019, August 27–30, 2019, Amsterdam, the Netherlands. LIPIcs, vol. 140, pp. 30:1–30:18. Schloss Dagstuhl - Leibniz-Zentrum für Informatik (2019). https://doi.org/10.4230/LIPIcs.CONCUR.2019.30

4. Beillahi, S.M., Bouajjani, A., Enea, C.: Checking robustness between weak transactional consistency models. In: ESOP 2021. LNCS, vol. 12648, pp. 87–117. Springer, Cham (2021). https://doi.org/10.1007/978-3-030-72019-3_4

5. Bernardi, G., Gotsman, A.: Robustness against consistency models with atomic visibility. In: Desharnais, J., Jagadeesan, R. (eds.) 27th International Conference on Concurrency Theory, CONCUR 2016, August 23–26, 2016, Québec City, Canada. LIPIcs, vol. 59, pp. 7:1–7:15. Schloss Dagstuhl - Leibniz-Zentrum für Informatik (2016). https://doi.org/10.4230/LIPIcs.CONCUR.2016.7

6. Bouajjani, A., Enea, C., Guerraoui, R., Hamza, J.: On verifying causal consistency. In: Castagna, G., Gordon, A.D. (eds.) Proceedings of the 44th ACM SIGPLAN Symposium on Principles of Programming Languages, POPL 2017, Paris, France, 18–20 January 2017, pp. 626–638. ACM (2017). https://doi.org/10.1145/3009837.3009888

7. Brutschy, L., Dimitrov, D.K., Müller, P., Vechev, M.T.: Serializability for eventual consistency: criterion, analysis, and applications. In: Castagna, G., Gordon, A.D. (eds.) Proceedings of the 44th ACM SIGPLAN Symposium on Principles of Programming Languages, POPL 2017, Paris, France, 18–20 January 2017, pp. 458–472. ACM (2017). https://doi.org/10.1145/3009837.3009895

8. Brutschy, L., Dimitrov, D.K., Müller, P., Vechev, M.T.: Static serializability analysis for causal consistency. In: Foster, J.S., Grossman, D. (eds.) Proceedings of the 39th ACM SIGPLAN Conference on Programming Language Design and Implementation, PLDI 2018, Philadelphia, PA, USA, 18–22 June 2018, pp. 90–104. ACM (2018). https://doi.org/10.1145/3192366.3192415

9. Burckhardt, S.: Principles of eventual consistency. Found. Trends Program. Lang. **1**(1-2), 1–150 (2014). https://doi.org/10.1561/2500000011

10. Burckhardt, S., Gotsman, A., Yang, H., Zawirski, M.: Replicated data types: specification, verification, optimality. In: Jagannathan, S., Sewell, P. (eds.) The 41st Annual ACM SIGPLAN-SIGACT Symposium on Principles of Programming Languages, POPL 2014, San Diego, CA, USA, 20–21 January 2014, pp. 271–284. ACM (2014). https://doi.org/10.1145/2535838.2535848

11. Burckhardt, S., Leijen, D., Protzenko, J., Fähndrich, M.: Global sequence protocol: a robust abstraction for replicated shared state. In: Boyland, J.T. (ed.) 29th European Conference on Object-Oriented Programming, ECOOP 2015, 5–10 July 2015, Prague, Czech Republic. LIPIcs, vol. 37, pp. 568–590. Schloss Dagstuhl - Leibniz-Zentrum für Informatik (2015). https://doi.org/10.4230/LIPIcs.ECOOP.2015.568

12. Cerone, A., Bernardi, G., Gotsman, A.: A framework for transactional consistency models with atomic visibility. In: Aceto, L., de Frutos-Escrig, D. (eds.) 26th International Conference on Concurrency Theory, CONCUR 2015, Madrid, Spain, September 1.4, 2015. LIPIcs, vol. 42, pp. 58–71. Schloss Dagstuhl - Leibniz-Zentrum für Informatik (2015). https://doi.org/10.4230/LIPIcs.CONCUR.2015.58

13. Cerone, A., Gotsman, A.: Analysing snapshot isolation. J. ACM **65**(2), 11:1–11:41 (2018). https://doi.org/10.1145/3152396

14. Gilbert, S., Lynch, N.A.: Brewer's conjecture and the feasibility of consistent, available, partition-tolerant web services. SIGACT News **33**(2), 51–59 (2002). https://doi.org/10.1145/564585.564601

15. Houshmand, F., Lesani, M.: Hamsaz: replication coordination analysis and synthesis. Proc. ACM Program. Lang. **3**(POPL), 74:1–74:32 (2019). https://doi.org/10.1145/3290387

16. Kaki, G., Priya, S., Sivaramakrishnan, K.C., Jagannathan, S.: Mergeable replicated data types. Proc. ACM Program. Lang. 3(OOPSLA) **154**, 1–154:29 (2019). https://doi.org/10.1145/3360580

17. Kleppmann, M., Mulligan, D.P., Gomes, V.B.F., Beresford, A.R.: A highly-available move operation for replicated trees. IEEE Trans. Parallel Distributed Syst. **33**(7), 1711–1724 (2022). https://doi.org/10.1109/TPDS.2021.3118603

18. Lahav, O., Boker, U.: Decidable verification under a causally consistent shared memory. In: Donaldson, A.F., Torlak, E. (eds.) Proceedings of the 41st ACM SIGPLAN International Conference on Programming Language Design and Implementation, PLDI 2020, London, UK, 15–20 June 2020, pp. 211–226. ACM (2020). https://doi.org/10.1145/3385412.3385966

19. Lahav, O., Margalit, R.: Robustness against release/acquire semantics. In: McKinley, K.S., Fisher, K. (eds.) Proceedings of the 40th ACM SIGPLAN Conference on Programming Language Design and Implementation, PLDI 2019, Phoenix, AZ, USA, 22–26 June 2019, pp. 126–141. ACM (2019). https://doi.org/10.1145/3314221.3314604

20. Lamport, L.: Time, clocks, and the ordering of events in a distributed system. Commun. ACM **21**(7), 558–565 (1978). https://doi.org/10.1145/359545.359563

21. Li, C., Porto, D., Clement, A., Gehrke, J., Preguiça, N.M., Rodrigues, R.: Making geo-replicated systems fast as possible, consistent when necessary. In: Thekkath, C., Vahdat, A. (eds.) 10th USENIX Symposium on Operating Systems Design and Implementation, OSDI 2012, Hollywood, CA, USA, 8–10 October 2012, pp. 265–278. USENIX Association (2012), https://www.usenix.org/conference/osdi12/technical-sessions/presentation/li
22. Nagar, K., Jagannathan, S.: Automated detection of serializability violations under weak consistency. In: Schewe, S., Zhang, L. (eds.) 29th International Conference on Concurrency Theory, CONCUR 2018, 4–7 September, 2018, Beijing, China. LIPIcs, vol. 118, pp. 41:1–41:18. Schloss Dagstuhl - Leibniz-Zentrum für Informatik (2018). https://doi.org/10.4230/LIPIcs.CONCUR.2018.41
23. Papadimitriou, C.H.: The serializability of concurrent database updates. J. ACM 26(4), 631–653 (1979). https://doi.org/10.1145/322154.322158
24. Perrin, M., Mostéfaoui, A., Jard, C.: Causal consistency: beyond memory. In: Asenjo, R., Harris, T. (eds.) Proceedings of the 21st ACM SIGPLAN Symposium on Principles and Practice of Parallel Programming, PPoPP 2016, Barcelona, Spain, 12–16 March 2016, pp. 26:1–26:12. ACM (2016). https://doi.org/10.1145/2851141.2851170, https://doi.org/10.1145/2851141.2851170
25. Preguiça, N.M., Baquero, C., Shapiro, M.: Conflict-free replicated data types (crdts). CoRR abs/1805.06358 (2018). http://arxiv.org/abs/1805.06358
26. Shapiro, M., Ardekani, M.S., Petri, G.: Consistency in 3d. In: Desharnais, J., Jagadeesan, R. (eds.) 27th International Conference on Concurrency Theory, CONCUR 2016, August 23–26, 2016, Québec City, Canada. LIPIcs, vol. 59, pp. 3:1–3:14. Schloss Dagstuhl - Leibniz-Zentrum für Informatik (2016). https://doi.org/10.4230/LIPIcs.CONCUR.2016.3

Security and Privacy

Encrypted Search: Not Enough to Ensure Privacy*

Achraf Nia[1]($\boxtimes$), Hossam Tarouchi[1], and Mohammed Erradi[2]

[1] Henceforth, Rabat, Morocco
a.nia@henceforth.ma
[2] ENSIAS, Mohammed V University of Rabat, Rabat, Morocco

Abstract. The success of most recent end-to-end encrypted messaging applications (such as whatsApp, signal, etc...) is due to the fact that they rely on sound cryptographic primitives and protocols to provide a high level of data protection. The massive use of these applications leads to an abundance of encrypted messages that need to be stored and retrieved upon user requests. This leads to a heavy burden on mobile phones storage resources which could be solved by using a server store.

However, the server store could not be trusted, and message encryption is not enough to ensure privacy protection. Indeed, even if the content is encrypted, the underlying metadata (such as the number of which a keyword has been searched, Timestamps, which user searched for which keyword) can reveal private and confidential information which can be exploited against the user will.

In this work, we suggest an approach using the private information retrieval technique widely used in the area of information retrieval. Private Information Retrieval (PIR) provides a way to retrieve encrypted content from a server. Initially, an encrypted search query is sent to the server. Then, the server replies without knowing neither the keyword to be searched for, nor the identity of the user conducting the search. Thus, we adapt PIR technique to provide an algorithm for searching encrypted messages without revealing Metadata.

Keywords: Encrypted search · Privacy · Metadata · Private information retrieval

1 Introduction

Instant messaging applications are gaining more attention than ever. Their popularity is mainly due to the protection of users privacy by mean of end-to-end encryption. Making them widely used, not only by individuals, but also by public organizations and businesses seeking privacy and confidentiality of the exchanged information among their employees. This blind trust for these messaging application results in the tremendous increase of users.

To search and retrieve messages, these instant messaging applications provide a built in feature for this purpose. Such encrypted search feature performs its

---

* Supported by Henceforth

D. Mohaisen and T. Wies (Eds.): NETYS 2023, LNCS 14067, pp. 81–89, 2023.
https://doi.org/10.1007/978-3-031-37765-5_6

computation on those messages stored in the mobile phone while using a local search process. However, the huge quantity of exchanged messages leads to a saturation of phones storage. In addition to the storage burden, when a user loses his/her phone, he loses all his messages. While most end-to-end encrypted instant messaging applications store an encrypted copy in the cloud, the search feature isn't available until all of the messages are fetched, which is time and storage consuming. Indeed, integrating such functionality requires storing all messages in the user mobile store as plain text. Thus compromising the security of the conversations if the phone ends up in the wrong hands.

In this work, we present an approach where we store users data over servers with a consequent storage capacity. And thus, the limitation given by popular instant messaging application such as weekly backup creation, and searching for messages only available locally on the mobile phone, can be solved.

The main contribution of this work is providing both content and metadata privacy for encrypted search. For content privacy, the content -the message being searched and the server response- must remain unknown to the server and adversaries. As for the metadata, the system must provide *relationship unobservability* between users and the desired retrieved item from the server.

In the following, Sects. 2 presents the goals and threat model of the suggested approach. Section 3 proposes an architecture and describe the protocol by giving a brief introduction to the PIR scheme and explaining the main phases of our approach.

2   Goals and Threat Model

In this section, we present the goals and threat model of our proposed work. Thus, by explaining how to guaranty privacy of users while hiding metadata from adversaries, whom may compromise the entirety of the system.

2.1   Goals

Content Privacy. Only the user searching for a message should have access to the message content. Searching for a message must provide a user with full privacy, without the server knowing the content of the message.

Metadata Privacy. Guarantee *relationship unobservability* and hide metadata from malicious adversaries. Relationship unobservability refers to the ability to conceal and obscure the connections and relationship between different individuals or entities. Its goal is to prevent identification of sensitive or personal information that could be used to compromise the privacy or security of individuals.

Metadata related to encrypted search provides information about the data itself even if encrypted, such as:

- *Users personal information:* Information about the user conducting the search, his username, email and IP address. Which helps to identify and track him.

- *Timestamps:* Reveals when a message has been searched, sent and received. Which can provide information about the timing of a communication or the activity of the parties involved.
- *Message size and attachments:* The size of a message and attachments can indicate the type and amount of data being transmitted. Which can help deduct its content
- *Metadata embedded in attachments:* Attachments contain metadata such as file name, creation date, author username. Which can reveal information about the content and the sender.

Metadata can reveal information about the communication and the content of messages. This metadata can be exploited by malicious parties to gain insight into the activity of an individual or a company, leading to privacy breach and confidential data disclosure. Thus, securing it is a must to provide overall privacy.

2.2 Threat Model

In this proposed work, we give the following assumptions about the threat model.

- We assume a honest but curious adversary who can observe the network traffic, and perform traffic analysis (Fig. 1). This adversary doesn't have any malicious or harmful intentions, but has a desire to learn more about the system and exploit potential vulnerabilities.
- Users trust their own devices. More generally, an adversary can compromise a device, but the metadata and privacy of non-compromised devices must be provided.
- The adversary may not break standard cryptographic primitives such as public-key and symmetric-key encryption.

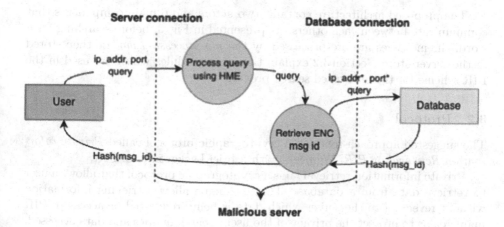

Fig. 1. Threat model.

3   Architecture and Protocol

3.1   Architecture

The architecture of the suggested approach relies on the interaction between user devices and a server which holds a mailbox structure as defined within the private information retrieval technique. The server runs over untrusted infrastructure which role is to facilitate encrypted search in a privacy-preserving manner.

The server uses the *mailbox* principle with n mailboxes, where n is the number of messages stored in the server. Each mailbox can store a message identifier and it has an ID, which is the word sent and stored. Basically, this mailbox is a virtual container used to store messages that users want to retrieve privately from the server without revealing the identity of the request data or the search query used to retrieve it. Figure 2 shows the basic communication between two users, where the message id column of the stored table represents the mailbox where user will store and retrieve the desired items.

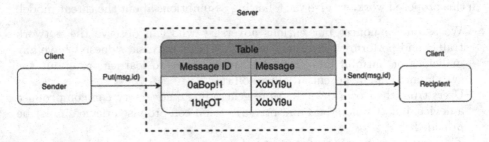

Fig. 2. Mailbox based communication.

The proposed architecture contains two actors and 6 main components that communicate between each others. As presented in Fig. 3, before searching for a word, the messages are pre-processed by the *pre-processing module* then stored in the server store. Section 3.2 explain the other modules which are used in the PIR scheme for the encrypted search process.

3.2   Protocol

The suggested approach relies on a cryptographic protocol called *Private information Retrieval* or *PIR*. We begin with a brief background of PIR.

Private information retrieval [4] is a cryptographic protocol that allows a user to retrieve data from a database. This technique allow retrieving information without revealing to the server which data is being requested or accessed. PIR main goal is to protect the privacy of the user's search queries and data accessed, while allowing efficient data retrieval.

In a PIR scheme, the user sends encrypted search queries to the server, which responses with encrypted data. By using encryption and other cryptohraphic

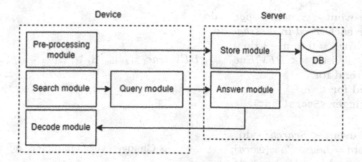

Fig. 3. Global architecture of the communication between the different components.

techniques, PIR ensures that the server cannot observe or infer the search queries or data being requested by the user.

A PIR Protocol has three main phases: *Query, answer, decode*. Using these three steps, we will try to adapt PIR to our problematic by beginning with pre-processing the messages before sending them to the server.

Pre-processing Phase. Upon sending a message, it will be split into distinct words (line 2 Fig. 5). Each word will be encrypted using an homomorphic encryption scheme and then stored with its message id. Even if this server is malicious, the content of the message won't be revealed. Homomorphic encryption enables computation to be performed on encrypted data without requiring the data to be decrypted first. Thus, using Brakerski-Fan-Vercauteren encryption offers the possibility to perform operations on the cipher text obtained in the pre-processing phase.

The user can later search for a specified message stored in the store by sending a query to the server. Figure 4 illustrate how the messages are pre-processes before being sent and stored in the server.

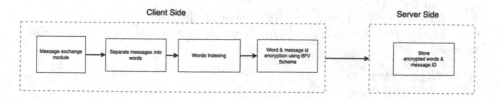

Fig. 4. Pre-processing module.

Query Phase. Upon searching for a word, using a query, the user will be able to retrieve a particular item from the store without revealing to the database which item is requested. After encoding and encrypting the query using homomorphic

```
1: upon event < SendMessage > do
2:     for each word in message do
3:         for i = 0 to n − 1 do
4:             list[i] =< BFV.Enc_(word), BFV.Enc_(messageID) >;
5:         end for
6:     end for
7:     Trigger <Store(list)>
8:
9: upon event < Search > do
10:     word = LowerCase(word);              ▷ Change every character to lower case
11:     for each char in word do
12:         if char = space then
13:             word = word.remove(char);     ▷ remove spaces from word
14:         end if
15:     end for
16:     Trigger <QUERY>
```

Fig. 5. Pre-processing phase algorithm

encryption (line 3 Fig. 6), the server will process the query so it can retrieve the message id of the desired word, without revealing or knowing the content of the query [1].

Using BFV homomorphic encryption scheme (line 6 Fig. 6), the query is encrypted and sent to the server to be processed. Homomorphic encryption [3] basically allows certain mathematical operations to be performed on encrypted data without decrypting it. In other words, homomorphic encryption allows computations to be performed on encrypted data directly, which makes it possible to keep the data private even while performing computations on it.

```
1: upon event < QUERY > do
2:     for i = 0 to n − 1 do
3:         f(i) = (i == word)?1 : 0;  ▷ Create a one-hot encoding of the desired word
4:     end for
5:     for i = 0 to N − 1 do // N is BFV plaintext dimension
6:         q_i = BFV.Enc(p_k, f_(i.n), ..., f_((i+1).N−1));  ▷ split and encrypt the one-hot
    vector
7:     end for
8:     Trigger <ANSWER>
```

Fig. 6. Query phase algorithm

Answer Phase. The answer phase in PIR is the phase where the database sends the requested information back to the user in a secure and private manner (Fig. 8). Once the server retrieve the specified message id using BFV homomorphic operation in the encrypted query and database (line 7,8,9,13 and 16 Fig. 7), the answer is encrypted once more to ensure that it can't be intercepted or modified in transit by a third party. The encrypted result, is then sent back to the user who can decrypt it to obtain the desired result.

```
 1: upon event < ANSWER > do
 2:    // L is a matrix of elements in Z_p : L ∈ Z^{n×m}
 3:    // q is the output of the Query function
 4:    for i = 0 to m - 1 do
 5:        sum_j = BFV.ENC(p_k, 0);
 6:        for j = 0 to N - 1 do
 7:            p_{ij} = BFV.SubMat(L);
 8:            t_{ij} = BFV.Mult(p_{ij}, q_i);
 9:            sum_j = BFV.ADD(sum_j, t_{ij});
10:        end for
11:    end for
12:    for j = 0 to N - 1 do
13:        sum_j = BFV.RowRotate(sum_j, j);        ▷ combine output from all columns
14:    end for
15:    for i = 0 to m - 1 do
16:        Answer = BFV.ADD(sum_i);                ▷ combine output from all rows
17:    end for
18:    Trigger <DECODE>
```

Fig. 7. *Answer* phase algorithm, (P_k, S_k) are (public, private) key pair for BFV scheme. SubMat extracts a sub matrix of a matrix

Decode Phase. After receiving the answer from the server, the client can decrypt and decode the result (line 2 Fig. 9), this result consists of the desired message id of the specified word given to the query. The client can then show each message containing the specified word. Figure 8 shows the interaction between the different PIR modules.

Using Private Information Retrieval, the server, even if malicious, doesn't know neither which word is being searched, nor information about the user.

At a high level architecture of Encrypted search using PIR. The client is responsible for the message pre-processing, the query creation and the decoding of the result. While the server stores the data and answer the query. Even if the server has access to the database, the content is encrypted and the privacy is ensured.

4   Related Work

Clusion [6] is an open source encrypted search library created and maintained by the Encrypted Systems Lab at Brown University. It focuses on the

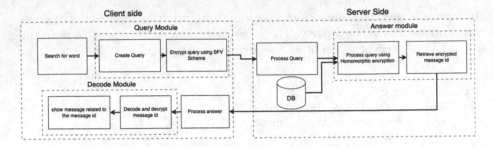

Fig. 8. Query, answer and decode module.

1: **upon event** $< DECODE >$ **do**
2:     Result $= BFV.DECODE(Answer, S_k)$;
3:     **Trigger <Display>**

Fig. 9. *Decode* phase algorithm.

encrypted search on the client side. It implements state-of-the-art and highly-efficient searchable symmetric encryption. Although the suggested approach provides a way for encrypted search over a server while securing users metadata, it doesn't replace local encrypted search solutions which doesn't involve a third party. Indeed, both local or remote encrypted search have their own limitation depending on the type of adversary and the intended use of it.

Addra [2] provides a way to secure metadata related to voice communication over fully untrusted servers. Addra uses FastPIR which is a computational private information retrieval (CPIR) library which is specialized to reduce response generation time by the PIR server. While Addra focuses on the voice communication privacy, this work uses PIR for the encrypted search privacy.

Spiral [7] is a demo which allows private access to 6 GB (30%) of English Wikipedia. In theory, even if the server is malicious, it will be unable to learn which articles the user request. Spiral consist of retrieving a whole document from a single word without revealing the user interest (latency is 4 sec after the first query). In the proposed approach, the latency can be greatly improved thanks to the size of the response which is a simple encrypted message id instead of a whole document.

5   Conclusion and Future Work

Encryption alone can't guarantee the privacy of the users of End to End encryption messaging applications. Even without knowing the content of the data, metadata provides enough information to provide context, describe the characteristics of the data and who has access to it. Thus, providing confidentiality and privacy is crucial in the majority of professional fields [5], such as health care or private instant messaging, where users can query their private information without compromising their own privacy and indentity. In this work, we have shown how to ensure privacy in encryption search by using Private Information Retrieval scheme.

Future work involves using new PIR schemes, such as FastPIR [2], in instant messaging applications in order to provide a new way to search over encryted messages so as to improve the performance while improving privacy for users.

References

1. Ahmad, I., Sarker, L., Agrawal, D., El Abbadi, A., Gupta, T.: Coeus: a system for oblivious document ranking and retrieval. In: Proceedings of the ACM SIGOPS 28th Symposium on Operating Systems Principles, pp. 672–690 (2021)
2. Ahmad, I., Yang, Y., Agrawal, D., El Abbadi, A., Gupta, T.: Addra: metadata-private voice communication over fully untrusted infrastructure. In: 15th USENIX Symposium on Operating Systems Design and Implementation, OSDI2021, 14–16 July 2021 (2021)
3. Albrecht, M., et al.: Homomorphic encryption security standard. Homomorphic Encryption. org, Toronto, Canada, Technical report 11 (2018)
4. Chor, B., Kushilevitz, E., Goldreich, O., Sudan, M.: Private information retrieval. J. ACM (JACM) 45(6), 965–981 (1998)
5. Greschbach, B., Kreitz, G., Buchegger, S.: The devil is in the metadata-new privacy challenges in decentralised online social networks. In: 2012 IEEE international conference on Pervasive Computing and Communications Workshops, pp. 333–339. IEEE (2012)
6. Kamara, S., Moataz, T.: Boolean searchable symmetric encryption with worst-case sub-linear complexity. In: Coron, J.-S., Nielsen, J.B. (eds.) EUROCRYPT 2017. LNCS, vol. 10212, pp. 94–124. Springer, Cham (2017). https://doi.org/10.1007/978-3-319-56617-7_4
7. Menon, S.J., Wu, D.J.: Spiral: Fast, high-rate single-server pir via fhe composition. In: 2022 IEEE Symposium on Security and Privacy (SP), pp. 930–947. IEEE (2022)

Case Study on the Performance of ML-Based Network Intrusion Detection Systems in SDN

Adnane Mzibri[✉], Redouane Benaini, and Mouad Ben Mamoun

ANISSE, Faculty of Sciences, Mohammed V University in Rabat, Agdal,
10000 Rabat, Morocco
adnane_mzibri@um5.ac.ma

Abstract. SDN enables centralized control of network services by separating control and data planes, providing greater flexibility and scalability in network traffic management. However, this architecture also creates new security challenges, such as a single point of failure that can compromise the entire network. Furthermore, the dynamic environment of SDN makes it difficult to adapt an effective and efficient anomaly-based IDS. A high-performance Machine Learning (ML)-based IDS can meet these challenges, but careful consideration is required in algorithm selection, data preprocessing, feature engineering, and model architecture. In this article, we conducted a comparative study of several ML models on the InSDN dataset. The results showed that the DT model performs well with only 7 out of the 83 features in the InSDN dataset, reducing the training time from 10 to 0.5 s.

Keywords: Machine Learning · SDN · IDS · Decision Tree Classifier

1 Introduction

SDN [1] is a modern networking architecture that offers increased agility, flexibility, and scalability compared to traditional networks [2,3]. However, it is also vulnerable to cyber attacks. In fact, SDN networks may be more susceptible to malicious traffic than traditional environments, as attackers can potentially target the SDN controller and cause damage to the entire network.

Traditional security measures like firewalls are no longer sufficient to ensure system security, and IDSs are essential for monitoring network traffic and detecting malicious activities or policy violations. However, IDSs have limitations such as false positives, false negatives, complex configuration, and a limited scope. Machine learning models can overcome these drawbacks by classifying abnormal traffic as an anomaly with self-learning capabilities. Many supervised learning models have been adopted for detecting network traffic anomalies [6–10].

Developing IDSs for SDN networks using machine learning techniques is an active area of research [4]. ML-based IDSs can dynamically adjust their behavior in response to changing traffic patterns within the network, enabling them to be more adaptable to evolving security threats.

D. Mohaisen and T. Wies (Eds.): NETYS 2023, LNCS 14067, pp. 90–95, 2023.
https://doi.org/10.1007/978-3-031-37765-5_7

This paper aims to compare the Random Forest (RF), Adaboost, and Decision Tree (DT) ML models to determine the best candidate for developing a high-performance and resource-efficient ML-based IDS capable of detecting potential security threats in SDNs in real-time. The remainder of this paper is organized as follows: Sect. 2 is devoted to some works on the performance of ML-based IDS. Section 3 presents the tools used and simulation results. Finally, we provide some conclusions in Sect. 4.

2   Related Work

Machine learning techniques are commonly used to develop IDSs for SDN networks. Almseidin et al. [6] evaluated the performance of different classification algorithms using public datasets and found that DT had the lowest false negative rate and a low time demand. Ajaeiya et al. [7] proposed an IDS solution for SDN networks that utilizes statistical information from OF switches and SVM algorithm to detect potential attacks. Yang et al. [8] proposed a 3-module based IDS model for DDoS attack detection in SDN networks using SVM algorithm. Aiken et al. [9] proposed an IDS for SDN that utilizes an anomaly-based network IDS module named Neptune and an adversarial test module named Hydra, and they found that RF achieved the best outcome in terms of detection accuracy. Santos et al. [10] compared the performance of four ML methods in detecting DDoS attacks in a simulated SDN environment and found that RF achieved the best accuracy while DT had the best efficiency in processing time. All the previous works cited utilize datasets based on a traditional network, our study is conducted on the InSDN dataset [5], which is based on an SDN network.

3   Case Study and Experimental Results

In this study, we employed three supervised ML algorithms: DT, RF and AdaBoost. To select the algorithms for the comparative study, we conducted several tests on different ML algorithms using the InSDN dataset and chose the aforementioned three for their reduced execution time and their high performance based on F1-score, accuracy, recall, and precision. We used the feature selection method to keep only the relevant features for each algorithm. The selected features for each model are described in Table 2, while the default parameters are used for all implemented algorithms. To train the classifiers, we used the cross-validation technique with K = 4, where the training and test data were split into 80% and 20%, respectively.

3.1   Data Collection and Preparation

The InSDN dataset contains network traffic data collected from a virtual SDN testbed that simulates various types of attacks, including DoS, DDoS, port scans, and botnet attacks, among others. The dataset also includes normal network traffic, we refer to ElSayed et al. [5]. In order to improve the suitability of our dataset, first, we removed all features that consistently had a value of null. Additionally, we encoded the normal and abnormal labels as 0 and 1, respectively, since ML classifiers cannot handle strings.

Table 1. A list of features of the InSDN dataset.

N	Feature	N	Feature	N	Feature	N	Feature
1	Flow ID	22	Flow Pkts/s	43	Fwd Pkts/s	64	Fwd Blk Rate Avg
2	Src IP	23	Flow IAT Mean	44	Bwd Pkts/s	65	Bwd Byts/b Avg
3	Src Port	24	Flow IAT Std	45	Pkt Len Min	66	Bwd Pkts/b Avg
4	Dst IP	25	Flow IAT Max	46	Pkt Len Max	67	Bwd Blk Rate Avg
5	Dst Port	26	Flow IAT Min	47	Pkt Len Mean	68	Subflow Fwd Pkts
6	Protocol	27	Fwd IAT Tot	48	Pkt Len Std	69	Subflow Fwd Byts
7	Timestamp	28	Fwd IAT Mean	49	Pkt Len Var	70	Subflow Bwd Pkts
8	Flow Duration	29	Fwd IAT Std	50	FIN Flag Cnt	71	Subflow Bwd Byts
9	Tot Fwd Pkts	30	Fwd IAT Max	51	SYN Flag Cnt	72	Init Fwd Win Byts
10	Tot Bwd Pkts	31	Fwd IAT Min	52	RST Flag Cnt	73	Init Bwd Win Byts
11	TotLen Fwd Pkts	32	Bwd IAT Tot	53	PSH Flag Cnt	74	Fwd Act Data Pkts
12	TotLen Bwd Pkts	33	Bwd IAT Mean	54	ACK Flag Cnt	75	Fwd Seg Size Min
13	Fwd Pkt Len Max	34	Bwd IAT Std	55	URG Flag Cnt	76	Active Mean
14	Fwd Pkt Len Min	35	Bwd IAT Max	56	CWE Flag Count	77	Active Std
15	Fwd Pkt Len Mean	36	Bwd IAT Min	57	ECE Flag Cnt	78	Active Max
16	Fwd Pkt Len Std	37	Fwd PSH Flags	58	Down/Up Ratio	79	Active Min
17	Bwd Pkt Len Max	38	Bwd PSH Flags	59	Pkt Size Avg	80	Idle Mean
18	Bwd Pkt Len Min	39	Fwd URG Flags	60	Fwd Seg Size Avg	81	Idle Std
19	Bwd Pkt Len Mean	40	Bwd URG Flags	61	Bwd Seg Size Avg	82	Idle Max
20	Bwd Pkt Len Std	41	Fwd Header Len	62	Fwd Byts/b Avg	83	Idle Min
21	Flow Byts/s	42	Bwd Header Len	63	Fwd Pkts/b Avg	84	**Label**

3.2   Feature Selection

We utilized feature selection to reduce the number of input variables in predictive modeling, which can improve performance and reduce computational cost. Specifically, we used the SelectKBest.f-classif() function from Python's SciKit-Learn library to eliminate non-informative features. The best features selected for DT model using this method are shown in Fig. 1. Similar procedures were used to select the best variables for other algorithms, and the results are summarized in Table 2. In this table, "Id of selected features" refers to the attribute number instead of its name. To see the mapping of numbers to names of the selected features, refer to Table 1.

Table 2. Feature selection.

ML model	ID of selected features	Nbr of selected features
RF	42 - 17 - 18 - 19 - 61 - 26 - 41 - 30 - 13 - 14 - 15 - 60 - 73 - 45 - 46 - 47 - 48 - 49 - 59 - 6 - 51 - 68 - 69 - 68 - 69 - 10 - 9 - 11	28
DT	26 - 42 - 44 - 46 - 49 - 73 - 79	7
Adaboost	54 - 78 - 79 - 42 - 35 - 36 - 44 - 58 - 50 - 21 - 26 - 41 - 28 - 29 - 13 - 43 - 80 - 73 - 45 - 46 - 47 - 48 - 51	24

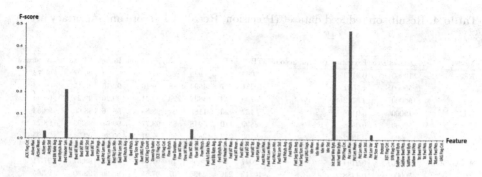

Fig. 1. Bar chart of DTC feature importance scores.

3.3 Experimental Results

All experiments were conducted on a workstation machine with the following specifications: Intel(R) UHD Graphics 620, I7-8650U CPU @ 1.90GHz (8 cores), 2.1 GHz, running Windows 10 Pro 64-bit with 16 GB of RAM. Table 3 given below presents the results of ML models (RF, DT and Adaboost) on the entire InSDN dataset.

Table 3. Results on entire InSDN dataset (Precision, Recall, F1_score and Accuracy are in %).

Model	Dataset size	execution time [in Second]	TP	FP	TN	FN	Precision	Recall	F1_score	Accuracy
RFC	10000	0.5466	2054	2	943	1	99.90	99.95	99.93	99.90
	50000	3.0521	10316	2	4679	3	99.98	99.97	99.98	99.97
	150000	10.8060	30925	5	14066	4	99.98	99.99	99.99	99.98
DTC	10000	0.0778	2055	4	939	2	99.81	99.90	99.85	99.80
	50000	0.4146	10315	9	4672	4	99.91	99.96	99.94	99.91
	150000	1.7378	30928	11	14058	3	99.96	99.99	99.98	99.97
	300000	10.1761	72254	6	17734	6	99.99	99.99	99.99	99.98
ADABOOST	10000	0.8521	2054	3	942	2	99.85	99.90	99.88	99.83
	50000	4.1684	10316	8	4673	3	99.92	99.97	99.95	99.93
	150000	13.4573	30910	23	14048	19	99.93	99.94	99.93	99.91

Table 4 given below presents the results of ML models (RF, DT and Adaboost respectively) on the reduced datasets consisting of (28, 7 and 24 features respectively).

The results show that reducing the number of available features (83) to a much smaller number (7) does not significantly degrade performance in terms of precision, recall, and F1-score measures. However, it does significantly reduce execution time. In the case of 150,000 rows, RF, Adaboost, and DT display in Table 3 respective execution times of 10.8, 14.45, and 1.73 s for the entire dataset, compared to 4.87, 12.3, and 0.1 s respectively with the reduced datasets displayed in Table 4. Even with 300,000 rows, the DT model takes only 0.52 s

Table 4. Results on reduced dataset (Precision, Recall, F1_score and Accuracy are in %).

Model	Dataset size	Execution time [in Second]	TP	FP	TN	FN	Precision	Recall	F1_score	Accuracy
RF	10000	0.3182	2033	14	929	24	99.32	98.83	99.07	98.73
	50000	1.6031	10231	87	4594	88	99.16	99.15	99.15	98.83
	150000	4.8722	30700	243	13837	229	99.21	99.26	99.24	98.95
DT	10000	0.0169	162	26	1188	24	98.55	98.66	98.60	98.33
	50000	0.0568	8859	110	5948	83	98.77	99.07	98.92	98.71
	150000	0.1362	30700	243	13837	229	99.21	99.26	99.24	98.95
	300000	0.5216	72172	88	17653	87	99.87	99.87	99.87	99.80
ADABOOST	10000	0.2194	2047	58	858	10	97.24	99.51	98.37	97.71
	50000	0.7388	10212	246	4435	107	97.65	98.96	98.30	97.65
	150000	2.3582	30735	758	13313	176	97.59	99.43	98.50	97.92

in execution time. This indicates that the DT-based model outperformed other models in terms of performance and training time when a reduced number of features were used.

4   Conclusion

In this study, we performed a comparative analysis of various machine learning techniques for network intrusion detection using the InSDN dataset. The results obtained from the experiments on the full and reduced datasets showed that algorithms do not depend on all 83 features, and a reduced number of features can yield better results while requiring fewer resources. The study concluded that the DT classifier outperformed other models by using only 7 features, resulting in a significant reduction in training time. Further research will explore newer techniques to enhance the classification and detection of unknown attacks.

References

1. McKeown, N.: Software-defined networking. INFOCOM keynote talk **17**(2), 30–32 (2009)
2. Bilal, O., Ben mamoun M., Benaini, R.: An overview on SDN architectures with multiple controllers. Comput. Networks Commun. (2016). Article ID 9396525 (2016). https://doi.org/10.1155/2016/9396525
3. Benamrane, F., Ben mamoun, M., Benaini, R.: An east-west interface for distributed SDN control plane: implementation and evaluation. Comput. Electr. Eng. **57**, 162–175 (2017)
4. Chica, J. C. C., Imbachi, J. C., Vega, J. F. B.: Security in SDN: a comprehensive survey. J. Network Comput. Appl. **159** (2020). https://doi.org/10.1016/j.jnca.2020.102595
5. Elsayed, M. S., Le-Khac, N. -A., Jurcut, A. D.: InSDN: A Novel SDN Intrusion Dataset. IEEE Access **8**, 165263–165284 (2020). https://doi.org/10.1109/ACCESS.2020.3022633

6. Almseidin, M., Alzubi, M., Kovacs, S., Alkasassbeh, M.: Evaluation of machine learning algorithms for intrusion detection system. In: Procedings of 15th International Symposium on Intelligent Systems and Informatics (SISY) IEEE, Subotica, Serbia, pp. 000277–000282 (2017). https://doi.org/10.1109/SISY.2017.8080566
7. Ajaeiya, G. A., Adalian, N., Elhajj, I. H., Kayssi, A., Chehab, A.: Flow-based intrusion detection system for SDN. In: Proceedings of 2017 IEEE Symposium on Computers and Communications (ISCC), Heraklion, Greece, pp. 787–793 (2017). https://doi.org/10.1109/ISCC.2017.8024623
8. Yang, L., Zhao, H.: DDoS attack identification and defense using SDN based on machine learning method. In: Proceedings of 15th International Symposium on Pervasive Systems, Algorithms and Networks (I-SPAN), Yichang, China, pp. 174–178 (2018). https://doi.org/10.1109/I-SPAN.2018.00036
9. Aiken, J., Sandra, S.-H.: Investigating adversarial attacks against network intrusion detection systems in SDNs. In: IEEE Conference on Network Functions Virtualization and Software Defined Networks (NFV-SDN), Dallas, TX, USA, pp. 1–7 (2019)
10. Santos, R., Souza, D., Santo, W., Ribeiro, A., Moreno, E.: Machine learning algorithms to detect DDoS attacks in SDN. Concurr. Comput. Pract. Exp. **16**, 1–14, (32) (2020)

Beyond Locks and Keys: Structural Equation Modeling Based Framework to Explore Security Breaches Through the Lens of Crime Theories

Narjisse Nejjari[1,2]([✉]), Karim Zkik[3], Houda Benbrahim[1], and Mounir Ghogho[2]

[1] IRDA, Rabat IT Center, ENSIAS, Mohammed V University, Rabat, Morocco
v-narjisse.nejjari@uir.ac.ma
[2] TicLAB, International University of Rabat, Sale El Jadida, Morocco
[3] ESAIP, Ecole d'Ingenieur, CERADE Angers, Saint-Barthélemy-d'Anjou, France

Abstract. The current evolution of the cyber-threat ecosystem shows that no organization can be considered invulnerable against security breach. It is therefore important to highlight exogenous factors other than those related to an organization's security posture to predict security breach incidents.

We present "Beyond Locks and Keys", a framework that analyzes the projection of crime theories applied in science of victimology, to study the risk of victimization to security breach in cyber space. Factors that could be associated to information security breach in organizations are studied through hypotheses extracted from crime theories. Victimization risk analysis is built by creating a comprehensive profile for each organization, capturing its characteristics, and grouping them in constructs used to measure the likelihood of data breach. We use structural equation modeling and statistical hypothesis testing approach to build our framework. We evaluate the validity of our model on a dataset of 4868 organizations based in the United states (US) collected between the years 2018 and 2020.

"Beyond Locks and Keys" highlights the importance of exogenous factors, besides the technical security ones, that contribute to the understanding of victimization risk to security breach.

Keywords: Security breach · Crime theory · Structural equation modeling

1 Introduction

The United States has seen a notable increase in data theft incidents in 2022, with an average cost per breach of $4.35 million [1,2]. Nearly two-thirds of US companies suffered at least one data breach in recent years [3]. To mitigate the consequences, the US federal agency recommends that organizations engage with academic researchers and experts to develop effective solutions for assessing and mitigating the damages caused by security breaches [4]. While many studies have investigated the type and location of data breaches [5–11], few have considered the exogenous factors that may contribute to victimization.

© The Author(s), under exclusive license to Springer Nature Switzerland AG 2023
D. Mohaisen and T. Wies (Eds.): NETYS 2023, LNCS 14067, pp. 96–101, 2023.
https://doi.org/10.1007/978-3-031-37765-5_8

In the field of crime theory, previous research has mainly focused on "lifestyle" or "routine activity" theories but has not explicitly addressed the connection between the victim's behavior and opportunities for victimization in the realm of data security [12–17]. This research aims to fill this gap by employing modern crime theory to identify and explore factors that may increase the likelihood of security breach.

In this research work, we examine whether constructs derived from crime theory, including attractiveness, visibility, and the level of guardianship, can be used to predict the occurrence of data breaches. To evaluate the validity of our model, we collecte multivariate data on both victim and non-victim organizations, and analyze them using the theories proposed by crime theory.

The remainder of this paper is organized as follows. In the next section, we present the research methodology. We evaluate and asses the validity of our model in the next section. Finally, we conclude and present limitations.

2   Research Methodology

In this section, we present the scenario of the research methodology conducted to build Beyond Locks and Keys framework (see Fig. 1).

2.1   Data Collection and Processing

To test the proposed model, we utilized web scraping techniques to collect data from various publicly available sources. The dataset covers the period between January 2018 and November 2020 and includes 4868 organizations. We collect over 60 variables that detailed various characteristics of each organization.

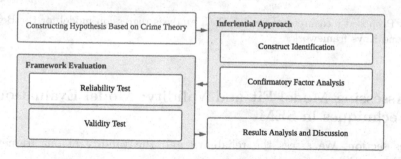

Fig. 1. Beyond Locks and Keys framework: Scenario of the research methodology

2.2   Structural Equation Modeling

This section explains Structural Equation Modeling (SEM), used to examine relationships between latent constructs and observed variables. The goal is to estimate factor loadings, structural path coefficients, and error variances that fit the data. Factor Analysis of Mixed Data (FAMD) is used for construct identification, and Confirmatory Factor Analysis (CFA) estimates factor loadings through Maximum Likelihood Estimation.

2.3 Proposed Measurement Model

The measurement model used to examine the causal relationships is:

$$Y = \text{Likelihood of security breach occurrence} =$$
$$\varepsilon + \Lambda_1(\text{Atractiveness}) + \Lambda_2(\text{Visibility}) + \Lambda_3(\text{Guardianship})$$

where Y is the likelihood of security breach occurrence which is the outcome endogenous variable, and the X_i variables are the independent predictor variables affecting Y, and the Λ_i values, the beta values, are the coefficients of the predictor's contribution to the outcome variable's variation. The model error terms residual is represented by ε.

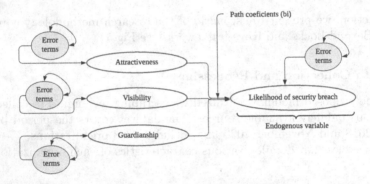

Fig. 2. Proposed measurement model: Path analysis regression model for the Beyond Locks and Keys framework

3   Assessing Model Fit and Validity: Model Evaluation Techniques in SEM

In this section, We assess the reliability and the validity of our framework throught multiple statistical tests.

3.1 Reliability Tests

Cronbach's alpha measures the degree to which items in the scale are interrelated, or how consistently they measure the same underlying construct [18]. Cronbach's alpha test can be mathematically formulated as follows:

$$\alpha = K(K-1)/\left[K - \Sigma\lambda_i + \Sigma(\lambda_i)^2\right]$$

where K is the number of items in the scale, λ_i i is the factor loading of the i-th item on the latent construct, and Σ represents the summation across all i items.

Composite reliability we use this test to evaluate the stability and consistency of our proposed model. Composite reliability can be mathematically formulated as follows [19]:

$$\rho c = \Sigma(\lambda_i)^2 / \left[\Sigma(\lambda_i)^2 + \Sigma(\sigma_i)^2 \right]$$

where λ_i is the standardized factor loading of the i-th item on the latent construct, $(\sigma_i)^2$ is the residual variance of the i-th item, and Σ represents the summation across all i items. Results suggested in Table 1 demonstrate an acceptable reliability for the items in the three constructs.

Table 1. Reliability tests and Average Variance Extracted (AVE).

Likelihood of security breach			
	Cronbach's Alpha	Composite Reliability	Average Variance Extracted (AVE)
Attractiveness	0.877	0.902	0.715
Visibility	0.784	0.781	0.542
Level of guardianship	0.817	0.827	0.503

3.2 Validity Tests

The fit of our over-identified model can be evaluated through a variety of fit indices, including the Chi-square test, Comparative Fit Index (CFI), Tucker-Lewis Index (TLI), Root Mean Square Error of Approximation (RMSEA), and Standardized Root Mean Squared Residual (SRMR) [20] (Table 2).

Table 2. CFA model fit measures.

	Comparative Fit Index (CFI)	Tucker-Lewis index (TLI)	Root Mean Square Error of Approximation (RMSEA)	Standardized Root Mean Squared Residual (SRMR)
Value	0.937	0.942	0.078	0.076
Threshold value	>0.90	>0.90	<0.08	<0.08

4 Conclusion

This research proposes a statistical framework based on structural equation modeling to study exogenous factors that may contribute to data breach incidents. The proposed measurement model is evaluated through reliability and validity tests, and the results show that the constructs used in the model are satisfactory in predicting the likelihood of data breaches. Future research can address limitations related to dataset's bias and explore the effectiveness of different security measures in preventing data breaches.

References

1. Mansfield-Devine, S.: IBM: cost of a data breach (2022)
2. Data Breach Report, Tech. rep., Ponemon Institute, IBM (2019)
3. Thales Data Threat Report, Tech. rep., Thales (2022)
4. Straub, J.: Evaluating the use of technology readiness levels (TRLS) for cybersecurity systems. In: 2021 IEEE International Systems Conference (SysCon), pp. 1–6. IEEE (2021)
5. Da Veiga, A., Astakhova, L.V., Botha, A., Herselman, M.: Defining organisational information security culture—perspectives from academia and industry. Comput. Secur. **92**, 101713 (2020)
6. Gupta, R., Tanwar, S., Tyagi, S., Kumar, N.: Machine learning models for secure data analytics: a taxonomy and threat model. Comput. Commun. **153**, 406–440 (2020)
7. Harris, D., Khan, L., Paul, R., Thuraisingham, B.: Standards for secure data sharing across organizations. Comput. Stand. Interfaces **29**(1), 86–96 (2007)
8. Hammouchi, H., Nejjari, N., Mezzour, G., Ghogho, M., Benbrahim, H.: Strisk: a socio-technical approach to assess hacking breaches risk. IEEE Trans. Depend. Secure Comput. **20**(2), 1074–1087 (2022)
9. Hu, J., Vasilakos, A.V.: Energy big data analytics and security: challenges and opportunities. IEEE Trans. Smart Grid **7**(5), 2423–2436 (2016)
10. Wieringa, J., Kannan, P., Ma, X., Reutterer, T., Risselada, H., Skiera, B.: Data analytics in a privacy-concerned world. J. Bus. Res. **122**, 915–925 (2019)
11. Nejjari, N., Lahlou, S., Fadi, O., Zkik, K., Oudani, M., Benbrahim, H.: Conflict spectrum: an empirical study of geopolitical cyber threats from a social network perspective. In: 2021 Eighth International Conference on Social Network Analysis, Management and Security (SNAMS), pp. 01–07. IEEE (2021)
12. Natarajan, M.: Crime opportunity theories: routine activity, rational choice and their variants. Routledge (2017)
13. Felson, M., Clarke, R.V.: Opportunity makes the thief, police research series, paper 98 (1–36) (1998) 10
14. Miethe, T.D., Meier, R.F.: Crime and its social context: toward an integrated theory of offenders, victims, and situations. Suny Press (1994)
15. Hindelang, M.J., Gottfredson, M.R., Garofalo, J.: Victims of personal crime: an empirical foundation for a theory of personal victimization. Ballinger Cambridge, MA (1978)
16. Cohen, L.E., Felson, M.: Social change and crime rate trends: a routine activity approach, American sociological review 588–608 (1979)
17. Alshalan, A.: Cyber-crime fear and victimization: an analysis of a national survey
18. Yang, Y., Green, S.B.: Coefficient alpha: a reliability coefficient for the 21st century? J. Psycho Educ. Assess. **29**(4), 377–392 (2011)

19. Canatay, A., Emegwa, T., Lybolt, L.M., Loch, K.D.: Reliability assessment in SEM models with composites and factors: a modern perspective. Data Anal. Perspect. J. **3**(1), 1–6 (2022)
20. Babin, B.J., Svensson, G.: Structural equation modeling in social science research: issues of validity and reliability in the research process. Eur. Bus. Rev. **24**(4), 320–330 (2012)

Fault Tolerance

Consensus on an Unknown Torus with Dense Byzantine Faults

Joseph Oglio, Kendric Hood, Gokarna Sharma, and Mikhail Nesterenko(✉)

Department of Computer Science, Kent State University, Kent, OH 44242, USA
{joglio,khood5,sharma,mikhail}@cs.kent.edu

Abstract. We present a solution to consensus on a torus with Byzantine faults. Any solution to classic consensus that is tolerant to f Byzantine faults requires $2f + 1$ node-disjoint paths. Due to limited torus connectivity, this bound necessitates spatial separation between faults. Our solution does not require this many disjoint paths and tolerates dense faults.

Specifically, we consider the case where all faults are in one column. We address the version of consensus where only processes in fault-free columns must agree. We prove that even this weaker version is not solvable if the column may be completely faulty. We then present a solution for the case where at least one row is fault-free. The correct processes share orientation but do not know the identities of other processes or the torus dimensions. The communication is synchronous.

To achieve our solution, we build and prove correct an all-to-all broadcast algorithm $\mathcal{BAT}$ that guarantees delivery to all processes in fault-free columns. We use this algorithm to solve our weak consensus problem. Our solution, $\mathcal{CBAT}$, runs in $O(H + W)$ rounds, where H and W are torus height and width respectively. We extend our consensus solution to the fixed message size model where it runs in $O(H^3 W^2)$ rounds. Our results are immediately applicable if the faults are located in a single row, rather than a column.

1 Introduction

A Byzantine process [16,21] may arbitrarily deviate from the prescribed algorithm. This is the strongest fault that can affect a process in a distributed system. The fault is powerful enough to straddle the realm of fault tolerance and security as it may model either a device failure or a malicious intruder.

In the presence of Byzantine faults, the common task for correct processes is to come to an agreement or consensus. The power of the faults may be abridged with cryptography [1,9,14] or randomization [4,10,24]. If neither primitive is available, the solutions require that the number of correct processes is large enough to overwhelm the faulty ones.

If the topology of a network is considered, the consensus problem is further complicated as faulty processes, even small in absolute number may isolate some correct processes and prevent them from achieving consensus. In a general topology, it is known that consensus is solvable only if the network is at least

D. Mohaisen and T. Wies (Eds.): NETYS 2023, LNCS 14067, pp. 105–121, 2023.
https://doi.org/10.1007/978-3-031-37765-5_9

$2f+1$-connected [8,11,16]. However, such connectivity demands a dense network with large node degree which limits the scalability of a solution achieved this way.

In this paper, we study Byzantine-robust consensus on a torus. Its fixed degree and small diameter makes torus an attractive architecture for distributed computing and storage tasks [3,12]. Torus connectivity is 4. Hence, according to classic connectivity bounds, it may not tolerate more than 1 fault. To increase tolerance, the fault locations must be restricted. One approach is to make the faults sparse. That is, the faulty processes need to be positioned far enough apart so that $2f+1$ connectivity is preserved [17]. Such a solution fails if the faults are located close to each other. In this paper, we address dense Byzantine faults on a torus of unknown dimensions. However, to achieve tolerance, we restrict fault location to a single column.

Related Work. There are a number of solutions optimizing consensus in incomplete topologies [2,7,18,25,26]. Chlebus et al. [7] optimize the speed of achieving Byzantine consensus in arbitrary topologies. The connectivity is subject to $2f+1$ bound. Alchieri et al. [2] study synchronous Byzantine consensus with unknown participants. They use participant detectors to establish network membership. Tseng and Vaidya [25] explore consensus in directed graphs. Winkler et al. [26] study consensus in directed dynamic networks. Oglio et al. [19] solve Byzantine consensus in Euclidean space.

Potentially, network topology may be discovered despite Byzantine faults. This simplifies consensus solution. Nesterenko and Tixeuil present two generic Byzantine-tolerant topology discovery algorithms [18]. However, neither algorithm is suitable for our task: their first algorithm raises an alarm once an inconsistency is discovered without completing the task. Their second algorithm requires $2f+1$ connectivity.

Let us discuss consensus on toruses and related topologies. Several papers [5, 15,22] consider the problem of Byzantine-tolerant reliable broadcast on an infinite grid or a torus in radio networks. In such a network, all processes within a particular distance from the sender receive the message simultaneously. Due to this limitation, their results are not immediately applicable to our model.

Kandlur and Shin [13] consider a synchronous Byzantine-tolerant broadcast on a torus. In their approach, each message is delivered over a fixed number of node-disjoint paths. The correct message is recovered so long as the majority of paths bypass faulty nodes. Since torus connectivity is 4, this approach may tolerate at most one fault. Maurer and Tixeuil [17] study a Byzantine-tolerant broadcast on a torus. In their model, the byzantine torus dimensions are not known. Their solution assumes that the faulty nodes are sparse, i.e. they are located far enough apart such that there is sufficiently many node disjoint paths between the sender and any of the receivers to ensure that the influence of the faulty nodes is countered.

Thus, to the best of our knowledge, previous work has not addressed dense Byzantine faults on a torus.

Paper Contribution and Approach. We consider the synchronous model, bidirectional communication, no cryptographic primitives or randomization. The topology we study is a torus whose dimensions: height H and width W are unknown to the processes. All processes share orientation. We assume that all faults are located in a single column.

We consider the weaker consensus where only processes in fault-free columns must agree on a value. We prove that even this version is not solvable if a single column is completely faulty.

We examine the case where at least one row is fault-free. To counter faulty column influence, we assume that $W \geq 5$. To solve this weak consensus problem, we first present an all-to-all broadcast algorithm $\mathcal{BAT}$ that guarantees delivery to fault-free columns. We prove it correct and show that it runs in $O(H + W)$ rounds in the LOCAL model [21] where messages are of arbitrary size. We then use $\mathcal{BAT}$ to build the consensus algorithm $\mathcal{CBAT}$. We prove it correct and show that it runs in $O(H + W)$ rounds in LOCAL.

We then extend $\mathcal{BAT}$ and $\mathcal{CBAT}$ to use fixed-size messages and estimate their running time in the CONGEST model [23]. We determine that the fixed-size message $\mathcal{BAT}$ runs in $O(H^2W)$ rounds and $\mathcal{CBAT}$ runs in $O(H^3W^2)$ rounds. Our results are immediately applicable to the case of faults located in a single row rather than column.

Let us now introduce our solution approach. To counter the faults, we leverage the processes' shared knowledge of the network topology. The data is first propagated along the column and the influence of possibly densely packed column of faults is neutralized. The single correct process is guaranteed to relay data across the faulty column. This horizontally propagated data is then disseminated through the fault-free columns to reach all correct processes there.

Paper Organization. In Sect. 2, we introduce our notation, state the problem and prove the necessity of a fault-free row. In Sect. 3, we present and prove correct our all-to-all broadcast algorithm $\mathcal{BAT}$. In Sect. 4, we use $\mathcal{BAT}$ to construct and prove correct our consensus algorithm $\mathcal{CBAT}$. In Sect. 5, we describe how the algorithms can be modified for fixed message size and estimate their run time. We conclude the paper by describing further research directions in Sect. 6.

2   Notation, Problem Statement, Fault Constraints

Computation Model. A process p contains variables and actions. We denote variable var of process p as $var.p$. If process p maintains variable var about process q, we denote it as $var.q.p$. A rectangular grid graph of processes is a Cartesian product of two chain graphs. Such a grid graph is embedded on a plane as a matrix of rows and columns. A *torus grid graph*, or *torus* for short, is formed by starting with a grid graph and connecting corresponding leftmost/rightmost and top/bottom processes with edges.

Every process in the torus has a unique identifier. An adjacent process is a *neighbor*. In a torus, every process has exactly four neighbors. Each process knows the identifiers of its neighbors: *left*, *right*, *up* and *down*. All processes share the orientation. That is, for any two processes p and q if $up.p = q$ then $down.q = p$ and if $left.p = q$ then $right.q = p$. We refer to the shared orientation as North, East, West and South. The torus dimensions are unknown to the processes. That is, they do not know the height H or the width W of the torus.

The system is completely synchronous. The operation proceeds in rounds. In every round, each process receives all pending messages sent to it, does local calculations and sends messages to its neighbors to be received in the next round. In one round, a process may thus receive multiple messages from the same or from different neighbors and then send multiple messages to neighbors. A *computation* is an infinite sequence of such rounds.

For most of the paper, we assume that size of the message is arbitrary. We lift this assumption later in the paper.

Process Faults. Processes are either correct or faulty. A *correct* process follows the algorithm while a *faulty* process behaves arbitrarily. A faulty process is always *black*. A correct process is *grey* if it has at most one black process in its column, it is *white* otherwise. The colors of individual processes are applied to the rows and columns of the torus: grey-white, black-white, etc. Refer to Fig. 1 for torus depiction and fault location.

Broadcast. Consider the problem where each process p is input an arbitrary initial value *initVal.p*, and p must share this value with every other process q so that $val.q.p = initVal.p$

Definition 1. *In the* Weak Synchronous All-to-All Broadcast Problem *every white process p must stop and for each white process q, p must output $val.q.p$ such that $val.q.p = initVal.q$.*

Consensus. In *Binary Consensus*, the input value *initVal.p* is restricted to either 0 or 1. Each process must output an irrevocable decision v with the following three properties:

- *agreement* – no two correct processes decide differently;
- *validity* – if there are no faults and for every process p, $initVal.p = v$, then p decides v;
- *termination* – every correct process eventually decides.

Definition 2. *In* strong consensus, *the above properties apply to every grey and white process, i.e. to each correct process. In* weak consensus, *the properties apply only to white processes.*

Impossibility. Let us outline the area of the possible. Strong consensus requires $2f + 1$ connectivity [8]. The connectivity of torus is 4, so there is no algorithm that solves strong consensus on a torus with $f > 1$ and arbitrary fault location.

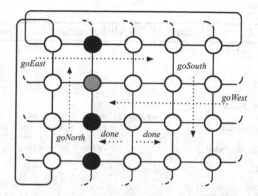

Fig. 1. Torus orientation, fault location, message types and message propagation direction in $\mathcal{BAT}$.

If faults are restricted to a single column but may occupy the complete column, consensus is still impossible. This holds true even if the processes know the torus dimensions. Intuitively, even if correct processes are connected, they may not be able to distinguish their faulty and non-faulty neighbors and agree on a value. The below theorem formalizes this observation.

Theorem 1. *There is no algorithm that solves consensus, weak or strong, on a torus with a faulty column.*

Proof. Assume the opposite: there is such an algorithm $\mathcal{A}$ hat solves weak consensus on a torus with a completely faulty column. Since there are no grey processes, the requirements of weak and strong consensuses are identical. Consider a torus T of height 1 and some width W. Since the algorithm $\mathcal{A}$ is a solution the consensus problem on a torus, it should be able to solve it on T. However, this topology is a ring. Its connectivity is 2. According to Dolev et al. [8], the consensus is solvable only if the connectivity of the network is at least $2f + 1 = 3$. That is, contrary to our initial assumption, $\mathcal{A}$ may not solve consensus on T. Hence the theorem.   □

3 $\mathcal{BAT}$: Byzantine-Tolerant Broadcast to All-to-All on a Torus

Overview. We present algorithm, we call $\mathcal{BAT}$, that solves the Weak Synchronous All-to-All Broadcast Problem. The code for $\mathcal{BAT}$ is shown in Algorithm 1. The functions used in $\mathcal{BAT}$ are in Algorithm 2. Our notation is loosely based on UNITY programming language [6]. Each process starts $\mathcal{BAT}$ by sending initial messages in Line 14. The execution of the rest of the actions are *receive actions*. Such an action is guarded by the corresponding message receipt. It is executed only when this message is sent to the receive process. The actions of the algorithm are grouped into phases: North, East-West, South and Decision. The algorithm is designed such that white processes synchronize their transitions through these phases.

Algorithm 1: $\mathcal{BAT}$: Byzantine All-to-All broadcast on a Torus

---

Input: *initVal*

1 **Constants:**
2   p `// process identifier`
3    $up, down, left, right$ `// neighbor identifiers`

4 **Variables:**
5   *northDone*, initially **false**
6   *column*, initially $\langle\rangle$ `// seq. of value-id pairs received from down neighbor`
7   *rowLeft, rowRight*, initially $\langle\rangle$ `// columns from resp. left and right neighbors`
8   *matrix*, initially $\langle\rangle$ `// results matrix to output`
9   *eastWestDone*, initially **false**   `// one of horizontal neighbors decided`

10 **Phases:**
11 **North:**
12   **Initial action:**
13   add $\langle initVal, p\rangle$ to *column*   `// initiate North Phase`
14   send $goNorth(initVal, p)$ to up

15   **Receive action:**
16   receive $goNorth(v, id)$ from $down \longrightarrow$
17   **if** not *northDone* **then**   `// has not started East-West Phase`
18   **if** $id \neq p$ **then**
19   add $\langle v, id\rangle$ to *column*
20   send $goNorth(v, id)$ to up
21   **else**   `// p receives its own value back`
22   *northDone* $\leftarrow$ **true**
23   send $goEast(column, left, p, right)$ to $right$
24   send $goWest(column, left, p, right)$ to $left$

25 **East-West, Receive actions:**
26   receive $goEast(c, l, id, r)$ from $left \longrightarrow$
27   **if** $id \neq p$ **then**
28   add $\langle c, l, id, r\rangle$ to head of *rowLeft*
29   send $goEast(c, l, id, r)$ to $right$
30   **else**
31        $m \leftarrow$ **match**($\langle column, left, p, right\rangle + rowLeft$,
32                   $\langle column, left, p, right\rangle + rowRight$)
33   **if** $matrix = \langle\rangle$ and $m \neq \langle\rangle$ **then**
34          $matrix \leftarrow m$
35   **Output:** *matrix*
36   send $goSouth(matrix, p)$ to $down$ `// start South Phase`
37   send *done* to $right$ and $left$ `// start Decision Phase`
38   **if** *eastWestDone* **then** **stop**

39   receive $goWest(c, l, id, r)$ from $right \longrightarrow$
     `// handle similar to goEast, add` $\langle c, l, id, r\rangle$ `to tail of rowRight`

40 **South, Receive action:**
41   receive $goSouth(m, id)$ from $up \longrightarrow$
42   **if** $id \neq p$ **then**
43   send $goSouth(m, id)$ to $down$
44   **if** $matrix = \langle\rangle$ **then**   `// South Phase did not reach p yet`
45          $matrix \leftarrow m$
46   **Output:** *matrix*
47   send *done* to $right$ and $left$ `// start Decision Phase`
48   **if** *eastWestDone* **then** **stop**

49 **Decision, Receive action:**
50   receive *done* from $direction \longrightarrow$
51   **if** not *eastWestDone* **then**
52   *eastWestDone* $\leftarrow$ **true**
53   **if** $matrix \neq \langle\rangle$ **then** **stop**

Algorithm 2: $\mathcal{BAT}$ functions

```
54  Functions:
55  match(rleft, rright):
56      cleft ← consistent(rleft)
57      cright ← consistent(rright)
58      if cleft ≠ ⟨⟩ and cright ≠ ⟨⟩ then
            // cleft = cright
59          if |cleft| = |cright| and
60          (∀i : 1 ≤ i < |cleft| :
61              s(i) ≡ ⟨lci, lli, lidi, lri⟩ ∈ cleft
62              s(i) ≡ ⟨rci, rli, ridi, rri⟩ ∈ cright :
63              lci = rci and lli = rli and lidi = ridi and lri = rri) then
                    // return columns of cleft
64                  return ⟨∀i : 1 < i ≤ |cleft| : s(i) ≡ ⟨ci, li, idi, ri⟩ ∈ cleft : ci⟩
65      return ⟨⟩

66  consistent(clmn):
67      if s ≡ ⟨·, ·, id, ·⟩ is unique in clmn and
68      exists at most one i : 1 ≤ i < |clmn| : cminus = clmn \ s(i) and
69      exists at most one j : 1 ≤ j ≤ |clmn| :
70          cplus = cminus insert ⟨⊥, l, id, r⟩ at position j in cminus
71      ∀i : 1 ≤ i < |cplus|, j = (i + 1 mod |cplus|) :
72          s(i) ≡ ⟨ci, li, idi, ri⟩ ∈ cplus
73          s(j) ≡ ⟨cj, lj, idj, rj⟩ ∈ cplus :
74          idi = lj and ri = idj then
75          return cplus
76      else
77          return ⟨⟩
```

Once done, each process sends the collected column data to its *left* and *right* neighbors in the East-West Phase. The data is sent in both directions for verification to counteract the actions of the grey and black processes in the row. If the data received from both directions match, each process starts the South Phase where the confirmed data is sent to *down* neighbor. This data is a matrix of values from all processes in the torus.

Due to the actions of the black processes in the black-white rows, the white processes may receive corrupted values and fail to complete the South Phase on time. Once the data starts propagating down the column in the South Phase, the white processes synchronize, receive correct matrix and output it. After output, processes enter the Decision Phase. This phase ensures termination of white processes.

$\mathcal{BAT}$ **Details.** The input for each process in the algorithm is an arbitrary value *initVal*. Each process p in $\mathcal{BAT}$ has its own identifier as well as the ids of its up, down, left and right neighbors.

Each process p maintains the following variables. The process has *column*, where it gathers pairs $\langle v, id \rangle$ of values and identifiers of its column in the North Phase. Boolean *doneNorth* signifies whethe p completed its North Phase. After it is done, the column values are exchanged across the row in two directions: left and right in the East-West Phase. These column values are collected in *rowLeft* and *rowRight*. Once the values are matched across the row, they are propagated through the column in the South Phase and collected in *matrix*.

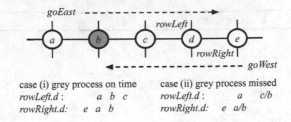

case (i) grey process on time   case (ii) grey process missed
rowLeft.d :   *a b c*   *rowLeft.d* :   *a   c/b*
rowRight.d: *e a b*   *rowRight.d:*   *e a/b*

Fig. 2. Matrix accumulation during the East-West Phase of $\mathcal{BAT}$. The matrix is accumulated at process d as it collects messages *goEast* and *goWest* from its left and right neighbors respectively. In case (i), the grey process b starts East West Phase together with white processes. In case (ii), b starts it one round earlier.

Variable *doneNeighbor* records the neighbor identifiers that made the decision to ensure proper termination.

Let us discuss $\mathcal{BAT}$ operation during each phase in detail. Refer to Fig. 1 for the messages that processes send and their propagation directions. All non-black processes simultaneously initiate the North Phase by sending their input values to the *up* neighbors in a *goNorth* message (see Line 15). Then, each process p starts collecting the values of its column processes by receiving *goNorth* from the *down* neighbor and propagating it upward. This continues until p receives its own message back. Once received, p initiates the East-West Phase (Line 23).

For that, p sends the collected column to its *left* and *right* neighbor in messages *goWest* and *goEast*, respectively. Together with the column, p sends its own identifier and the identifiers of *left* and *right*. This allows the recipients to reconstruct the sequence of the processes in the row if one of the entries is missing. Flag *northDone* ensures that each process sends *goWest* and *goEast* at most once.

Due to the actions of the black processes in its column, even if some grey process completes its own North Phase, it may do so out of sync with the White processes. However, the receipt of *goEast* or *goWest* from its neighbor, enables g's corresponding receive action of the East-West phase. Thus, even though g itself is out of sync, it relays these messages to the white processes in its row allowing them to proceed with the execution the East-West Phase.

The East-West Phase is the most complicated part of the algorithm. Let us illustrate its operation with an example. Please see Fig. 2. Assume a torus row contains processes a, b, c, d and e. All of them are white, except for b which is grey. Each white process completes the North Phase in the same round and starts the East-West Phase by sending the collected column to its right neighbor in a *goEast* message and to its left neighbor in *goWest* message. The grey process may (i) complete its North Phase together with the white processes or (ii) miss it and either complete it in a different round or not at all.

Let us first describe case (i). Once a process receives either *goEast* or *goWest*, the process records what the message carries and sends it further in the same direction. Thus, in the first round of the East-West Phase, d receives messages from c and e, in the second b and a and so on. As *goEast* message arrives to d from its left neighbor, d inserts its contents to the head of *rowLeft.d*.

When *goWest* message arrives to d from the right, d adds its contents to the tail of *rowRight.d*. Figure 2 shows the contents *rowLeft.d* and *rowRight.d* after three rounds of the East-West Phase when d received messages from c, b, and a from the left and e, a, and b from the right. The East-West Phase proceeds until the process receives a message from itself. In the example in Fig. 2, this happens in two more rounds, after d receives messages from e then d from the left and c then, possibly, d from the right.

In case (ii), the grey process b completes the North Phase in a round different from the white processes. In Fig. 2, b completes its North Phase one round earlier. Therefore, this message reaches d together with a message from a from the right, and together with message from c from the left.

After the process receives the message from itself, either from the right or the left, it compares the contents of *rowLeft* and *rowRight* by invoking function **match()** (Line 32). The operation of this function is somewhat complex since grey process may be out of synchrony with the rest of its row. If the contents of the two variables do not match, Function **match()** returns the data stripped of a mismatched column of the grey process. The resultant list of columns: *matrix* is the output of $\mathcal{BAT}$. This *matrix* is sent to the *down* process in a *goSouth* message. This begins the South Phase (Line 36).

$\mathcal{BAT}$ operation is such that all white processes either initiate the South Phase in the same round or do not initiate the South Phase at all. Indeed, due to the actions of the black processes in the black-white rows, the white processes may not get the matching data and fail to start their own South Phase. However, the white processes in the grey-white row are guaranteed to start the South Phase. The South Phase started by these processes, re-synchronizes white processes and propagates the correct *matrix* information in *goSouth* message. Once a process receives the missing information, it outputs it (Line 44).

Yet, the processes should not terminate. Indeed, black processes may force a grey process in the black-grey column to receive a *goSouth* message at any time. The grey processes may output the result and consider its mission accomplished. If a grey process terminates, its halting prevents it from forwarding messages from white processes in the East-West Phase.

To ensure proper termination, processes execute the Decision Phase. After outputting the decision matrix, each process sends *done* message to its horizontal, i.e. left and right, immediate neighbors. The process stops if it receives at least one of them (Line 52) and it has the decision matrix. One of the horizontal neighbors is guaranteed to be white. Thus, if a process obtains the decision matrix and gets one *done*, then its white neighbors may not be in the middle of the East-West Phase and this process may safely stop.

Discussion on $\mathcal{BAT}$ Functions. Let us now discuss the functions used in $\mathcal{BAT}$. They are shown in Algorithm 2. Function **match()** accepts the input received from the West – *left*, and East – *right* during the East-West Phase. The entries of *left* and *right* are of the following format: the column c received by the original sender, its left neighbor identifier l, its own identifier id and its right neighbor id r.

First, *left* and *right* are individually checked for internal consistency in function **consistent()**. As process p receives data from either East or West, the left and right neighbors of the subsequent entries should match. In grey-white row, this is true for all entries except for possibly the grey process that may start its East-West phase earlier or later than the white ones. In this case, the grey process entry may arrive out of order. That is, it may arrive together with another white process entry while its own spot in the sequence remains empty.

Function **consistent()** finds a potential single entry that is out of sequence as well as a single process gap (Line 69). Specifically, **consistent()** checks whether there exists at most one element in its parameter *clmn* such that if it is removed, *cminus* is produced, and then another element is possibly added to *cminus* producing *cplus*. This added entry contains $\bot$ for the column values and the l, id, r tuple are such that the left and right neighbors in the consequent entries in resultant *cplus* match. In this case **consistent()** returns *cplus*. Consider case (ii) shown in Fig. 2. Observe what *rowLeft* and parameter *left* contain:

$$(1)\langle\cdot,c,d,e\rangle,(2)\langle\cdot,d,e,a\rangle,(3)\langle\cdot,e,a,b\rangle,(4)\bot,(5)\langle\cdot,b,c,d\rangle/\langle\cdot,a,b,c\rangle$$

That is, the third round entry is empty and the fifth round entry contains the data originated by process c and the grey process b. Process b sends its data out of sync with the white processes. Function **consistent()**, on the basis of the adjacent entries, reconstructs the fourth entry and drops the extra fifth entry sent by b:

$$(1)\langle\cdot,c,d,e\rangle,(2)\langle\cdot,d,e,a\rangle,(3)\langle\cdot,e,a,b\rangle,(4)\langle\bot,a,b,c\rangle,(5)\langle\cdot,b,c,d\rangle$$

The corrected entry is stored in *cleft* by **match()**. Similar manipulation by **consistent()** yields *cright*. Function **match()** determines that *cleft* is equal to *cright*. That is, the process p gets the same data from both East and West. In this case **match()** returns the matrix of columns stored by *cleft* and *cright*.

Theorem 2. *Algorithm $\mathcal{BAT}$ solves the* Weak Synchronous All-to-All Broadcast Problem *on an unknown torus with Byzantine faults in at most one column with at least one correct row in at most $2H+2+W$ rounds.*

The above theorem states the correctness and efficiency of $\mathcal{BAT}$. See [20] for proof details. Let us discuss the intuition for the correctness proof. It is relatively straightforward to show that all white processes complete the first, North, Phase in $H+1$ round and collect the true contents of their respective columns. By induction on the number of rounds, we show that each process p collects a column of true data about any process q in the same row, so long as the processes between p and q, in the direction of information propagation are non-black. Indeed, the non-black processes do not impede data propagation.

We then separately consider white processes in (a) grey-white rows and (b) black-white rows. In the East-West Phase, the information propagates in two directions. We show that during this phase, in a grey-white row, in round $H + 1 + W$, the information spreading in two directions matches. The match is up to the potentially misplaced data from the single grey process. We prove that this information is true to the original white process data throughout the matrix. In the black-white row, we show that a white process either completes the phase in $H + 1 + W$ round with correct white process data or not at all.

That is, we show that each white process, regardless of the row location, that complete the East-West Phase, holds correct information about all the white processes in the matrix. Moreover, each white process in the grey-white row is guaranteed to complete this phase.

We then consider the South Phase. There, we show that it is completed in an additional H rounds, and all the white processes are updated with the correct matrix information before termination. This completes the proof of Theorem 2.

The computation model that we consider $\mathcal{BAT}$ is called LOCAL. It assumes unlimited size messages. Theorem 2 shows that $\mathcal{BAT}$ completes in $O(H + W)$ rounds in LOCAL.

4 $\mathcal{CBAT}$: Consensus Using $\mathcal{BAT}$

Description. Observe that $\mathcal{BAT}$ cannot immediately be used to solve consensus since, after its completion, the outputs of each process differ by the values of black and grey processes. An individual white process is not able to determine the color of the senders. Therefore, if the white process makes the consensus decision on the basis of the single execution of $\mathcal{BAT}$, the Byzantine senders may cause white processes to disagree on their outputs.

Instead we use $\mathcal{BAT}$ to select a leader process and agree on the input value of this leader. A particular difficulty is presented if the selected leader process is faulty. In this case, the leader may send different values to different processes. To prevent that, the processes use $\mathcal{BAT}$ again to exchange received values, determine whether the leader is consistent in its transmission of its initial value, and, if not, replace the leader . This determination has to proceed despite the inconsistent information provided by the faulty processes in this second exchange.

Let us describe the algorithm $\mathcal{CBAT}$ that achieves consensus. It is shown in Algorithm 3. We assume that the number of columns $W \geq 5$. The algorithm has three sequentially executing stages: Broadcast, Confirm and Decide. In the first two stages $\mathcal{CBAT}$ executes $\mathcal{BAT}$.

In the Broadcast Stage, the processes exchange the initial input values. In the Confirm Stage, they transmit the complete matrix they received during Broadcast. At the end of Confirm, each white process receives $H \times W$ matrices of such values. In the Decide Stage, every white process independently arrives at the consensus decision.

Let us describe how this decision is computed. Each process p deterministically selects a leader process ldr. In the algorithm, it is the process with the highest identifier. Then, out $H \times W$ matrices that process p receives in the second stage, p composes the matrix M_L of values sent to all other processes

---

Algorithm 3: $\mathcal{CBAT}$

    Input: v boolean   `// consensus input value`

78 **Variables:**
79    $M_B \equiv \{v_{ij} : 1 \leq i \leq H, 1 \leq j \leq W\}$ `// matrix of votes received by each process`
80    $M_C \equiv \{M_{ij} : 1 \leq i \leq H, 1 \leq j \leq W\}$ `// votes reported as received by each process`
81   M_B and M_C are initially $\perp$

82 **Stages:**
83 **Broadcast:**
84    $M_B \leftarrow \mathcal{BAT}(v)$

85 **Confirm:**
86    $M_C \leftarrow \mathcal{BAT}(M_B)$

87 **Decide:**
     `// deterministically select leader`
88    $ldr \leftarrow highestID(M_B)$
89   let $v_{mn} \in M_B$ be the input value of ldr
90   let $C_L \in M_B$ `// leader's column in` M_B
91   let $M_L = \{v_{ij} : v_{mn} \in M_{ij} \in M_C\}$ `// v sent by ldr, received by every process`
92

     `// two columns with ⊥ elements or`
     `// two columns with 1/0 elements or`
     `// two columns whose values differ from rest`
93   **if** $\exists\, q \neq r$ *and* $\exists\, e, f$:
94      $v_{qe}, v_{rf} \in M_L \setminus C_L$:
95      $v_{qe} = v_{rf} = \perp$
96   *or*
97      $\exists\, w \neq x,\ y \neq z$ *and* $\exists\, a, b, c, d$:
98      $v_{wa}, v_{xb}, v_{yc}, v_{zd} \in M_L \setminus C_L$:
99      $v_{wa} = v_{xb} = 0$ *and* $v_{yc} = v_{zd} = 1$ **then**
       `// select a new leader from a different column`
100      $ldr \leftarrow highestID(M_B \setminus C_L)$
       `// recompute` M_L `and` C_L
101   **Output:** $majority(M_L \setminus C_L)$

---

by the leader as these processes report to p. Process p examines these values for inconsistencies. The inconsistencies are as follows: either the values differ in more than one column; or the values contain $\perp$, a sign that $\mathcal{BAT}$ detected faulty values, in more than one column; or the values in at least two columns differ from the rest. In the latter case, since the total number of columns is at least 5, and the leader column is not considered, there are at least two columns that are different from at least two other columns. In all cases, these inconsistencies can be determined by all correct processes. Once the faulty process is detected, the whole column where all the faulty processes may be located is also discovered. Therefore, p selects a new leader from a different column. Once each process selects the leader, that leader may still be faulty and send arbitrary values to other processes. However, these values are consistently stored in the M_L matrix. Each process decides on the majority of values in this matrix.

Correctness Proof. Note that the below discussion relies on correctness of $\mathcal{BAT}$ proved in Theorem 2. Denote $val.a$ the input value $initVal$ of some fixed process that is reported by process a after the Broadcast Stage of $\mathcal{CBAT}$. Denote $val.a.b$ the same fixed process value received by process b from process a after the Confirm Stage.

Lemma 1. *Let v, w, x be white processes executing $\mathcal{CBAT}$ and distributing the value input to some process u. Then, after the Confirm Stage of $\mathcal{CBAT}$, if u is white then $val.v.x = val.w.x$; and $val.v.x = val.v.y$ regardless of the color of u.*

Proof. Let us address the first claim of the lemma where u is white. In the Broadcast Stage, processes are sending their individual input values using $\mathcal{BAT}$. This includes $initVal$ of process u. If the sender u is white and the recipients v and w are white, then, according to Theorem 2, $initVal = val.v = val.w$. During the Confirm Stage, each process, including v and w, sends the complete matrix of received values, including $val.v$ and $val.w$ to all processes, including x using $\mathcal{BAT}$. Since v, w, and x are white, according to Theorem 2, $val.v = val.v.x$ and $val.w = val.w.x$. That is, $val.v.x = val.w.x$. This proves the first claim of the lemma.

Let us consider the second claim that should hold regardless of the color of u. Consider the value $val.v$ stored at v after the Broadcast Stage. During Confirm, this value is sent to all processes including x and y. If v, x and y are white, according to Theorem 2 $val.v = val.v.x = val.v.y$. Hence the second claim of the lemma also holds.   □

Lemma 2. *Every white process selects the same leader in the Decide Stage of $\mathcal{CBAT}$.*

Proof. For each white process p, algorithm $\mathcal{BAT}$ is guaranteed to produce a matrix that has the same identifiers, configuration and size. This means that all processes select the same ldr in Line 88 of $\mathcal{CBAT}$.

Let us consider whether each process changes its leader in Line 100. This happens if process p detects inconsistencies in at least two columns excluding the leader column. Process ldr is either correct or faulty.

If ldr is correct, then according to the first claim of Lemma 1, the entries for ldr in M_L at p are the same, except for possibly a single column of faulty processes. This means that if ldr is correct, none of the white processes changes its leader after initial selection.

If ldr is faulty, then according to the second claim of Lemma 1, the corresponding entries for ldr in M_L for all white processes are equal. That is, if processes p and q are white, then if entry $m_{ij} \in M_L$ in p is equal to $m_{ij} \in M_L$ in q.

That is, if two non-leader columns are inconsistent, then all white processes detect that. That is, if one white process changes leader, all white processes change leaders also. If the processes change leaders, by the operation of the algorithm, they select the same leader. Hence the lemma.   □

Lemma 3. *All white processes in $\mathcal{CBAT}$ output the same value. If the selected leader ldr is correct, they input $initVal.ldr$.*

Proof. Every white process p outputs the majority of values in $M_L \setminus C_L$. Due to Lemma 2, white processes in $\mathcal{CBAT}$ select the same leader. The leader may be either correct or faulty.

If the leader is correct, then, According to Lemma 1, all white entries in $M_L \setminus C_L$ are equal to $initVal.ldr$. Only one column in $M_L \setminus C_L$ may be non-white with potentially arbitrary values. Since we assume that the torus contains at least 5 columns, the majority of $M_L \setminus C_L$ is equal to $initVal.ldr$ and that is what the white process p outputs.

Let us consider the case of faulty leader. White processes change the leader only when they detect that the original leader is faulty. They select it from a different column, therefore, the new leader is correct and the previous reasoning to the output value applies.

The remaining case is that of a faulty leader and no leader change. According to the operation of the algorithm, after leader selection at most one column in $M_L \setminus C_L$ has inconsistencies. The rest of the entries hold the same value $x \in 0, 1$. According to the second claim of Lemma 1, the inconsistencies are in the same column of $M_L \setminus C_L$ for each white process. This means that the rest of the values in the matrix are x. Since white processes output the majority value and the number of columns is at least 5, all white processes output the same value x. □

Theorem 3. $\mathcal{CBAT}$ *solves weak consensus on an unknown torus whose width is at least 5 with Byzantine faults in at most one column and with at least one correct row.*

Proof. We prove the theorem by showing that $\mathcal{CBAT}$ satisfies all three properties of consensus. The agreement property of the consensus requires that all white processes output the same value. Lemma 3 indicates that $\mathcal{CBAT}$ satisfies that property. The validity property states that in case there are no faults and all processes are input the same value, they should all output the same value. According to Lemma 3, if the leader is correct, all correct processes output its input value. Hence, if all processes are correct, and they are all input the same value, they select one process as the leader and output this value. Therefore, $\mathcal{CBAT}$ satisfies validity.

Let us address termination. The consensus requires that each correct process terminates. $\mathcal{CBAT}$ sequentially executes three stages. The first two stages are executions of $\mathcal{BAT}$ and the last one is a finite computation. According to Theorem 2, $\mathcal{BAT}$ terminates. Hence, all three stages of $\mathcal{CBAT}$ terminate and this algorithm satisfies the termination property of the consensus.   □

Algorithm $\mathcal{CBAT}$ sequentially executes $\mathcal{BAT}$. Each $\mathcal{BAT}$ completes in $O(H + W)$ rounds in LOCAL. This means that $\mathcal{CBAT}$ also completes in $O(H + W)$ rounds.

5   Extension to Fixed Message Size

As presented, $\mathcal{BAT}$ is assumed to operate with unlimited size messages. However, it can be modified to operate with fixed size messages as follows. Observe that the messages get progressively larger as they accumulate the data about the torus. In the first phase, the North Phase, the messages are fixed size since each process only transmits its identifier and its input value. At most one message is sent per link per round. After the completion of this phase, the white processes discover the height H of the torus. In the next phase, the East-West Phase, the processes exchange messages whose size is proportional to the height of the torus. Since white processes know the torus size, this message may be replaced by H fixed size messages transmitted over H rounds. Due to the operation of the algorithm, at most 2 messages are transmitted per round in the East-West Phase. In the fixed size implementation, each process waits for $2H$ rounds to receive appropriate messages. The black processes may deceive the grey process and assume the larger torus height. This would make the grey process transmit a message larger than H rounds during the East-West Phase. This, in turn, may prevent the correct message from being transmitted in the same round. To eliminate that, the blocks of the two messages need to be transmitted in the round-robin manner. The South Phase message transmits the complete matrix. So the fixed size implementation has to wait for $H \cdot W$ rounds to receive a single matrix.

The fixed message size model is called CONGEST. Let us estimate the running time of the modified algorithm in CONGEST. The four phases of the original $\mathcal{BAT}$ take $O(H)$, $O(W)$, $O(H)$ and $O(1)$ rounds, respectively. The above argument shows that in each respective phase, the modified $\mathcal{BAT}$ needs to send $O(1)$, $O(H)$, $O(HW)$ and $O(1)$ sequential fixed-size messages per round. Hence, the number of rounds in fixed-size message $\mathcal{BAT}$ is dominated by the third phase and is in $O(H^2W)$.

Let us now discuss the fixed message size modification of $\mathcal{CBAT}$. In the first stage, $\mathcal{CBAT}$ uses $\mathcal{BAT}$ to broadcast constant-size decision values. Hence, its run time is in $O(H^2W)$. In the second stage, each process sends a complete $H \cdot W$ matrix. Hence, the run time of this stage, and of the whole algorithm is in $O(H^3W^2)$.

6   Conclusion and Future Work

Algorithm $\mathcal{BAT}$ assumes that all the faults are in the same column. In future research, the following conjectures are worth investigating. We believe that solving the problem with faulty processes spread across multiple columns, one fault per row, is possible but requires substantial modification of the algorithm. We suspect that solving the problem for the case of more than one fault per row is not possible.

To achieve the solution presented in this paper, we assumed shared process orientation. It is interesting to explore how important this assumption is to the solution. That is, whether it is possible to solve the problem without shared orientation.

In this paper we presented a Byzantine-tolerant consensus algorithm that exploits the knowledge of the network type – torus, to exceed the tolerance bound presented by the general consensus algorithm. Our study then opens the following question: what network types have similar properties? To put another way, what specifically makes torus Byzantine-fault resistant and can this property be generalized? We believe that this is a fruitful avenue of future research.

References

1. Abraham, I., Devadas, S., Nayak, K., Ren, L.: Brief announcement: practical synchronous byzantine consensus. In: 31st International Symposium on Distributed Computing (DISC 2017). Schloss Dagstuhl-Leibniz-Zentrum fuer Informatik (2017)
2. Alchieri, E.A.P., Bessani, A.N., da Silva Fraga, J., Greve, F.: Byzantine consensus with unknown participants. In: Baker, T.P., Bui, A., Tixeuil, S. (eds.) OPODIS 2008. LNCS, vol. 5401, pp. 22–40. Springer, Heidelberg (2008). https://doi.org/10.1007/978-3-540-92221-6_4
3. Alchieri, E.A.P., Bessani, A.N., da Silva Fraga, J., Greve, F.: Byzantine consensus with unknown participants. In: Baker, T.P., Bui, A., Tixeuil, S. (eds.) OPODIS 2008. LNCS, vol. 5401, pp. 22–40. Springer, Heidelberg (2008). https://doi.org/10.1007/978-3-540-92221-6_4
4. Ben-Or, M.: Another advantage of free choice (extended abstract) completely asynchronous agreement protocols. In: Proceedings of the Second Annual ACM Symposium on Principles of Distributed Computing, pp. 27–30 (1983)
5. Bhandari, V., Vaidya, N.H.: On reliable broadcast in a radio network. In: Proceedings of the Twenty-fourth Annual ACM Symposium on Principles of Distributed Computing, pp. 138–147 (2005)
6. Chandy, K., Misra, J.: Parallel program design: a foundation. Addison Wesley Publishing Co., (1988)
7. Chlebus, B.S., Kowalski, D.R., Olkowski, J.: Fast agreement in networks with byzantine nodes. In: 34th International Symposium on Distributed Computing (DISC 2020) (2020)
8. Dolev, D.: The byzantine generals strike again. J. Algorithms 3(1), 14–30 (1982)
9. Dolev, D., Strong, H.R.: Authenticated algorithms for byzantine agreement. SIAM J. Comput. 12(4), 656–666 (1983)
10. Feldman, P., Micali, S.: An optimal probabilistic protocol for synchronous byzantine agreement. SIAM J. Comput. 26(4), 873–933 (1997)
11. Fischer, M.J., Lynch, N.A., Merritt, M.: Easy impossibility proofs for distributed consensus problems. Distrib. Comput. 1, 26–39 (1986)
12. Ganesan, P., Yang, B., Garcia-Molina, H.: One torus to rule them all: multidimensional queries in P2P systems. In: Proceedings of the 7th International Workshop on the Web and Databases: colocated with ACM SIGMOD/PODS 2004, pp. 19–24 (2004)
13. Kandlur, D.D., Shin, K.G.: Reliable broadcast algorithms for harts. ACM Trans. Comput. Syst. (TOCS) 9(4), 374–398 (1991)
14. Katz, J., Koo, C.-Y.: On expected constant-round protocols for byzantine agreement. J. Comput. Syst. Sci. 75(2), 91–112 (2009)
15. Koo, C.-Y.: Broadcast in radio networks tolerating byzantine adversarial behavior. In: Proceedings of the Twenty-third Annual ACM Symposium on Principles of Distributed Computing, pp. 275–282 (2004)
16. Lamport, L., Shostak, R., Pease, M.: The byzantine generals problem. ACM Trans. Program. Lang. Syst. 4(3), 382–401 (1982)
17. Maurer, A., Tixeuil, S.: Byzantine broadcast with fixed disjoint paths. J. Parallel Distrib. Comput. 74(11), 3153–3160 (2014)

18. Nesterenko, M., Tixeuil, S.: Discovering network topology in the presence of byzantine faults. In: International Colloquium on Structural Information and Communication Complexity, pages 212–226. Springer, Berlin, Heidelberg (2006). https://doi.org/10.1007/11780823_17

19. Oglio, J., Hood, K., Sharma, G., Nesterenko, M.: Byzantine Geoconsensus. In: Echihabi, K., Meyer, R. (eds.) NETYS 2021. LNCS, vol. 12754, pp. 19–35. Springer, Cham (2021). https://doi.org/10.1007/978-3-030-91014-3_2

20. Oglio, J., Hood, K., Sharma, G., Nesterenko, M.: Consensus on unknown torus with dense byzantine faults. arXiv preprint arXiv:2303.12870 (2023)

21. Pease, M., Shostak, R., Lamport, L.: Reaching agreement in the presence of faults. J. ACM (JACM) **27**(2), 228–234 (1980)

22. Pelc, A., Peleg, D.: Broadcasting with locally bounded byzantine faults. Inf. Process. Lett. **93**(3), 109–115 (2005)

23. Peleg, D.: Distributed computing: a locality-sensitive approach. SIAM (2000)

24. Rabin, M.O.: Randomized byzantine generals. In: 24th Annual Symposium on Foundations of Computer Science (SFCS 1983), pp. 403–409. IEEE (1983)

25. Tseng, L., Vaidya, N.H.: Fault-tolerant consensus in directed graphs. In: Proceedings of the 2015 ACM Symposium on Principles of Distributed Computing, pp. 451–460 (2015)

26. Winkler, K., Schwarz, M., Schmid, U.: Consensus in rooted dynamic networks with short-lived stability. Distrib. Comput. **32**(5), 443–458 (2019). https://doi.org/10.1007/s00446-019-00348-0

Distributed Systems

Approximation Algorithms for Drone Delivery Scheduling Problem

Saswata Jana [ID] and Partha Sarathi Mandal[(✉)] [ID]

Indian Institute of Technology Guwahati, Guwahati 781039, India
{saswatajana,psm}@iitg.ac.in

Abstract. The coordination among drones and ground vehicles for last-mile delivery has gained significant interest in recent years. In this paper, we study *multiple drone delivery scheduling problem* (MDSP) [3] for last-mile delivery, where we have a set of drones with an identical battery budget and a set of delivery locations, along with profit for delivery, cost and delivery time intervals. The objective of the MDSP is to find conflict-free schedules for each drone such that the total profit gained is maximum subject to the battery constraint of the drones. In this paper, we propose a fully polynomial time approximation scheme (FPTAS) for the single drone delivery scheduling problem (SDSP) and a $\frac{1}{3}$-approximation algorithm for MDSP with a constraint on the number of drones. We also describe a deterministic rounding algorithm for the problem by relaxing the *integer linear programming*(ILP) formulation of the problem.

Keywords: Approximation Algorithm · Drone Delivery Scheduling · Truck · Last-mile Delivery

1 Introduction

Motivation: The rapid demand for commercial deliveries motivates logistics to provide more efficient services to customers. In delivery, the *last-mile delivery* [6], which involves collecting the goods from the distribution center to the customer's door, is the most costly and time-consuming process. This type of delivery necessitates a lot of human interaction. However, advances in drone technology have created a miniature. Large corporations have started planning for efficient parcel delivery via drones [1]. Also, drones can bypass traffic congestion on traditional networks by flying. This ability enables the drone to travel faster than the usual delivery truck and reduces transportation costs. Drones are carried by truck in the last mile delivery for better efficiency. In this collaboration, drones take off from the truck to deliver the package to customers and then return to the truck

Saswata Jana acknowledges financial support from the Prime Minister's Research Fellowship (PMRF) scheme of the Govt. of India (PMRF-ID: 1902165).
Partha Sarathi Mandal acknowledges partially financial support from the SERB project under MATRICS, Govt. of India, Grant Number: MTR/2019/001528.

for the next delivery. In addition, drones have enormous applications in the field of agriculture [10], healthcare [15], defense and disaster response [11], resource monitoring and assessment [17], manufacturing [12], and many more.

Challenges: Despite the broad application of drones, it has certain limitations. A drone can only deliver small packages due to capacity constraints. Since customers' locations are geographically distributed, safety and reliability are critical issues. Package delivery by drones with the help of a truck has many challenges. For a given set of customer locations, we need to know the best route for the truck, the launching points for drones, and the rendezvous points for drones and the truck to make deliveries. Furthermore, the limited battery budget of the available drones and the limited number of drones in the company's warehouse prevent us from making a desirable number of deliveries. Various companies have introduced preferences among customers (like prime customers). For this reason, they want to maximize their profit by preferring those prime deliveries over others. At a time, a drone can deliver at most one package. All these complexities influence logistics to make those deliveries, for which the profit is maximized.

But, for a large set of customers, designing an algorithm to find the optimal route or to schedule the deliveries to a set of drones optimally is a big challenge. Furthermore, all these problems are NP-hard [3,13]. It motivates us to look for some approximation algorithms toward the optimal results of the problems in polynomial time. FPTAS (fully polynomial time approximation scheme) is one of the best schemes in this approximation. FPTAS is an algorithm that takes the instance of the maximization (minimization) problem and an arbitrary $\epsilon > 0$ as it's input and returns a solution within factor $(1 - \epsilon)$ $((1 + \epsilon))$ of the optimal solution. The running time of this algorithm is polynomial in both the instance size and $\frac{1}{\epsilon}$. In addition, an algorithm called a pseudo-polynomial algorithm if the algorithm's running time is polynomial in the numeric value of the input but not necessarily in the number of bits to represent the input.

Drone Delivery Scheduling Problem: This paper considers last-mile delivery to customers with a truck moving in a prescribed route containing a set of drones. For a given set of deliveries and their delivery time intervals with cost, reward (or profit) for each delivery, and battery budget of the drones, the goal is to schedule the drones for the deliveries to make the total profit maximum. This problem was introduced by Sorbelli et al. [4]. The authors proved that the problem is NP-hard and proposed an optimal algorithm for the single drone case and approximation algorithms for multiple drone cases. This paper presents three approximation algorithms with better approximation factors, as mentioned below.

1.1   Contributions

In this paper, our contributions are the following.

- We propose a deterministic rounding algorithm for the *drone delivery scheduling problem* with approximation factor $\frac{1}{6}$.

- For the *single drone delivery scheduling problem*, we propose an optimal algorithm with running time $\mathcal{O}(n \log n + nP)$, where n is the number of deliveries and P is the sum of all the profits.
- For the *single drone delivery scheduling problem*, we propose an FPTAS with running time $\mathcal{O}(n \log n + n \lfloor \frac{n^2}{\epsilon} \rfloor)$, for $\epsilon > 0$.
- For the *multiple drone delivery scheduling problem* with m drones, we propose an $\frac{1}{3}$-approximation algorithm with running time $\mathcal{O}(n^2)$ if $m \geq \Delta$, Δ being the maximum degree of the interval graph derived from the delivery intervals.

1.2   Related Works

The drone delivery scheduling problem has been studied by Sorbeli et al. [3,4]. The most relevant results of this paper are listed in Table 1. Related works are mostly classified into two categories. In the *first category*, the studies [8,9,13,14], considered the delivery scenario where each *package delivered either by the truck or by a drone*. In the *second category*, the studies [3–5] considered the delivery scenario where each *package deliver by drone only*.

First Category: Murray and Chu [13] first introduced *flying sidekicks traveling sales associate problem*, an extension of the traveling salesman problem (TSP) where they considered delivery of the packages either by the drone operating in coordination with the truck or by the delivery-truck itself. In this model, the drone can launch from the depot or any customer location to deliver the package. Then it returns to the truck at any customer location or the depot. In addition, the truck can also deliver the packages and make synchrony for launching and landing the drone. This paper aims to reduce the total time to make all the deliveries. They proposed an optimal *mixed integer linear programming* (MILP) formulation and two heuristic solutions with numerical testing for this purpose. Furthermore, Murray and Raj [14] extended the above problem for multiple drones, referred to as *multiple flying sidekicks traveling salesman problem*. Here, the authors designed MILP formulation for the problem and a heuristic solution with simulation. Using the solution for the TSP, Crisan and Nechita [8] suggested another competent heuristic for the *flying sidekicks traveling salesman problem*. The mobility of drones came into the literature when Daknama and Kraus [9] took a policy for recharging the drones on the truck's roof. With this, a drone can deliver more packages than the usual methods. In addition, a heuristic algorithm has been proposed by the authors for the schedule of the truck and drones.

Second Category: Delivery by drone is only considered by Boysen et al. [5]. Their objective is to find the drone's launching and rendezvous points among a set of given stop points in the truck's route such that the total makespan to complete all the deliveries becomes minimum. Sorbelli et al. [4] proposed another drone delivery model. They proposed a Multiple Drone-Delivery Scheduling Problem (MDSP), where a truck and multiple drones cooperate among themself to deliver packages. Here authors assumed that each delivery's launching and rendezvous location is given. This problem aims to find the schedule for the available drones

Table 1. Comparing existing literature with our proposed algorithms, where n and m are the number of deliveries and drones, respectively. B is the battery budget, P is the sum of all the profits, and $\epsilon > 0$.

No of Drones	Paper	Approx. Factor	Time Complexity
$m = 1$	Sorbelli et al. [4]	1 (Optimal)	$\mathcal{O}(n \log n + nB)$
	Pferschy and Schauer [16]	1 (Optimal)	$\mathcal{O}((n + n_e)P^2)$
	Theorem 2	1(Optimal)	$\mathcal{O}(n \log n + nP)$
	Sorbelli et al. [4]	Not Constant	$\mathcal{O}(n \log n)$
	Theorem 3	FPTAS	$\mathcal{O}(n \log n + n\lfloor \frac{n^2}{\epsilon} \rfloor)$
$m > 1$	Sorbelli et al. [4]	Not Constant	$\mathcal{O}(mn \log n)$
	Chekuri and Khanna [7]	$0.632 - \mathcal{O}(\epsilon)$	$\mathcal{O}(m(n \log n + n\lfloor \frac{n^2}{\epsilon} \rfloor))$
	Theorem 6	$\frac{1}{3}$	$\mathcal{O}(n^2)$

to maximize profit. The authors propose NP-hardness proof of the problem, and ILP formulation, In addition, the authors gave an optimal algorithm for the single drone case with time complexity depending on the drone's battery budget (B), and approximation algorithms for the multiple drone case with non-constant approximation factor. In this paper, we study this problem (MDSP). The time complexity of our proposed optimal algorithm for the single drone depends on the sum of all the profits (P) and the approximation factors of the proposed algorithms for the multiple drone are constant. Additionally, the drone delivery problem is related to the well-studied *0-1 knapsack problem* [2,7,16], where we have a knapsack associated with a capacity and a set of items associated with some profit and cost. The objective is to choose a subset of items such that the profit is maximized constraint to the knapsack capacity. In addition, if there is a conflict graph representing the conflict between items, the problem is known as *knapsack problem with conflicts*. The objective for this problem is to choose the conflict-free subset of items to maximize the profit subject to the knapsack capacity. The MDSP is related this problem if we consider each delivery as one of the items in the knapsack and the drone's battery budget as the knapsack's capacity. For the *knapsack problem with conflicts*, Pferschy and Schauer [16] presented an optimal pseudo-polynomial algorithm for the problem if the conflict graph is a chordal graph with running time $\mathcal{O}((n + n_e)P^2)$, where n is the number of items, n_e is the number of edges in the conflict graph and P is the sum of all the profits. The result holds for the interval graph, as it is a subclass of the chordal graph. Also, the authors mentioned the existence of FPTAS to the problem from their formulated exact algorithm. Our proposed exact algorithm and FPTAS have better time complexity than this. Basnet [2] proposed some heuristics for the problem *multiple knapsack problem with conflicts*. In this problem, the number of knapsacks is more than one and the objective is the same as the earlier. But, the author did not give any approximation factor for the problem. Although, a greedy approach can be taken for the multiple drones case by successfully applying FPTAS for the single drone for each drone on the remaining items. The approximation factor for this algorithm $(Greedy(\epsilon))$ is calculated by Chekuri and Khanna [7]. If we use our proposed FPTAS for this greedy approach, we have the overall time complexity for $Greedy(\epsilon)$ is $\mathcal{O}(m(n\log n + n\lfloor\frac{n^2}{\epsilon}\rfloor))$, where $\epsilon > 0$, n is the number of deliveries and m is the number of drones. Whereas, our proposed approximation algorithm for MDSP is $\mathcal{O}(n^2)$, far better than the time complexity for $Greedy(\epsilon)$. Table 1 compares our works with the related results.

The rest of the paper is organized as follows. The model with the problem formulation and a deterministic rounding algorithm is presented in Sect. 2. An approximation algorithm for a single drone is proposed in Sect. 3 and for multiple drones is presented in Sect. 4. We conclude the paper in Sect. 5.

2 Model and Problem Formulation

In this section, we describe the model of the Multiple Drone-Delivery Scheduling Problem (MDSP) and integer linear programming (ILP) formulation [3] of it. Later on, a deterministic rounding algorithm is proposed by relaxing the ILP.

2.1 Model

Let $\mathcal{M} = \{1, 2, \cdots, m\}$ be the set of drones, each having equal battery budget B and $\mathcal{N} = \{1, 2, \cdots, n\}$ be the set of customers or deliveries with prescribed location δ_j for each $j \in \mathcal{N}$.

For each customer j, there is associate *cost* c_j and *profit* p_j, which are incurred by a drone for completing the delivery j. Initially, all the drones are at the depot. A truck starts it's journey containing all the drones on a prescribed route for delivering customers. A drone takes off from the truck at the given launch point (δ_j^L) to complete the delivery to the customer j at the position δ_j, and after completing the delivery, it meets the truck again at the given rendezvous point (δ_j^R). Let at time t_0 the truck starts it's journey and t_j^L, t_j^R be the time when it comes to the points δ_j^L, δ_j^R, respectively.

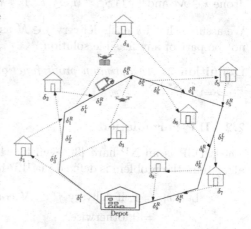

Fig. 1. A drone-delivery model.

So, $I_j = [t_j^L, t_j^R]$ is the *delivery time interval* for the delivery j. Any delivery j can be performed by at most one drone, and that drone cannot be assigned to any other delivery at the time interval I_j. Also, note that the truck cannot move back at any time, i.e., if P and Q are two points on the route of the truck, where Q is located after P, then $t_P < t_Q$, where t_P and t_Q are the times when the truck passes through the points P and Q, respectively.

Figure 1 shows an example of a drone-delivery model with eight delivery locations (δ_i) and two drones. The solid lines in the figure represent the truck's route, while the dotted lines represent the paths of the drone.

Any two intervals I_j and I_k are said to be *compatible* if $I_j \cap I_k = \emptyset$; else they are *conflicting*, where $1 \leq j \neq k \leq n$. Let $I = \{I_1, I_2, \cdots, I_n\}$ be the set of delivery time intervals corresponding to the set of deliveries $\mathcal{N}$. Without loss of generality, we assume that intervals $I_1, I_2, \cdots, I_n$ are sorted in non-decreasing order according to their launching time, i.e., $t_1^L \leq t_2^L \leq, \cdots, \leq t_n^L$. A set $S \subseteq I$ is said to be *compatible* if all pairs of intervals in it are *compatible*. A compatible set S is said to be *feasible*, if the energy cost of S, which is defined as $\mathcal{W}(S) = \sum_{I_j \in S} c_j \leq B$. One drone $i \in \mathcal{M}$ can be utilized for multiple deliveries (S), provided S is feasible. The profit for the set S defined as $\mathcal{P}(S) = \sum_{I_j \in S} p_j$.

Definition 1. *An assignment S of the deliveries for a drone is defined as $S = \{I_{k_1}, I_{k_2}, \cdots, I_{k_l}\} \subseteq I$, where $1 \leq k_i \leq n$.*

We are formally rewriting the definition of the Multiple Drone-Delivery Scheduling Problem [3] as follows.

Problem 1. (Multiple Drone-Delivery Scheduling Problem (MDSP))
Given a set of drones $\mathcal{M}$ with identical battery budget B and an interval set I corresponding to a set of deliveries $\mathcal{N}$, the objective is to find a family of assignment $\mathcal{S}^* = \{S_1^*, S_2^*, \cdots, S_m^*\}$ corresponding to m drones such that $\sum_{i=1}^m \mathcal{P}(S_i^*)$ is maximized, where $S_i^* \subseteq I$ is the feasible assignment corresponding to the drone $i \in \mathcal{M}$ and $S_k^* \cap S_l^* = \emptyset; \forall k, l : 1 \leq k \neq l \leq m$.

We assume that for each delivery $j \in \mathcal{N}$ associate cost, $c_j \leq B$, otherwise it will not be part of any feasible solution.

Definition 2. *An optimum profit function f for m drones is defined as $f(m) = \sum_{i=1}^m \mathcal{P}(S_i^*)$.*

2.2 ILP Formulation

The MDSP is an NP-hard [3], even for the single drone case. For the optimal algorithm, the problem is defined via ILP formulation according to [3] as follows:

$$\text{Let, } x_{ij} = 1, \text{ if delivery } j \in \mathcal{N} \text{ completed by the drone } i \in \mathcal{M} \tag{1}$$
$$= 0, \text{ otherwise.}$$

$$\max \sum_{i \in \mathcal{M}} \sum_{j \in \mathcal{N}} p_j x_{ij} \tag{2}$$

$$\text{subject to, } \sum_{j \in \mathcal{N}} c_j x_{ij} \leq B, \, \forall \, i \in \mathcal{M} \tag{3}$$

$$\sum_{i \in \mathcal{M}} x_{ij} \leq 1, \, \forall \, j \in \mathcal{N} \tag{4}$$

$$x_{ij} + x_{ik} \leq 1, \ \forall i \in \mathcal{M}; \ \forall j, k \in \mathcal{N} : I_j \cap I_k \neq \emptyset \tag{5}$$

$$x_{ij} \in \{0, 1\}, \ \forall i \in \mathcal{M}, \ \forall j \in \mathcal{N} \tag{6}$$

The objective function (2) is about maximizing the profit by scheduling the deliveries with m drones. Constraint (3) depicts that a drone cannot have an assignment that exceeds it's battery budget B. Constraint (4) says that each delivery can be completed by at most one drone. Constraint (5) says that if two deliveries conflict, a drone can choose at most one of them.

The aforementioned formulation is only suitable for solving the problem optimally for small-sized instances. But for large instances, we need some approximation. In the next Sect. 2.3, we derive a deterministic rounding algorithm for the ILP and calculate the approximation factor of the algorithm.

2.3 Deterministic Rounding Algorithm

An *integer linear programming* (ILP) is not solvable optimally in polynomial time. To reduce the time complexity, we proposed a deterministic rounding method for the MDSP in this section.

We can formulate a *linear programming* (LP) from the ILP formulation of the MDSP (as stated in Sect. 2.2) by replacing the constraints (6) by (7).

$$0 \leq x_{ij} \leq 1, \ \forall i \in \mathcal{M}, \ \forall j \in \mathcal{N} \tag{7}$$

This replacement changed the ILP to an LP. An LP can be solved optimally in polynomial time. But a solution of the LP is not feasible for the corresponding ILP as there are fraction values (in this problem between 0 and 1) to the LP solution, whereas the ILP solution contains only integers. Thus we need the rounding of the LP solution to get a feasible solution for the ILP.

Let $x(x_{ij})$ be an optimal solution for the LP. Now we construct another solution $x'(x'_{ij})$ from x by defining $x'_{ij} = 1$, if $x_{ij} > 1/2$ and $x'_{ij} = 0$, if $x_{ij} \leq 1/2$. With this setting, we have the following lemmata.

Lemma 1. *x' is a feasible solution for the MDSP by violating the constraint (3) by $2B$.*

Proof. Let us assume that $x'_{ij} + x'_{ik} > 1$, for any arbitrary $i \in \mathcal{M}$, $j \in \mathcal{N}$ and $k \in \mathcal{N}$ such that $I_j \cap I_k \neq \emptyset$. Then, $x'_{ij} = 1$ and $x'_{ik} = 1$, implies $x_{ij} > 1/2$ and $x_{ik} > 1/2$, implies $x_{ij} + x_{ik} > 1$, which is a contradiction, as x is a feasible solution to the LP.

Thus $x'_{ij} + x'_{ik} \leq 1$, $\forall i \in \mathcal{M}$, $j \in \mathcal{N}$ and $k \in \mathcal{N}$ such that $I_j \cap I_k \neq \emptyset$, which is the constraint (5). A similar proof can be done to show that x' satisfies the constraint (4). Constraint (6) holds from the construction of x'. Now for any $i \in \mathcal{M}$, define X_i as $X_i = \{j \in \mathcal{N} : x'_{ij} = 1\}$ and $\overline{X_i}$ as $\overline{X_i} = \mathcal{N} \setminus X_i$. Then,

$$\sum_{j \in \mathcal{N}} c_j x'_{ij} = \sum_{j \in X_i} c_j x'_{ij} + \sum_{j \in \overline{X_i}} c_j x'_{ij} < \sum_{j \in X_i} 2c_j x_{ij} + \sum_{j \in \overline{X_i}} c_j x_{ij} \leq 2 \sum_{j \in \mathcal{N}} c_j x_{ij} \leq 2B.$$

Thus x' violates the constraint (3) by $2B$. Hence the proof.   □

Let $\mathcal{OPT}_{LP}$ be the profit corresponding to the optimal solution (x) of the LP. Let $\mathcal{S}_{ILP}$ be the collection of assignments associated with the solution of the ILP after rounding. Any assignment $S \in \mathcal{S}_{ILP}$ corresponds to the drone $i \in \mathcal{M}$ defined as, $S = \{I_j : x'_{ij} = 1\}$. Then we have the following lemma.

Lemma 2. $\mathcal{P}(\mathcal{S}_{ILP}) \geq \frac{1}{2}\mathcal{OPT}_{LP}$.

Proof.

$$
\mathcal{P}(\mathcal{S}_{ILP}) = \sum_{i \in \mathcal{M}} \sum_{j \in X_i} p_j x'_{ij} + \sum_{i \in \mathcal{M}} \sum_{j \in \overline{X_i}} p_j x'_{ij} \geq \sum_{i \in \mathcal{M}} \left(\sum_{j \in X_i} p_j x_{ij} + \sum_{j \in \overline{X_i}} p_j \left(x_{ij} - \frac{1}{2}\right) \right)
$$

$$
\geq \sum_{i \in \mathcal{M}} \sum_{j \in \mathcal{N}} p_j x_{ij} - \frac{1}{2} \sum_{i \in \mathcal{M}} \sum_{j \in \overline{X_i}} p_j x_{ij} \geq \mathcal{OPT}_{LP} - \frac{1}{2}\mathcal{OPT}_{LP} = \frac{1}{2}\mathcal{OPT}_{LP}.
$$

$\square$

Algorithm 1. PARTITION(S, S^1, S^2, S^3)

1: **Initially:-** $S = \{I_{t_1}, I_{t_2}, \cdots, I_{t_l}\}$; $S^1 = S^2 = S^3 = \emptyset$.
2: **for** $j \leftarrow 1, l$ **do**
3:     **if** $\mathcal{W}(S^1) \leq B$ **then**
4:         Move the delivery I_{t_j} to S^1
5:     **else**
6:         break
7:     **end if**
8: **end for**
9: Move the delivery I_{t_j} to S^2
10: **for** $j \leftarrow j + 1, l$ **do**
11:     Move the delivery I_{t_j} to S^3
12: **end for**

But $\mathcal{S}_{ILP}$ is not a feasible solution for the ILP of the MDSP, as every assignment of $\mathcal{S}_{ILP}$ has cost at most $2B$, which violates the constraint (3). So we need to modify the solution. Every assignment $S \in \mathcal{S}_{ILP}$ is partitioned into three assignments greedily. Each of them has cost at most B. We have formulated the greedy approach for the partition in Algorithm 1.

Lemma 3. PARTITION(S, S^1, S^2, S^3) *partitions the assignment S into three disjoint assignments, S^1, S^2, S^3, each having cost at most B.*

Proof. From the step (3), we have $\mathcal{W}(S^1) \leq B$.
From the model's assumption, every delivery has cost at most B. So, $\mathcal{W}(S^2) \leq B$.
Let $S^2 = \{t_j\}$. Then, $\mathcal{W}(S^1) + c_{t_j} > B$.
Now, let us assume that $\mathcal{W}(S^3) > B$, then $\mathcal{W}(S) = \mathcal{W}(S^1) + c_{t_j} + \mathcal{W}(S^3) > 2B$. This is a contradiction, as $\mathcal{W}(S) \leq 2B$. So, $\mathcal{W}(S^3) \leq B$. Hence the proof. $\square$

Algorithm 2. ROUNDING($\mathcal{N}, \mathcal{M}, I, B$)

1: Construct the ILP formulation of the problem as stated in section 2.2.
2: Relaxing the constraint (6) of the ILP by (7) to get the corresponding LP.
3: Solve the LP optimally, say $x(x_{ij})$ is a solution for the LP and $\mathcal{OPT}_{LP}$ is the corresponding profit to the solution.
4: Define $x'(x'_{ij})$ by $x'_{ij} = 1$, if $x_{ij} > 1/2$, otherwise $x_{ij} = 0$.
5: Find the collection of assignments ($\mathcal{S}_{\mathcal{ILP}}$) corresponding to the solution x'_{ij}.
6: Partition each assignment $S \in \mathcal{S}_{ILP}$ into three assignments S^1, S^2, S^3 by using Algorithm 1.
7: Take m most profitable assignments among $3m$ assignments $\bigcup_{S \in \mathcal{S}_{ILP}} (S^1 \cup S^2 \cup S^3)$ and assign to the drones in $\mathcal{M}$.

So, we have $3m$ assignments (some of them may be empty) after partitioning each assignment in $S \in \mathcal{S}_{ILP}$, each having cost at most B. From these assignments, we will take m most profitable assignments, as per the problem's requirement. Thus, we can have our rounding algorithm as stated in Algorithm 2.

Theorem 1. *Algorithm 2 gives $\frac{1}{6}$ approximation factor to the optimal solution of the MDSP with polynomial running time.*

Proof. Let $\mathcal{S}'$ be the collection of m assignments returned by Algorithm 2. Then,

$$\mathcal{P}(\mathcal{S}') \geq \frac{1}{3}\mathcal{P}(\mathcal{S}_{ILP}) \geq \frac{1}{6}\mathcal{OPT}_{LP} \geq \frac{1}{6}f(m). \tag{8}$$

The first inequality is straightforward from the step 7 of the algorithm. The second inequality holds from Lemma 2. The last inequality follows from the observation that an optimal solution to a problem formulated by ILP is also a feasible solution to the corresponding relaxed LP problem.

An LP can be solved in polynomial time. Construction of an ILP, PARTITION() and finding m maximum elements among $3m$ elements can also be done in polynomial time. So, the time complexity of Algorithm 2 is polynomial. □

The approximation factor derived from the above deterministic rounding algorithm is very high. In the next section, we propose the following two approximation algorithms with better approximation factors for solving the problem; one for the single drone and the other for the multiple drones case.

3 Delivery with Single Drone

In this section, we design an approximation algorithm (APPROXALGOFORS-DSP) to solve the above problem for the single drone case, i.e., $|\mathcal{M}| = 1$, which is referred to as *single drone-delivery scheduling problem* (SDSP).

According to the model, intervals $I_1, I_2, \cdots, I_n$ are sorted in non-decreasing order as per their launching time. Now, we can find the previous nearest conflict-free interval $I_{L(j)}$ for each $I_j \in I$ by computing $L(j)$ as follows.

$L(j) := \max\{k : k \in \mathcal{N}, k < j \text{ and } t_k^R < t_j^L\}, \forall j \in \mathcal{N}$ and $L(j) = 0$ if there is no such k exists for the delivery j.

This procedure informs us which intervals we need to take out from the previous assignment if we add the current interval to it.

Now, we design a pseudo-polynomial dynamic programming (Algorithm 3) for SDSP and then an approximation algorithm (Algorithm 4) based on the FPTAS for the *0-1 knapsack problem* [18].

3.1 Dynamic Programming Formulation

Let $P = \sum_{j \in \mathcal{N}}(p_j)$, then P is an upper bound of the optimal profit. We define $S(j,p) \subseteq \{I_1, I_2, \cdots, I_j\}$, a compatible subset of I such that the cost $\mathcal{W}(S(j,p))$ is minimized subject to $\mathcal{P}(S(j,p)) = p$, where $1 \le j \le n$ and $0 \le p \le P$.
Set $A(j,p) = \mathcal{W}(S(j,p))$.
Basis:- $A(1,p) = c_1$, if $p = p_1$; otherwise $A(1,p) = \infty$.
$A(j,0) = 0; \forall j \in \mathcal{N} \cup \{0\}$. $A(0,p) = \infty; \forall p : 1 \le p \le P$.
For given $A(j,p)(1 \le j < n \text{ and } 0 \le p \le P)$, compute $A(j+1,p)$ as follows.

Case 1 ($I_{j+1} \in S(j+1,p)$): All the deliveries between $(L(j+1)+1)$ and j do not be the part of $S(j+1,p)$. So, for this case $A(j+1,p) = c_{j+1} + A(L(j+1), p - p_{j+1})$, if $p \ge p_{j+1}$; else $A(j+1,p) = A(j,p)$.
Case 2 ($I_{j+1} \notin S(j+1,p)$): For this case we always have $A(j+1,p) = A(j,p)$.

From the above two cases, we can infer that

$$A(j+1,p) = \min\{A(j,p), (c_{j+1} + A(L(j+1), p - p_{j+1}))\}, \text{ if p } \ge p_{j+1}, \tag{9}$$
$$= A(j,p), \text{ otherwise.}$$

Using the equation (9), we design an optimal dynamic programming Algorithm 3 (DPALGOFORSDSP) as follows. The optimal feasible intervals $S^* = \{S^*\}$ is an assignment for the drone to be delivered to make the profit maximum.

Algorithm 3. (DPALGOFORSDSP)

1: **for** $j \leftarrow 1, n-1$ **do**
2:    **for** $p \leftarrow 1, P$ **do**
3:        compute $A(j+1,p)$ using the formula at the equation (9).
4:    **end for**
5: **end for**
6: Find p: $p = \max\{p : A(n,p) \le B\}$ ▷ Maximum profit p subject to the budget B.
7: Find the feasible intervals (S^*) by backtracking to the array A for the value p.

Theorem 2. *Algorithm 3 is a pseudo-polynomial time optimal algorithm for SDSP.*

Proof. Intervals are sorted according to their launching time as per the model assumption. Although, this assumption can be dropped by sorting the intervals. So we can find the $L(j)$ for each $j \in \mathcal{N}$ in $\mathcal{O}(n \log n)$ time. For Algorithm 3, we can compute the 2D array (A) by $\mathcal{O}(nP)$ time. Also, step 6 of this algorithm can be done by $\mathcal{O}(P)$ time. So, running time is $\mathcal{O}(n \log n + nP)$ and correctness follows from the equation (9). Thus it is a pseudo-polynomial time algorithm. $\square$

Now, we propose a fully polynomial time approximation scheme (FPTAS) which is described via Algorithm 4 (ApproxAlgoForSDSP) to solve SDSP. Algorithm 4 uses Algorithm 3 as a subroutine.

Algorithm 4. (ApproxAlgoForSDSP)

1: Set $K = \frac{\epsilon P}{n^2}$, for $\epsilon > 0$.
2: Set a new profit $p'_j = \lfloor \frac{p_j}{K} \rfloor$ for each delivery $j \in \mathcal{N}$.
3: Find the optimum solution (S') of the same problem (SDSP) using Algorithm 3, with the new profit p'_j $(j \in \mathcal{N})$ and replacing P by $P' = \sum_{j \in \mathcal{N}}(p'_j)$

Theorem 3. *Algorithm 4 gives an FPTAS for SDSP with running time* $\mathcal{O}(n \log n + n \lfloor \frac{n^2}{\epsilon} \rfloor)$ *for* $\epsilon > 0$.

Proof. Let S^* and S' be the optimum feasible intervals for the SDSP with profit values p_j and p'_j $(\forall j \in \mathcal{N})$, respectively.
    Also let $\mathcal{P}(S^*) = \sum_{j \in S^*} p_j$; $\mathcal{P}'(S^*) = \sum_{j \in S^*} p'_j$; $\mathcal{P}'(S') = \sum_{j \in S'} p'_j$.
As $(p_j - K.p'_j) \leq K$, we have $\mathcal{P}(S^*) - K\mathcal{P}'(S^*) \leq nK$.
As Algorithm 4 gives us the optimum solution for the problem with new profit values and S', S^* both being feasible sets, $\mathcal{P}'(S') \geq \mathcal{P}'(S^*)$.
Also we have $\mathcal{P}(S') \geq K.\mathcal{P}'(S')$, as $p_j \geq K.p'_j$. Thus,

$$\mathcal{P}(S') \geq K.\mathcal{P}'(S') \geq K.\mathcal{P}'(S^*) \geq \mathcal{P}(S^*) - nK = \mathcal{P}(S^*) - \frac{\epsilon P}{n}$$

$$\geq \mathcal{P}(S^*) - \epsilon \mathcal{P}(S^*), \text{ (as } \mathcal{P}(S^*) \geq \max_{j \in \mathcal{N}}(p_j) \geq \frac{P}{n}) \tag{10}$$

$$= (1 - \epsilon)\mathcal{P}(S^*)$$

The running time for this algorithm is $\mathcal{O}(n \log n + nP')$ (from Theorem 2), where $P' = \sum_{j \in \mathcal{N}}(p'_j) = \sum_{j \in \mathcal{N}}(\lfloor \frac{n^2 p_j}{\epsilon P} \rfloor) \leq \sum_{j \in \mathcal{N}}((\lfloor \frac{n^2}{\epsilon} \rfloor + 1)\frac{p_j}{P}) = \lfloor \frac{n^2}{\epsilon} \rfloor + 1$.
Thus the running time for Algorithm 4 is $\mathcal{O}(n \log n + n \lfloor \frac{n^2}{\epsilon} \rfloor)$. $\square$

4 Delivery with Multiple Drones

In this section, based on a greedy approach, we formulate an approximation algorithm for the *multiple drone delivery scheduling problem* (MDSP). Please note that, unlike SDSP, MDSP does not have an FPTAS, as stated below.

Theorem 4. *MDSP does not admit an FPTAS.*

Proof. MDSP is a generalized version of *multiple knapsack problem* (MKP). If we remove the conflicting condition of MDSP, it becomes MKP. *Chekuri and Khanna* [7] proved that MKP does not admit FPTAS. From this, it is straightforward to conclude that MDSP also does not admit FPTAS.   □

In the following part, we propose a constant factor approximation algorithm to solve the MDSP by restricting the number of drones. Now, we define some definitions and lemmata for the MDSP.

Definition 3. *The density of a delivery $j \in \mathcal{N}$ defined as the ratio between profit (p_j) and cost (c_j), which is denoted by $d_j = \frac{p_j}{c_j}$.*

Definition 4. *An assignment $S = \{I_{k_1}, I_{k_2}, \cdots, I_{k_l}\} \subseteq I$ of the deliveries with density $d_{k_1} \geq d_{k_2} \geq \cdots \geq d_{k_l}$, is called a critical assignment for a drone with battery budget B, if $\mathcal{W}(S) > B$ and $\mathcal{W}(S \setminus \{k_l\}) \leq B$.*

Lemma 4. *If $S = \{I_{k_1}, I_{k_2}, \cdots, I_{k_l}\} \subseteq I$ with l largest densities $d_{k_1} \geq d_{k_2} \geq \cdots \geq d_{k_l}$ is a compatible and critical assignment for any SDSP then $\mathcal{P}(S) \geq f(1)$.*

Proof. We prove the lemma by contradiction. In contradictory, let $\mathcal{P}(S) < f(1)$. Let T be the optimal assignment for the chosen SDSP, i.e., $\mathcal{P}(T) = f(1)$.
Then $\mathcal{P}(S) < \mathcal{P}(T)$ implies $\mathcal{P}(S \setminus T) < \mathcal{P}(T \setminus S)$.
But every item in $(S \setminus T)$ has a density at least the density of any item in $(T \setminus S)$, implies $\mathcal{W}(S \setminus T) < \mathcal{W}(T \setminus S)$, implies $\mathcal{W}(S) < \mathcal{W}(T)$, which is a contradiction as $\mathcal{W}(T) \leq B$ and $\mathcal{W}(S) > B$. Hence, the statement of the lemma follows.   □

From the above lemma, we can state the following result.

Corollary 1. $\max(\mathcal{P}(\{I_{k_l}\}), \mathcal{P}(S \setminus \{I_{k_l}\})) \geq \frac{f(1)}{2}$.

Theorem 5. *Let $\mathcal{S} = \{S_1, S_2, \cdots, S_{m'}\}$ be a collection of assignment for MDSP with $m'(m' \geq m)$ drones, where S_i is a compatible assignment for the drone $i(1 \leq i \leq m')$ and $S_k \cap S_l = \emptyset; \forall k, l : 1 \leq k \neq l \leq m'$. If $\mathcal{S}$ is the set of first $\sum_{i=1}^{m'} |S_i|$ largest density intervals of I and among m' assignments of $\mathcal{S}$ at least m are critical, then $\mathcal{P}(\mathcal{S}) = \sum_{i=1}^{m'} \mathcal{P}(S_i) \geq f(m)$.*

Proof. We prove the theorem by contradiction.
In contradictory, let $\mathcal{P}(\mathcal{S}) < f(m)$. Let $\mathcal{T}$ be the optimal family of assignment for the MDSP with m drones, then $\mathcal{P}(\mathcal{T}) = f(m)$.
    Let $S = \cup_{i=1}^{m'} S_i$ and T be the set of all deliveries in $\mathcal{T}$. Then $\mathcal{P}(S) < \mathcal{P}(T)$, implies $\mathcal{P}(S \setminus T) < \mathcal{P}(T \setminus S)$. But every item in $(S \setminus T)$ has a density at least the density of any item in $(T \setminus S)$. So, $\mathcal{W}(S \setminus T) < \mathcal{W}(T \setminus S)$, implies $\mathcal{W}(S) < \mathcal{W}(T)$, which is a contradiction as $\mathcal{W}(T) \leq mB$ and $\mathcal{W}(S) > mB$. Hence, the statement of the theorem follows.   □

We can construct an interval graph using the delivery intervals for a given instance of MDSP and find the graph's maximum degree Δ. With this knowledge of Δ, we propose Algorithm 5 (GREEDYALGOFORMDSP) to solve MDSP.

Algorithm 5. (GREEDYALGOFORMDSP)

1: **Initially:-** $M = \{1, 2, \cdots, m + \Delta\}$; $M' = \emptyset$; $\forall i \in M : L_i = \emptyset$; $P_i = 0$; $W_i = 0$; $S_i = \emptyset$.
2: Sort delivery intervals I according to their density. $\triangleright$ wlog let $d_1 \geq d_2 \geq, \cdots, \geq d_n$.
3: **for** $j \leftarrow 1, n$ **do**
4:     **if** $|M'| \neq m$ **then**
5:         Find $i \in M$ such that $S_i \cap I_j = \emptyset$
6:         **if** $W_i + c_j \leq B$ **then**
7:             $W_i = W_i + c_j$; $S_i = S_i \cup \{I_j\}$; $P_i = P_i + p_j$.
8:         **else**
9:             $W_i = W_i + c_j$; $S_i = S_i \cup \{I_j\}$; $P_i = P_i + p_j$
10:            $M = M \setminus \{i\}$; $M' = M' \cup \{i\}$; $L_i = \{j\}$.
11:        **end if**
12:    **else**
13:        break.
14:    **end if**
15: **end for**
16: **for** each i in M' **do**
17:    **if** $(P_i - \mathcal{P}(L_i)) \geq \mathcal{P}(L_i)$ **then**
18:        $W_i = W_i - \mathcal{W}(L_i)$; $P_i = P_i - \mathcal{P}(L_i)$; $S_i = S_i \setminus L_i$
19:    **else**
20:        $W_i = \mathcal{W}(L_i)$; $P_i = \mathcal{P}(L_i)$; $S_i = L_i$.
21:    **end if**
22: **end for**
23: Return m most profitable $i \in (M \cup M')$ along with it's S_i.

Lemma 5. *Algorithm 5 gives a feasible solution for MDSP with m drones.*

Proof. Instead of m drones, the algorithm starts with $(m+\Delta)$ drones. For assigning a delivery j (in the non-decreasing order of their densities) to a drone in M at step $3 - 15$, the algorithm checks whether there are m critical assignments (recorded by M') in the current schedule or not. If not (i.e., $M' \neq m$), then there is at least $(\Delta + 1)$ drones in M, because $|M| \geq (m + \Delta) - (m - 1)$, to assign the delivery j. In this schedule, j can conflict with the assignment of at most Δ many drones in M. Therefore, there always exists a drone i in M such that it's current assignment is compatible with I_j, i.e., $S_i \cap \{I_j\} = \emptyset$. Now, if the addition of delivery j to S_i does not exceed the battery budget, i.e., $W_i + c_j \leq B$, where $W_i = \mathcal{W}(S_i)$. Then drone i is feasible for the delivery j. So, in this case, we schedule the delivery j to drone i and update the current cost (W_i) and profit (P_i) value for the drone i at step 7. Otherwise $(W_i + c_j > B)$, the addition of delivery j to the current schedule (S_i) of i makes the assignment critical. So, in this case, we also update the current assignment (S_i), cost (W_i), and profit (P_i) value for the drone i at step 9. In addition, we remove drone i from the set M and add it to the set M' at step 10, as the assignment of i becomes critical.

So, there always exists a drone i whose current assignment is compatible with the delivery j. Therefore, we can find m critical assignments whose indices are recorded by M', or all the deliveries are assigned to the $(m + \Delta)$ drones. Whenever we find m critical assignment, we break the loop at step 13.

At the end of step 15, we have $(m+\Delta)$ compatible assignments. Among them, at most m are critical. To make those assignments feasible, we ignore either the last delivery or all the preceding deliveries of each assignment for which the profit is maximum. At last, we take m most profitable assignments among all $(m + \Delta)$ feasible assignments, as our objective is to find m feasible assignments. Thus Algorithm 5 finds a feasible solution for MDSP with m drones.   □

Lemma 6. *The time complexity of Algorithm 5 is $\mathcal{O}(n^2)$, where $n = |\mathcal{N}|$.*

Proof. Step-wise analysis of Algorithm 5 is given below. The n delivery intervals can be sorted at step 2 in $\mathcal{O}(n \log n)$ time. For assigning the delivery j according to their non-decreasing order of density to a drone in M, at most $(\Delta + 1)$ compatibility check to any of the $(\Delta+1)$ assignments of the drones in M is sufficient. Since there are at most $(j - 1)$ deliveries assigned to those drones, we can find one such drone i in M for which $S_i \cap I_j = \emptyset$ by $\mathcal{O}(j)$ many comparisons. Then all the update operations corresponding to S_i, W_i, P_i, M and M' take constant time. Hence, the total running time for steps (3-15) is $\leq \sum_{j=1}^{n} \mathcal{O}(j) = \mathcal{O}(n^2)$.

Step (16-22) runs in $\leq \mathcal{O}(|M'|) \leq \mathcal{O}(m)$ time. Last step can be done in $\mathcal{O}(m + \Delta) + \mathcal{O}(m \log(m + \Delta)) \leq \mathcal{O}(n^2)$ time. (as $m, \Delta \leq n$)
Thus, the overall running time is $\mathcal{O}(n^2)$.   □

Lemma 7. *Algorithm 5 gives an $\frac{m}{(2m+\Delta)}$ approximation factor of the MDSP with m many drones and Δ being the maximum degree of the interval graph.*

Proof. Let $OPT = f(m)$, be the optimum profit for the MDSP with m many drones. Let $\mathcal{S} = \{S_1, S_2, \cdots, S_{m+\Delta}\}$ be the family of assignments return by Algorithm 5 at the step 15. At this step, either all the deliveries are assigned to the $(m + \Delta)$ drones or m assignments are critical. For any case $\mathcal{P}(\mathcal{S}) = \sum_{i=1}^{m+\Delta} \mathcal{P}(S_i) \geq OPT$. ($m$ assignments are critical implies $\mathcal{P}(\mathcal{S}) \geq OPT$ from Theorem 5).

Without loss of generality, let $\{S_1, S_2, \cdots, S_t\}$ $(t \leq m)$ be a collection of critical assignment. The algorithm moderates each by omitting either the last delivery or all the remaining deliveries for which the profit is maximum to make those assignments feasible. Let $\{S_1', S_2', \cdots, S_t'\}$ be the moderate set. Then $\mathcal{P}(S_i') \geq \frac{\mathcal{P}(S_i)}{2}$, $\forall i : 1 \leq i \leq t$ (from Corollary 1).

The final solution returned by the algorithm is those assignments corresponding to the m largest profits among $\{\mathcal{P}(S_1'), \mathcal{P}(S_2'), \cdots, \mathcal{P}(S_t'), \mathcal{P}(S_{t+1}), \mathcal{P}(S_{t+2}), \cdots, \mathcal{P}(S_{m+\Delta})\}$. Let $\mathcal{S}_A$ be that collection, then,

$$\mathcal{P}(\mathcal{S}_A) \geq \frac{m}{m + \Delta}(\sum_{i=1}^{t} \mathcal{P}(S_i') + \sum_{i=t+1}^{m+\Delta} \mathcal{P}(S_i)) \geq \frac{m}{m + \Delta} \cdot \frac{1}{2}(\sum_{i=1}^{m+\Delta} \mathcal{P}(S_i) + \sum_{i=t+1}^{m+\Delta} \mathcal{P}(S_i))$$

$$\geq \frac{m}{2(m + \Delta)} \left(OPT + \sum_{i=t+1}^{m+\Delta} \mathcal{P}(S_i) \right)$$

Now we have the following two cases for a fixed $\epsilon > 0$.

Case 1 $\left(\sum_{i=t+1}^{m+\Delta} \mathcal{P}(S_i) \geq \epsilon OPT\right)$: Then, from the above inequality we have, $\mathcal{P}(S_A) \geq \frac{m}{2(m+\Delta)}(1+\epsilon)OPT$.

Case 2 $\left(\sum_{i=t+1}^{m+\Delta} \mathcal{P}(S_i) < \epsilon OPT\right)$: Then, $\sum_{i=1}^{t} \mathcal{P}(S_i) \geq (1-\epsilon)OPT$, otherwise $\sum_{i=1}^{m+\Delta} \mathcal{P}(S_i) < OPT$, which is a contradiction. So, $\mathcal{P}(S_A) \geq \sum_{i=1}^{t} \mathcal{P}(S_i')$ (as $t \leq m$), implies $\mathcal{P}(S_A) \geq \frac{1}{2}\sum_{i=1}^{t} \mathcal{P}(S_i) \geq \frac{(1-\epsilon)}{2}OPT$.

From the cases, we can conclude that, $\mathcal{P}(S_A) \geq \max\{\frac{m}{2(m+\Delta)}(1+\epsilon), \frac{(1-\epsilon)}{2}\}OPT$. We can have the best performance guarantee, if $\frac{m}{2(m+\Delta)}(1+\epsilon) = \frac{(1-\epsilon)}{2}$, implies $\epsilon = \frac{\Delta}{2m+\Delta}$. Thus, $\mathcal{P}(S_A) \geq \frac{m}{2m+\Delta}OPT$. Hence, the proof. □

Theorem 6. *For $m \geq \Delta$, Algorithm 5 gives an $\frac{1}{3}$-approximation factor for MDSP, where m is the number of drones and Δ is the maximum degree of the interval graph constructed from given delivery time intervals.*

Proof. Correctness of the algorithm follows from Lemma 5 and polynomial running time follows from Lemma 6.

Now, for $m \geq \Delta$, $\frac{m}{2m+\Delta} \geq \frac{1}{3}$.. Hence from Lemma 7, if S_A is the solution of MDSP, derived by using Algorithm 5 and OPT is optimum profit of that problem, then $\mathcal{P}(S_A) \geq \frac{1}{3}OPT$. Hence the proof. □

Corollary 2. *Algorithm 5 gives f-factor approximation for MDSP, if $m \geq (\frac{f}{1-2f})\Delta$, where $f < \frac{1}{2}$.*

5 Conclusion

This paper studied the drone-delivery scheduling problem for single and multiple drone cases. We propose an FPTAS for SDSP with running time $\mathcal{O}(n \log n + n\lfloor\frac{n^2}{\epsilon}\rfloor)$ for $\epsilon > 0$ and n being the number of deliveries. Also propose an $\frac{1}{3}$-approximation algorithm with running time $\mathcal{O}(n^2)$ for MDSP with m drones if $m \geq \Delta$, where Δ is the maximum degree of the interval graph constructed from given delivery time intervals. A deterministic rounding algorithm for this problem is also proposed by relaxing the ILP formulation. It would be interesting to find an asymptotic PTAS for MDSP without any constraints on the number of drones. Also, if drones are not identical concerning the battery budget, what would be the approach for an approximation algorithm?

References

1. Amazon: Amazon customers in Lockeford, California, will be among the first to receive prime air drone deliveries in the U.S. https://www.aboutamazon.com/news/transportation/amazon-prime-air-prepares-for-drone-deliveries
2. Basnet, C.: Heuristics for the multiple knapsack problem with conflicts. Int. J. Oper. Res. **32**, 514–525 (2018)

3. Betti Sorbelli, F., Corò, F., Das, S.K., Palazzetti, L., Pinotti, C.M.: Greedy algorithms for scheduling package delivery with multiple drones, pp. 31–39. ICDCN 2022, ACM, New York, NY, USA (2022)
4. Betti Sorbelli, F., Corò, F., Das, S.K., Palazzetti, L., Pinotti, C.M.: On the scheduling of conflictual deliveries in a last-mile delivery scenario with truck-carried drones. Pervasive Mob. Comput. **87**, 101700 (2022). https://www.sciencedirect.com/science/article/pii/S1574119222001134
5. Boysen, N., Briskorn, D., Fedtke, S., Schwerdfeger, S.: Drone delivery from trucks: drone scheduling for given truck routes. Networks **72**, 506–527 (2018)
6. Boysen, N., Fedtke, S., Schwerdfeger, S.: Last-mile delivery concepts: a survey from an operational research perspective. OR Spectrum **43**, 1–58 (2021)
7. Chekuri, C., Khanna, S.: A PTAS for the multiple knapsack problem. In: Proceedings of the Eleventh Annual ACM-SIAM Symposium on Discrete Algorithms, pp. 213–222. SODA 2000, Society for Industrial and Applied Mathematics, USA (2000)
8. Crişan, G.C., Nechita, E.: On a cooperative truck-and-drone delivery system. Procedia Comput. Sci. **159**, 38–47 (2019). knowledge-Based and Intelligent Information & Engineering Systems: Proceedings of the 23rd International Conference KES2019
9. Daknama, R., Kraus, E.: Vehicle routing with drones. ArXiv abs/1705.06431 (2017)
10. Dutta, G., Goswami, P.: Application of drone in agriculture: a review. Int. J. Chem. Stud. **8**, 181–187 (2020)
11. Kardasz, P., Doskocz, J.: Drones and possibilities of their using. J. Civil Environ. Eng. **6**, 1000233 (2016)
12. Maghazei, O., Netland, T.: Drones in manufacturing: exploring opportunities for research and practice. Journal of Manufacturing Technology Management (Forthcoming) (2019)
13. Murray, C.C., Chu, A.G.: The flying sidekick traveling salesman problem: optimization of drone-assisted parcel delivery. Transp. Res. Part C: Emerg. Technol. **54**, 86–109 (2015)
14. Murray, C.C., Raj, R.: The multiple flying sidekicks traveling salesman problem: Parcel delivery with multiple drones. Transport. Res. Part C: Emerg. Technol. **110**, 368–398 (2020)
15. Park, H.J., Mirjalili, R., Côté, M.J., Lim, G.J.: Scheduling diagnostic testing kit deliveries with the mothership and drone routing problem. J. Intell. Robotics Syst. **105**(2), 38 (2022)
16. Pferschy, U., Schauer, J.: The knapsack problem with conflict graphs. J. Graph Algorithms Appl. **13**, 233–249 (2009)
17. Sibanda, M., et al.: Application of drone technologies in surface water resources monitoring and assessment: a systematic review of progress, challenges, and opportunities in the global south. Drones **5**(3), 84 (2021)
18. Vazirani, V.V.: Approximation Algorithms. Springer, Heidelberg (2001). https://doi.org/10.1007/978-3-662-04565-7

Pebble Guided Treasure Hunt in Plane

Adri Bhattacharya[1]($\boxtimes$) (iD), Barun Gorain[2] (iD), and Partha Sarathi Mandal[1] (iD)

[1] Indian Institute of Technology Guwahati, Guwahati, India
{a.bhattacharya,psm}@iitg.ac.in
[2] Indian Institute of Technology Bhilai, Bhilai, India
barun@iitbhilai.ac.in

Abstract. We study the problem of treasure hunt in a Euclidean plane by a mobile agent with the guidance of pebbles. The initial position of the agent and position of the treasure are modeled as special points in the Euclidean plane. The treasure is situated at a distance at most $D > 0$ from the initial position of the agent. The agent has a perfect compass, but an adversary controls the speed of the agent. Hence, the agent can not measure how much distance it traveled for a given time. The agent can find the treasure only when it reaches the exact position of the treasure. The cost of the treasure hunt is defined as the total distance traveled by the agent before it finds the treasure. The agent has no prior knowledge of the position of the treasure or the value of D. An Oracle, which knows the treasure's position and the agent's initial location, places some pebbles to guide the agent towards the treasure. Once decided to move along some specified angular direction, the agent can decide to change its direction only when it encounters a pebble or a special point.

We ask the following central question in this paper:
"For given $k \geq 0$, what is cheapest treasure hunt algorithm if at most k pebbles are placed by the Oracle?"

We show that for $k = 1$, there does not exist any treasure hunt algorithm that finds the treasure with finite cost. We show the existence of an algorithm with cost $O(D)$ for $k = 2$. For $k > 8$ we have designed an algorithm that uses k many pebbles to find the treasure with cost $O(k^2) + D(\sin \theta' + \cos \theta')$, where $\theta' = \frac{\pi}{2^{k-8}}$. The second result shows the existence of an algorithm with cost arbitrarily close to D for sufficiently large values of D.

Keywords: Treasure Hunt · Mobile agent · Pebbles · Euclidean plane · Deterministic algorithms

The authors of the paper are thankful to Dr. Yoann Dieudonné for his valuable inputs and suggestions.

A. Bhattacharya—Supported by CSIR, Govt. of India, Grant Number: 09/731(0178)/ 2020-EMR-I

B. Gorain—Partially supported by SERB Govt. of India, Grant Number: CRG/2020/ 005964 and MTR/2021/000118

P. S. Mandal—Partially supoprted by SERB, Govt. of India, Grant Number: MTR/ 2019/001528.

1   Introduction

Treasure Hunt problem is the task of finding an inert target by a mobile agent in an unknown environment. The unknown environment can be modeled as a network or a plane. Initially placed at a point in the unknown environment, a mobile agent has to find an inert target, called the treasure. The target or the treasure can be a miner lost in a cave. The cave can be uninhabitable for humans to search for the lost miner, or it can be inundated with toxic waters henceforth, the person should be found as fast as possible. In computer science applications, a software agent must visit the computers connected by a local area network to find the computer affected by malware.

In this paper, we study the problem of treasure hunt in the Euclidean plane under a very weak scenario which assumes very little knowledge and control power of the mobile agent. Specifically, the agent does not have any prior knowledge about the position of the treasure or its distance from the treasure. Moreover, the agent has no control over the speed of its movement, and it is assumed an adversary completely controls the speed of the agent. In practice, for software agents in a network, the movement speed of the agent depends on various factors, such as congestion in the network. In the case of hardware mobile robots, their speeds depend on many mechanical characteristics as well as environmental factors. The agent is equipped with a perfect compass, which helps the agent to rotate and move in a prescribed direction. The agent is initially placed at a point P in the plane. The treasure T is located at most $D > 0$ distance (unknown to the agent) from P. The agent finds the treasure only when it reaches the exact position of the treasure. The agent's initial position is considered to be a special point, and the agent can detect this point whenever it visits P.

In the absence of control over its movement speed, once the agent decides to move along a particular angle, it is very important for the agent to learn when to stop its movement. Otherwise, the adversary can increase the speed arbitrarily high, and the agent ends up traversing an arbitrarily large distance. In order to enable the agent to have some control over its movement, an Oracle, knowing the position of the treasure, and the initial position of the agent, places some stationary pebbles on the plane. We assume a restriction on the pebble placement by the Oracle: any two pebbles must be placed at least 1 unit distance apart[1]. The agent can detect the existence of a pebble only when it reaches the position of the pebble where its placed by the Oracle.

These pebble placement helps the agent control its movement and rule out the possibility of traversing arbitrarily large distances. Starting from some position of the plane, the agent, moving along a specific direction, stops or changes its direction once it encounters a pebble along the path of its movement. Thus, the movement algorithm of the agent gives instruction to move along a specific angle α until it encounters a special point (i.e., the initial position P or the position of the treasure T) or hits a pebble.

---

[1] This is required if the sensing capability of the agent is weak, two pebbles placed very close to each other may not be distinguished by the agent.

Formally, for a given positive integer $k \geq 0$, the Oracle is a function $f_k : (E \times E) \to E^k$, where E is the set of all the points in the Euclidean Plane. The function takes two points as the input, the first one is the initial position of the agent, and the second one is the position of the treasure, and gives k points in the plane as output which represents the placement of a pebble at each of these k points.

The central question studied in this paper is: "For given $k \geq 0$, what is the minimum cost of treasure hunt if at most k pebbles are placed in the plane?"

1.1 Contribution

Our contributions in this paper are summarized below.

- For $k = 1$ pebbles, we have shown that it is not possible to design a treasure hunt algorithm that finds the treasure with finite cost.
- For $k = 2$ pebbles, we propose an algorithm that finds the treasure with cost at most $4.5D$, where D is the distance between the initial position of the agent and the treasure.
- For $k > 8$, we design an algorithm that finds the treasure using k pebbles with cost $O(k^2) + D\left(\sin\theta' + \cos\theta'\right)$, where $\theta' = \frac{\pi}{2^{k-8}}$. For sufficiently large values of D and $k \in o(\sqrt{D})$, the cost of this algorithm is arbitrarily close to D, the cost of the optimal solution in case the position of the treasure is known to the agent.

Due to the restrictions in the page limit, the proofs of many theorems and lemmas are omitted from the conference version. These proofs can be found in the full version of the paper [5].

1.2 Related Work

The task of searching for an inert target by a mobile agent has been rigorously studied in the literature under various scenarios. The underlying environment or the topology may be either a discrete or continuous domain, i.e., a graph or a plane. The search strategy can be either deterministic or randomized. The book by Alpern et al. [2] discusses the randomized algorithms based on searching for an inert target as well as the rendezvous problem, where the target and the agent are both dynamic, and they cooperate to meet. The papers by Miller et al. [20], and Ta-Shma et al. [23] relate the correlation between rendezvous and treasure hunt problem in graph.

The problem of searching on a line for an inert target was first initiated by Beck et al. [3]. They gave an optimal competitive ratio of 9. Further, Demaine et al. [8] modified the problem, in which there is a cost involved for each change in the direction of the searcher. In [18], the author surveys the searching problem in terms of search games where the target is either static or mobile. The search domain is either a graph, a bounded domain, or an unbounded set. Fricke et al. [16], generalized the search problem in a plane with multiple searchers.

Now, the paradigm of *algorithm with advice* has been introduced mainly in networks. These *advice* enhances the efficiency of the problems as discussed in

[1,4,6,7,9,11–15,17,19,21]. In this paradigm, the authors [14,15] mainly studied the minimum amount of advice required in order to solve the problem efficiently. In [10,12], the online version of the problems with advice was studied. The authors [6], considered the treasure hunt problem, in which they gave an optimal cost algorithm where the agent gets a hint after each movement. Pelc et al. [22], gave an insight into the amount of information required to solve the treasure hunt in geometric terrain at $O(L)$- time, where L is the shortest path of the treasure from the initial point. Bouchard et al. [7], studied how different kinds of initial knowledge impact the cost of treasure hunt in a tree network.

The two papers closest to the present work are [19,21]. Pelc et al. [21], provided a trade-off between cost and information of solving the treasure hunt problem in the plane. They showed optimal and almost optimal results for different ranges of vision radius. Gorain et al. [19], gave an optimal treasure hunt algorithm in graphs with pebbles, termed as advice. In [4], the authors studied a trade-off between the number of pebbles vs. the cost of the treasure hunt algorithm in an undirected port-labeled graph.

Organization: The paper is organized in the following manner. Section 2 gives a brief idea about the feasibility of the treasure hunt problem when a certain number of pebbles are placed. Section 3 has four subsections, in Subsect. 3.1 the high-level idea of the algorithm is described, in Subsect. 3.2, the pebble placement strategy is described, and in Subsect. 3.3 the treasure hunt algorithm is discussed. In Sect. 3.4, correctness and complexity are discussed. Further, in Sect. 4, possible future work and conclusion are explained.

2   Feasibility of Treasure Hunt

In this section, we discuss the feasibility of the treasure hunt problem, when the oracle places one and two pebbles, respectively.

Theorem 1. *It is not possible to design a treasure hunt algorithm using at most one pebble that finds the treasure at a finite cost.*

Proof. The agent initially placed at P and the pebble is placed somewhere in the plane by the oracle. Since the agent has no prior information about the location of the treasure, the treasure can be positioned anywhere in the plane by the adversary. The only possible initial instruction for the agent is to move along a certain angle from P. The agent along its movement, must encounter a pebble otherwise, it will continue to move in this direction for an infinite distance, as it has no sense of distance. After encountering the pebble, there are three possibilities: either it may return back to P and move at a certain angle from P or it may return back to P and move along the same path traversed by the agent previously to reach the pebble, or it may move at a certain angle from the pebble itself. The adversary may place the treasure at a location different from the possible path to be traversed by the agent. Hence, it is not possible to find the treasure at a finite cost.   □

In this part, we discuss the strategy of pebble placement and respective traversal of the agent toward the treasure when two pebbles are placed by the oracle.

Pebble Placement: Based on the location of the treasure, two pebbles are placed as follows. Let the coordinates of the treasure T be (x_T, y_T). If either of x_T or y_T is positive, place one pebble at $(z+1, z+1)$, where $z = \max\{|x_T|, |y_T|\}$. Place another pebble at $(x_T, z+1)$. Otherwise, if both x_T and y_T are negative, place one pebble at $(1, 1)$ and another pebble at $(x_T, 1)$.

Treasure Hunt by the Agent: The agent initially at P, moves at an angle $\frac{\pi}{4}$ with the positive x axis until it encounters treasure or a pebble (i.e., p_1). If a pebble is encountered, then from this position, the agent moves along an angle $\pi - \frac{\pi}{4}$ until it encounters the treasure or reaches a pebble (i.e., p_2). If a pebble is encountered (i.e., from p_2), the agent further moves along an angle $\frac{\pi}{2}$ until it reaches the treasure T.

Theorem 2. *The agent finds the treasure with cost $O(D)$ using the above algorithm.*

3   Improved Solution for Treasure Hunt

In this section, we propose a faster algorithm which requires at least 9 pebbles to perform the treasure hunt.

3.1   High Level Idea

Before we give the details of the pebble placement algorithm, we describe the high-level idea of the same. Intuitively, depending on the number of pebbles available, the Oracle divides the plane into multiple sectors as described in Sect. 3.2. Then it identifies the sector number m in which the treasure is located and 'encode' this number by placing the pebbles. The agent, looking at the pebble placements, 'decodes' this encoding, and move along the particular sector to find the treasure. There are certain challenges that need to be overcome to implement this idea.

Sector Detection: The first difficulty is how different placements of pebbles enable the agent to differentiate between the bit 0 and the bit 1. Since the agent has no sense of time and distance, two different pebble placements may look identical to the agent. On the other hand, since the agent has no prior information about the encoded integer, its movement should also be planned in a way that using the same movement strategy, it will be able to detect the bit zero for some instances and the bit 1 for other instances. The capability of detecting the initial point P as a special point is used to overcome this difficulty.

First, we place a pebble p_1 at the point $(1,0)$, and two additional fixed pebbles p_2 at $(1,1)$ and p_3 at $(2,1)$ are placed. The rest of the pebbles are placed based on the fact whether a particular bit of the encoding is a 0 or 1. Initially, consider the specific scenario of encoding only one bit 0 or 1. The idea is to place a particular pebble p in two possible positions on the x-axis such that the agent, starting from P, reach p, then moving at a certain fixed angle α from p will reach p_2 for one position and p_3 for the other. The agent can not distinguish between p_2 and p_3, but moving in a particular angle β from p_2 will reach P and from p_3 will reach p_1. These two different scenarios are distinguished as 0 and 1, respectively. In order to achieve and implement the idea, the pebble p is placed at the point $(3,0)$ in case of encoding 1 and $(4,0)$ in case of encoding 0. The advantage of these placements is that in case of placing p at $(3,0)$ is that, the agent moving from P to p, and then moving at an angle $\arctan\left(\frac{-1}{2}\right)$, reaches p_2 and then moving at an angle $\arctan(3)$, it reaches P. On the other hand, in the case of placing p at $(4,0)$, with same movement, the agent arrives at p_1. Hence, it learns these two different observations as two different bits 1 and 0, respectively (See Fig. 1).

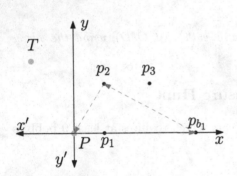

Fig. 1. Placement of pebble by oracle when first bit is 1

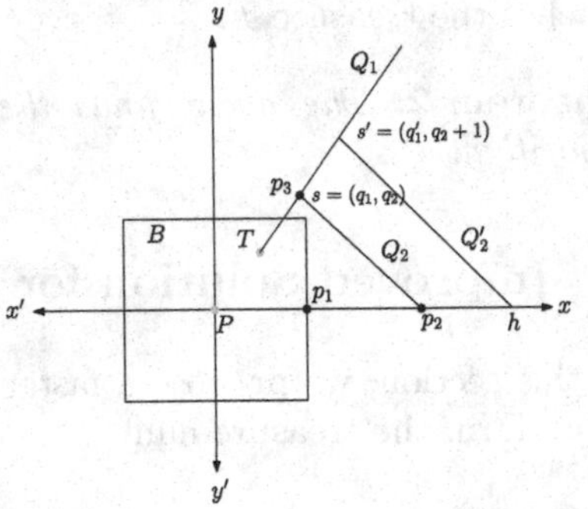

Fig. 2. Pebble placement when treasure inside B

We extend the above idea for encoding any binary string μ as follows. In addition to the pebbles p_1, p_2, and p_3, one additional pebble for each of the bits of μ are placed. To be specific, for $1 \leq i \leq |\mu|$, a pebble p_{b_i} is placed at $(2i + 1, 0)$ if the i-th bit is 1, else p_{b_i} is placed at $(2i + 2, 0)$. Starting from P to p_{b_i}, moving at an angle $\arctan\left(\frac{-1}{2i}\right)$ until a pebble is reached, then moving at an angle $\arctan\left(\frac{2i+1}{2i-1}\right)$, the agent reaches either P or p_1 depending on the i-th bit is 1 or 0 respectively.

A difficulty that remains to be overcome is how the agent detects the end of the encoding. This is important because if the termination is not indicated, then there is a possibility that the agent moves to find more pebbles p_{b_j}, $j > |\mu|$, and continues its movement for an infinite distance. We use two additional pebbles named p_{t_1} and p_{t_2} for the specific requirement of termination detection. The position of these two pebbles p_{t_1} and p_{t_2} are as follows. If the 1st bit of the binary string μ is 1, i.e., p_{b_1} is placed at $(3,0)$ then the pebbles p_{t_1} and p_{t_2} are placed at $(4, 1)$ and $(2|\mu| + 6, 0)$, respectively. Otherwise, if the 1st bit is 0 then these two pebbles are placed at $(5, 1)$ and $(2|\mu| + 7, 0)$, respectively. After visiting the pebble $p_{|\mu|}$ for the last bit of μ, the agent returns to P, and moves as usual to find a pebble expecting to learn more bits of the binary string. From P, once it reaches p_{t_2}, it moves at an angle $\arctan\left(\frac{-1}{2(|\mu|+1)}\right)$ until a pebble is reached. Note that the two pebbles p_{t_1} and p_{t_2} are placed in such a way that the angle $\angle Pp_{t_2}p_{t_1} = \arctan\left(\frac{-1}{2(|\mu|+1)}\right)$. Hence using the movement from p_{t_2} at angle $\arctan\left(\frac{-1}{2(|\mu|+1)}\right)$ the agent reaches p_{t_1} and from p_{t_1} moving at angle $\arctan\left(\frac{2(|\mu|+1)+1}{2(|\mu|+1)-1}\right)$, it reaches to p_{b_1}. Since the following specific movement mentioned above, the agent reaches to a pebble, it initially assumed that it learned the bit zero. However, moving west from p_{b_1}, it reaches another pebble (i.e., the pebble p_1), instead of origin. This special occurrence indicates the termination of the encoding to the agent. Hence, in this way, the agent learns the binary string μ, and the integer Δ whose binary representation is μ.

Finding the Treasure Inside the Sector: One more pebble p_T is placed on the foot of the perpendicular drawn from T on L_{j+1}. After learning the encoding of μ_j, the agent decodes the integer j, and correctly identifies the two lines L_j and L_{j+1} inside the sector, which helps agent to locate the exact location of T.

A difficulty arises here while placing the pebble p_T inside the sector as some pebbles that are already placed while the encoding of the sector number may be very close (at distance < 1) from the possible position of p_T. To resolve this, we do the placement of the pebbles for encoding on positive x-axis if the position of the treasure is at the left half plane, and the placement of the pebbles are done on the negative x-axis, if the position of the treasure is at the right half plane. To instruct the agent which way it must move to find the pebbles for learning the encoding, one additional pebble p_0 is placed at P.

Some specific cases need to be separately handled: If the treasure is in a position (x, y), such that $-1 \le x \le 1$ and $y \ge -1$, as this again may create a problem in placing p_T inside the prescribed position inside the sector. The details of these cases will be discussed while explaining the pebble placement strategy in Sect. 3.2.

3.2   Pebble Placement

The agent is initially placed at P, and the treasure is placed at T. The oracle, knowing the initial position P of the agent and the position $T = (x_T, y_T)$ of the treasure, places k pebbles in the Euclidean plane. Let B be the square region bounded by the lines $x = 1$, $x = -1$, $y = 1$, and $y = -1$. Based on the position of the treasure, the pebble placement is described using two different cases.

Case 1: If $x_T > 0$ and $T \notin B$, then the pebbles are placed as follows.

– Place a pebble p_0 at P.
– Draw 2^{k-8} half-lines $L_0, \cdots, L_{2^{k-8}-1}$, starting at the initial position P of the agent, such that L_0 goes North and the angle between consecutive half-lines is $\pi/2^{k-8}$ for $i = 0, \cdots, 2^{k-8} - 1$. The sector S_i is defined as the set of points in the plane between L_i and $L_{(i+1) \bmod 2^{k-8}}$, including the points

on L_i and excluding the points on $L_{(i+1) \mod 2^{k-8}}$. If $T \in S_j$, for some $j \in \{0, 1, \cdots, 2^{k-8} - 1\}$ then place pebbles as follows.

- Place the pebbles p_1 at $(-1,0)$, p_2 at $(-1,-1)$ and p_3 at $(-2,-1)$.
- Let μ_j be the binary representation of the integer j with leading $\lfloor \log k \rfloor - \lfloor \log j \rfloor$ many zeros. If $0 \le x_T \le 1$ and $y_T > 1$, then $\mu_j = 0 \cdot \mu_j$, else $\mu_j = 1 \cdot \mu_j$. For $1 \le \ell \le |\mu_j|$, if the ℓ-th bit of μ_j is 1, then place a pebble at $(-2\ell - 1, 0)$, else place a pebble at $(-2\ell - 2, 0)$.
- If the 1st bit of μ_j is 1, then place a pebble p_{t_1} at (-4,-1), else place p_{t_1} at (-5,-1).
- If the 1st bit of μ_j is 1, then place a pebble p_{t_2} at $(-2|\mu_j| - 6, 0)$, else place p_{t_2} at $(-2|\mu_j| - 7, 0)$.

- If $x_T < 0$ and $T \notin B$, then the placements of the pebbles are done as follows. For each pebble placed at (m, n), where $m \ne 0$ or $n \ne 0$ in the above case, place the corresponding pebble at $(-m, -n)$ in this case. Also, place no pebble at P.

- If the first bit of μ_j is 0, then let F be the foot of the perpendicular drawn from T to L_j, else let F be the foot of the perpendicular drawn from T to L_{j+1}. Place a pebble p_T at F (Lemma 1 ensures that the pebbles are placed at a distance of at least 1 in this scenario).

Case 2: If $x_T > 0$ and $T \in B$, then the pebbles are placed as follows.

- Place a pebble p_1 at $(1,0)$ (refer Fig. 2).
- Let $m_1 = \tan\left(\pi - \arctan(\frac{-1}{2}) - \arctan(3)\right)$ and $m_2 = \tan\left(\pi - \arctan\left(\frac{-1}{2}\right)\right)$. Draw a line Q_1 through T with slope m_1 and draw a line Q_2 through the point $(2,0)$ with slope m_2. Let $s = (q_1, q_2)$ be the point of intersection between these two lines. Let s' be the point on the line Q_1 whose y coordinate is $q_2 + 1$. Draw the lines Q_2' parallel to Q_2 and go through s'. Let h be the points of intersection of the lines Q_2' with x-axis.
Two additional pebbles p_2 and p_3 are placed as follows.

  - If $q_2 < 1$, then place p_2 at h and p_3 at s'. Otherwise, place p_2 at $(2,0)$ and p_3 at s.

Case 3: If $x_T < 0$ and $T \in B$, then the pebbles are placed as follows.

- Place the pebbles p_0 at P and p_1 at (-1,0).
- Let $m_1 = -\tan\left(\pi - \arctan(\frac{-1}{2}) - \arctan(3)\right)$ and $m_2 = -\tan(\pi - \arctan\left(\frac{-1}{2}\right))$. Draw a line Q_1 through T with slope m_1 and draw a line Q_2 through the point $(-2,0)$ with slope m_2. Let $r = (r_1, r_2)$ be the point of intersection between these two lines. Let r' be the point on the line Q_1 whose y coordinate is $r_2 + 1$. Draw the lines Q_2' parallel to Q_2 and go through r'. Let n be the points of intersection of the lines Q_2' with x-axis.
Two additional pebbles p_2 and p_3 are placed as follows.

  - If $r_2 < 1$, then place p_2 at n and p_3 at r'. Otherwise, place p_2 at $(-2,0)$ and p_3 at r.

Algorithm 1: PEBBLEPLACEMENT

---

1 Draw 2^{k-8} half lines $L_0, \cdots, L_{2^{k-8}-1}$ starting from P, where angle between two consecutive half-lines is $\frac{\pi}{2^{k-8}}$. Let Sector S_i be the sector bounded by the half lines L_i and L_{i+1} and let $T \in S_\Delta$, $\Delta \in \{0, 1, \cdots, 2^{k-8} - 1\}$

2 **if** $x_T \geq 0$ **then**

3   **if** $0 \leq x_T \leq 1$ *and* $-1 \leq y_T \leq 1$ **then**

4   SquarePlacement(2)

5   **else**

6   Place a pebble p_0 at P

7   **if** $x_T \leq 1$ *and* $y_T > 1$ **then**

8   NonSquarePlacement(1, 0)

9   Place a pebble p_T at the foot of the perpendicular drawn from T on L_Δ.

10   **else**

11   NonSquarePlacement(1, 1)

12   Place a pebble p_T at the foot of the perpendicular drawn from T on $L_{\Delta+1}$.

13 **else**

14   **if** $-1 \leq x_T \leq 0$ *and* $-1 \leq y_T \leq 1$ **then**

15   Place a pebble p_0 at P.

16   SquarePlacement(1)

17   **else**

18   **if** $-1 \leq x_T \leq 0$ *and* $y_T > 1$ **then**

19   NonSquarePlacement(2,0)

20   Place a pebble p_T at the foot of the perpendicular drawn from T on L_Δ.

21   **else**

22   NonSquarePlacement(2,1)

23   Place a pebble p_T at the foot of the perpendicular drawn from T on $L_{\Delta+1}$.

Algorithm 2: SQUAREPLACEMENT(*count*)

---

1 Place a pebble p_1 at $((-1)^{count}, 0)$.

2 **if** $q_2 < 1$ **then**

3   Place the pebbles p_2 at h and p_3 at s', respectively.

4 **else**

5   Place the pebbles p_2 at $((-1)^{count} \cdot 2, 0)$ and p_3 at s, respectively.

Algorithm 3: NONSQUAREPLACEMENT($count, bit$)

---

1 Initially $l = 2$

2 Place the pebbles p_1 at $((-1)^{count}, 0)$, p_2 at $((-1)^{count}, (-1)^{count})$ and p_3 at $((-1)^{count} \cdot 2, (-1)^{count})$, respectively.

3 μ_j be the binary representation of the integer j with leading $\lfloor \log k \rfloor - \lfloor \log j \rfloor$ many zeroes.

4 $\mu_j = bit.\mu_j$ ▷ Represents the concatenation of bit value with μ_j

5 **if** $bit = 1$ **then**

6   ⌊ Place a pebble at $((-1)^{count} \cdot 3, 0)$.

7 **else**

8   ⌊ Place a pebble at $((-1)^{count} \cdot 4, 0)$.

9 **while** $l \leq k + 1$ **do**

10   **if** l-th bit of μ_j is 1 **then**

11   ⌊ Place a pebble at $((-1)^{count} \cdot (2\ell + 1), 0)$.

12   **else**

13   ⌊ Place a pebble at $((-1)^{count} \cdot (2\ell + 2), 0)$.

14   ⌊ $l = l + 1$

15 **if** 1st bit of μ_j is 1 **then**

16   Place the pebbles p_{t_1} at $((-1)^{count} \cdot 4, (-1)^{count})$ and p_{t_2} at $((-1)^{count} \cdot (2|\mu_j| + 6), 0)$, respectively.

17 **else**

18   Place the pebble p_{t_1} at $((-1)^{count} \cdot 5, (-1)^{count})$ and p_{t_2} at $((-1)^{count} \cdot (2|\mu_j| + 7), 0)$, respectively.

Algorithm 4: AGENTMOVEMENT

---

1 If a pebble is found at P then set $angle = \pi$, otherwise set $angle = 0$.

2 $t = 2$, $\mu = \epsilon$.

3 Start moving at an angle $angle$ with the positive x axis.

4 **if** treasure is found **then**

5   ⌊ Terminate

6 **else**

7   Continue moving in the same direction until the t-th pebble or the treasure is found.

8   **if** treasure found **then**

9   ⌊ Terminate

10   **else**

11   ℓ=FindBit($t, angle$)

12   **if** $\ell \in \{0, 1\}$ **then**

13   Update $\mu = \mu \cdot \ell$ and $t = t + 1$.

14   ⌊ Go to Step 3

15   **else**

16   ⌊ FindTreasure($\mu, angle$)

Algorithm 5: FINDBIT($t, angle$)

1 Move at an angle $\pi - \theta_t$, where $\theta_t = \arctan(\frac{-1}{2t})$ until the treasure or a pebble is found.
2 **if** *treasure found* **then**
3 $\quad\lfloor$ Terminate
4 **else**
5 $\quad$ Move at an angle $\pi - \beta_t$, where $\beta_t = \arctan(\frac{2t+1}{2t-1})$.
6 $\quad$ **if** *treasure found* **then**
7 $\quad\quad\lfloor$ Terminate
8 $\quad$ **else if** *P is found* **then**
9 $\quad\quad\lfloor$ return 1
10 $\quad$ **else if** *a pebble is found at a point other than P* **then**
11 $\quad\quad$ **if** *angle = 0* **then**
12 $\quad\quad\quad\lfloor$ Move at an angle $\pi + \frac{\pi}{4}$.
13 $\quad\quad$ **else**
14 $\quad\quad\quad\lfloor$ Move at an angle $\pi - \frac{\pi}{4}$.
15 $\quad\quad$ **if** *P is found* **then**
16 $\quad\quad\quad\lfloor$ return 0
17 $\quad\quad$ **else**
18 $\quad\quad\quad\lfloor$ Continue its movement until P is reached and return 2.

Algorithm 6: FINDTREASURE($\mu, angle$)

1 Let Δ be the integer whose binary representation is μ
2 **if** *angle = π* **then**
3 $\quad$ **if** $\mu_1 = 0$ **then**
4 $\quad\quad\lfloor$ Set $val = \Delta$ and call SECTORTRAVEL($val, 1, 2$)
5 $\quad$ **else**
6 $\quad\quad\lfloor$ Set $val = \Delta + 1$ and call SECTORTRAVEL($val, 1, 1$).
7 **else**
8 $\quad$ **if** $\mu_1 = 0$ **then**
9 $\quad\quad\lfloor$ Set $val = \Delta$ and call SECTORTRAVEL($val, 2, 1$)
10 $\quad$ **else**
11 $\quad\quad\lfloor$ Set $val = \Delta + 1$ and call SECTORTRAVEL($val, 2, 2$)

Algorithm 7: SECTORTRAVEL($val, count, num$)

1 Move at an angle $\frac{\pi}{2} + (-1)^{count} \left(\frac{\pi \cdot val}{2^{k-8}} \right)$ until a pebble or treasure is found.
2 **if** *Treasure found* **then**
3 $\quad\lfloor$ Terminate.
4 **else**
5 $\quad\lfloor$ Move at an angle $\pi + (-1)^{num} \frac{\pi}{2}$ and terminate whenever treasure is found.

3.3   Treasure Hunt

Starting from P, the agent finds the treasure with the help of the pebble placed at different points on the plane. On a high level, the agent performs three major tasks: (1) Learn the direction of its initial movement (2) Learn the encoding of the sector number in which the treasure is located, and (3) Move inside the designated sector and find the treasure.

The agent learns the direction of its initial movement by observing whether a pebble is placed at P or not. If a pebble is placed, then it learns that the direction of its initial movement is west and pebble placement is done for the encoding of the sector number on the negative x axis. Otherwise, it learns that the direction of its initial movement is east and pebble placement is done for the encoding of the sector number on the positive x axis. Then for each $j = 1, 2, \cdots$, it continues its movement in a specific path (depending on the value of j) and learns the j-th bit of the encoding until it detects the termination of the encoding. To be specific, the j-th bit of the encoding is learned by the agent using the movements in the following order from P.

- Starting from P, move along x-axis until the $(j + 1)$-th pebble is reached,
- Move at angle $\arctan(\frac{-1}{2j})$, and continue moving in this direction until a pebble is reached
- Move at an angle $\arctan(\frac{2j+1}{2j-1})$ until P or a pebble is found.
- If P is found in the previous step, then the bit is 1.
- If a pebble is found, then move along x axis towards P. If P is encountered, then the bit is 0.
- If a pebble is encountered instead of P in the previous step, then the agent learns that the encoding is completed.

Let μ be the binary string learned by the agent in the above process and let Δ be the integer whose binary representation of μ. If the first bit of μ is 1, then the agent starts moving along $L_{\Delta+1}$ from P until it hits a pebble or reaches the treasure. Once the pebble is reached, the agent changes its direction at angle $\frac{\pi}{2}$ if its initial direction of movement was west, else the agent changes its direction at angle $\frac{3\pi}{2}$. It moves along the same direction until the treasure is reached.

The following lemma ensures that the pebbles are placed at a distance of at least 1 in step 4 of Case 1 in the above pebble placement strategy.

Lemma 1. *If $T = (x_T, y_T) \in B'$, where $B' = \{(x, y) |\ 0 \leq x \leq 1\ and\ y_T > 1\}$, the location of the foot of the perpendicular F on L_j is outside the square B.*

3.4   Correctness

In this section, we give the correctness and an upper bound on the cost of finding treasure from the proposed algorithms. The following two lemmas show the algorithm's correctness when the treasure is inside B and the upper bound of the cost of treasure hunt.

Lemma 2. *With 3 pebbles and the treasure located inside B, the agent successfully finds the treasure.*

Lemma 3. *When the treasure is located inside B, the agent starting from P successfully finds the treasure at cost $O(D)$.*

Lemmas 4, 5, 6 & 7 proves the correctness of the algorithm when the treasure is located outside B.

Lemma 4. *When the treasure is outside B, the agent successfully finds the j-th bit of the binary string μ at cost $O(j)$.*

Lemma 5. *Given k pebbles and the treasure located outside B, the agent successfully finds the binary string μ at cost $O(k^2)$.*

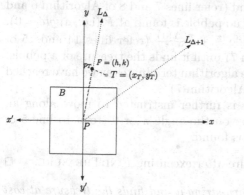

Fig. 3. To determine the location of pebble p_T

Fig. 4. Traversal of the agent inside the sector when $\mu_1 = 1$ of Γ

Lemma 6. *The agent obtains the binary string μ, and successfully finds the treasure by executing FINDTREASURE, when the treasure is outside B.*

Proof. After termination of AGENTMOVEMENT 4, the agent performs FIND-TREASURE 6 with obtained binary string μ to reach the treasure T if not reached.

The treasure is either located somewhere on the region $x \geq 0$ (i.e., right half of y-axis) or $x \leq 0$ (i.e., left half of y-axis) and accordingly, the oracle divides the whole left half or right half of y-axis into 2^{k-8} sectors (refer line 1 of Algorithm 1), where a sector S_i is bounded by half-lines L_i and L_{i+1} and angle between consecutive half lines is $\frac{\pi}{2^{k-8}}$. Suppose the treasure is located somewhere in sector S_Δ, so μ is the binary representation of Δ. The agent decodes this value Δ after executing AGENTMOVEMENT 4. The aim of the oracle is to align the agent either along the half-line L_Δ or $L_{\Delta+1}$. The alignment of the agent along the half-lines L_Δ or $L_{\Delta+1}$ depends on the first bit value of μ, i.e., on μ_1 (refer line 3 in Algorithm 6) in the following manner:

Case ($\mu_1 = 0$): If a pebble is found at P (i.e., $angle = \pi$ refer to line 2 of Algorithm 4) then the agent is instructed to move along an angle $\frac{\pi}{2} - \frac{\pi\Delta}{2^{k-8}}$, i.e., along the half-line L_Δ until the treasure or a pebble, i.e., p_T is found (refer Fig. 3 for placement of p_T). Otherwise, if no pebble is found at P (i.e., $angle = 0$ refer to line 4 of Algorithm 4) then the agent is instructed to move along an angle $\frac{\pi}{2} + \frac{\pi\Delta}{2^{k-8}}$ (refer to lines 11 and 12 of Algorithm 6 and line 1 of Algorithm 7) until it finds the treasure or a pebble.

  – *If the treasure is found*: Algorithm terminates as we have reached our goal (refer lines 2 and 3 of Algorithm 7).
  – *If a pebble is found*: The agent moves along an angle $\pi + \frac{\pi}{2}$ or $\pi - \frac{\pi}{2}$ depending on the angle π or 0 (line 5 of Algorithm 7) until treasure is found.

Case ($\mu_1 = 1$): If a pebble is found at P (i.e., $angle = \pi$) then the agent is instructed to move along an angle $\frac{\pi}{2} - \frac{\pi(\Delta+1)}{2^{k-8}}$, i.e., along the half-line $L_{\Delta+1}$ until the treasure or a pebble is found (refer lines 7 and 8 of Algorithm 6 and line 1 of Algorithm 7). Otherwise, if no pebble is found at P (i.e., $angle = 0$), then the agent moves along an angle $\frac{\pi}{2} + \frac{\pi(\Delta+1)}{2^{k-8}}$ (refer lines 14 and 15 of Algorithm 6 and line 1 of Algorithm 7) until it finds the treasure or a pebble.

  – *If the treasure is found*: Then the algorithm terminates as we have reached our goal (refer lines 2 and 3 of Algorithm 7).
  – *If a pebble is found*: The agent is further instructed to move along an angle $\pi - \frac{\pi}{2}$ or $\pi + \frac{\pi}{2}$ depending on the angle π or 0 (refer to line 5 of Algorithm 7) until the treasure is found.

In each case, the agent finds the treasure after executing FINDTREASURE.   □

Lemma 7. *The agent obtains the binary string μ and finds the treasure at cost $D(\sin\theta' + \cos\theta')$, where $\theta' = \frac{\pi}{2^{k'}}$ and $k' = k - 8$, when the treasure is outside B.*

Proof. The agent after gaining the binary string μ, executes AGENTMOVEMENT and FINDTREASURE, and reaches the treasure by following the path $PF \to FT$ from P (refer Fig. 4). Since the angle between L_Δ and $L_{\Delta+1}$ is $\frac{\pi}{2^{k-8}}$. Hence, $\angle FPT$ is at most $\frac{\pi}{2^{k-8}}$ (refer Fig. 4) which is θ' (say), also $\angle TFP = \frac{\pi}{2}$ (as F is the foot of perpendicular of T to $L_{\Delta+1}$ if $\mu_1 = 1$ otherwise, if $\mu_1 = 0$ then F is the foot of perpendicular of T to L_Δ) and $|PT| \leq D$. So we have $PF = D\cos\theta'$ and $FT = D\sin\theta'$. Hence, the cost of traveling along the sector S_Δ from P to reach T is $PF + FT$ which is $D(\sin\theta' + \cos\theta')$.   □

The following theorem can be summarized by using Lemmas 6 & 7.

Theorem 3. *Given k pebbles, the agent starting from P successfully finds treasure with $O(k^2) + D(\sin\theta' + \cos\theta')$-cost, where $\theta' = \frac{\pi}{2^{k'}}$ and $k' = k - 8$.*

Remark 1. Consider the function $f(k) = O(k^2) + D(\sin\theta' + \cos\theta')$, where $\theta' = \frac{\pi}{2^{k-8}}$. Note that for $D, k \to \infty$ and $k \in o(\sqrt{D})$, the value of $\frac{f(k)}{D} \to 1$. In order to demonstrate this fact, we plot the value of $\frac{f(k)}{D}$ for increasing values of D in

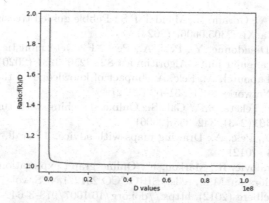

Fig. 5. The curve represents the ratio of $\frac{f(k)}{D}$ for different values of D

the range $[1000, 100000000]$ and for $k = \lfloor D^{\frac{1}{3}} \rfloor$. Figure 5 shows the values of $\frac{f(k)}{D}$ for different values of D in the above-mentioned range and for the fix value of k for each D. This figure shows that for a large value of D, the value of $\frac{f(k)}{D}$ is very close to 1.

4   Conclusion

We propose an algorithm for the treasure hunt that finds the treasure in an Euclidean plane using $k \geq 9$ pebbles at cost $O(k^2) + D(\sin\theta' + \cos\theta')$, where $\theta' = \frac{\pi}{2^{k-8}}$. Proving a matching lower bound remains an open problem to consider in the future. It can be noted that if the agent has some visibility, the problem becomes very trivial even with only one pebble: place a pebble on the line from P to T within a distance of r from P, where r is the visibility radius of the agent. Starting from P, the agent sees the position of the pebble, move to the pebble, and then continue until it hits the treasure. But the problem becomes challenging if the compass of the agent is not perfect: i.e., if the agent does not have ability to measure an angle accurately. This seems a nice future problem as an extension of the current work.

References

1. Abiteboul, S., Alstrup, S., Kaplan, H., Milo, T., Rauhe, T.: Compact labeling scheme for ancestor queries. SIAM J. Comput. **35**(6), 1295–1309 (2006)
2. Alpern, S., Gal, S.: The Theory of Search Games and Rendezvous, vol. 55. Springer, NY (2006). https://doi.org/10.1007/b100809
3. Beck, A., Newman, D.J.: Yet more on the linear search problem. Israel J. Math. **8**(4), 419–429 (1970)
4. Bhattacharya, A., Gorain, B., Mandal, P.S.: Treasure hunt in graph using pebbles. In: Devismes, S., Petit, F., Altisen, K., Di Luna, G.A., Fernandez Anta, A. (eds.) Stabilization, Safety, and Security of Distributed Systems. SSS 2022. Lecture Notes in Computer Science, vol. 13751, pp. 99–113. Springer, Cham (2022). https://doi.org/10.1007/978-3-031-21017-4_7

5. Bhattacharya, A., Gorain, B., Mandal, P.S.: Pebble guided treasure hunt in plane. arXiv preprint arXiv:2305.06067 (2023)
6. Bouchard, S., Dieudonné, Y., Pelc, A., Petit, F.: Deterministic treasure hunt in the plane with angular hints. Algorithmica **82**, 3250–3281 (2020)
7. Bouchard, S., Labourel, A., Pelc, A.: Impact of knowledge on the cost of treasure hunt in trees. Networks **80**(1), 51–62 (2022)
8. Demaine, E.D., Fekete, S.P., Gal, S.: Online searching with turn cost. Theoret. Comput. Sci. **361**(2–3), 342–355 (2006)
9. Dereniowski, D., Pelc, A.: Drawing maps with advice. J.Parall. Distrib. Comput. **72**(2), 132–143 (2012)
10. Dobrev, S., Královič, R., Markou, E.: Online graph exploration with advice. In: Even, G., Halldórsson, M.M. (eds.) SIROCCO 2012. LNCS, vol. 7355, pp. 267–278. Springer, Heidelberg (2012). https://doi.org/10.1007/978-3-642-31104-8_23
11. Emek, Y., Fraigniaud, P., Korman, A., Rosén, A.: Online computation with advice. Theoret. Comput. Sci. **412**(24), 2642–2656 (2011)
12. Fraigniaud, P., Gavoille, C., Ilcinkas, D., Pelc, A.: Distributed computing with advice: information sensitivity of graph coloring. Distrib. Comput. **21**, 395–403 (2009)
13. Fraigniaud, P., Ilcinkas, D., Pelc, A.: Tree exploration with advice. Inf. Comput. **206**(11), 1276–1287 (2008)
14. Fraigniaud, P., Ilcinkas, D., Pelc, A.: Communication algorithms with advice. J. Comput. Syst. Sci. **76**(3–4), 222–232 (2010)
15. Fraigniaud, P., Korman, A., Lebhar, E.: Local MST computation with short advice. In: Proceedings of the Nineteenth Annual ACM Symposium on Parallel Algorithms and Architectures, pp. 154–160 (2007)
16. Fricke, G.M., Hecker, J.P., Griego, A.D., Tran, L.T., Moses, M.E.: A distributed deterministic spiral search algorithm for swarms. In: 2016 IEEE/RSJ International Conference on Intelligent Robots and Systems (IROS), pp. 4430–4436. IEEE (2016)
17. Fusco, E.G., Pelc, A.: Trade-offs between the size of advice and broadcasting time in trees. In: Proceedings of the Twentieth Annual Symposium on Parallelism in Algorithms and Architectures, pp. 77–84 (2008)
18. Gal, S.: Search games. Wiley Encyclopedia of Operations Research and Management Science (2010)
19. Gorain, B., Mondal, K., Nayak, H., Pandit, S.: Pebble guided optimal treasure hunt in anonymous graphs. Theoret. Comput. Sci. **922**, 61–80 (2022)
20. Miller, A., Pelc, A.: Tradeoffs between cost and information for rendezvous and treasure hunt. J. Parall. Distrib. Comput. **83**, 159–167 (2015)
21. Pelc, A., Yadav, R.N.: Cost vs. information tradeoffs for treasure hunt in the plane. arXiv preprint arXiv:1902.06090 (2019)
22. Pelc, A., Yadav, R.N.: Advice complexity of treasure hunt in geometric terrains. Inf. Comput. **281**, 104705 (2021)
23. Ta-Shma, A., Zwick, U.: Deterministic rendezvous, treasure hunts and strongly universal exploration sequences. In: Symposium on Discrete Algorithms: Proceedings of the Eighteenth Annual ACM-SIAM Symposium on Discrete Algorithms, vol. 7, pp. 599–608 (2007)

Distance-2-Dispersion: Dispersion with Further Constraints

Tanvir Kaur and Kaushik Mondal$^{(\boxtimes)}$

Indian Institute of Technology Ropar, Rupnagar, Punjab, India
{tanvir.20maz0001,kaushik.mondal}@iitrpr.ac.in

Abstract. The aim of the dispersion problem is to place a set of k ($\leq n$) mobile robots in the nodes of an unknown graph consisting of n nodes such that in the final configuration each node contains at most one robot, starting from any arbitrary initial configuration of the robots on the graph. In this work, we propose a variant of the dispersion problem, namely Distance-2-Dispersion, in short, D-2-D, where we start with any number of robots, and put an additional constraint that no two adjacent nodes contain robots in the final configuration. However, if a maximal independent set is already formed by the nodes which contain a robot each, then any other unsettled robot, if exists, will not find a node to settle. Hence we allow multiple robots to sit on some nodes only if there is no place to sit. If $k \geq n$, it is guaranteed that the nodes with robots form a maximal independent set of the underlying network.

The graph $G = (V, E)$ is a port-labelled graph having n nodes and m edges, where nodes are anonymous. The robots have unique ids in the range $[1, L]$, where $L \geq k$. Co-located robots can communicate among themselves. We provide an algorithm that solves D-2-D starting from a rooted configuration (i.e., initially all the robots are co-located) and terminates after $2\Delta(8m - 3n + 3)$ synchronous rounds using $O(\log \Delta)$ memory per robot without using any global knowledge of the graph parameters m, n and Δ, the maximum degree of the graph. We also provide $\Omega(m\Delta)$ lower bound on the number of rounds for the D-2-D problem.

Keywords: Mobile robots · Collaborative dispersion · Deterministic algorithm

1 Introduction

The aim of the dispersion problem is to place a set of k ($\leq n$) mobile robots in the nodes of an unknown graph consisting of n nodes such that in the final configuration each node contains at most one robot, starting from any arbitrary initial configuration of the robots on the graph. This problem was introduced in the year 2018 by Augustine et al. [1]. Later, this problem is studied under various models and with different assumptions in the literature [2–10]. The main tool used for dispersion is Depth-First-Search traversal and since the robots are equipped with memory, they store the important information required to complete dispersion without getting stuck in a cycle. A natural question that arises

D. Mohaisen and T. Wies (Eds.): NETYS 2023, LNCS 14067, pp. 157–173, 2023.
https://doi.org/10.1007/978-3-031-37765-5_12

is what would happen if there are some extra constraints imposed on the dispersion problem. As an example, no robot can settle in the one-hop neighborhood of an already settled robot. This led to the generation of the Distance-2-Dispersion problem. In this problem, k robots arbitrarily placed on the graph need to attain a configuration such that the settled robots occupy no two adjacent nodes. Also, an unsettled robot can settle at a node that already contains a settled robot, only if for the unsettled robot there is no other node to settle maintaining the added constraint. With this, there can be *many* nodes without a settled robot, i.e., no robot to store any information at those nodes, and the nodes also do not have any memory, thus the problem becomes interesting if one aims to solve with *less* memory requirement at each robot.

The Model: Let G be an arbitrary connected undirected graph with n nodes, m edges, and maximum degree Δ. The nodes are anonymous, i.e., they have no id. It is a port-labelled graph, i.e., each node u assigns a distinct port number to each of its edges from a range $[0, \delta(u) - 1]$ where $\delta(u)$ is the degree of node u. The neighboring node of u that is reachable through port p from u is denoted by $u(p)$. Port numbers that are assigned at the two ends of any edge are independent of each other. Nodes do not have any memory and hence G is a zero storage graph.

A total of k movable entities are present in the system, which are called robots. Each robot has a unique id from the range $[1, L]$ and each robot knows its id. In any round, if two or more robots are at a single node, we call them co-located and such robots can share information via message passing[1]. Any robot present on some node knows the degree of that node as well as the port-numbers associated with each of the edges corresponding to that node. So, if some robot needs to leave its current node through any particular port number, it can do that. Besides this, whenever any robot moves from a node u to another node v, it learns the port number through which it enters the node v.

Our algorithm proceeds in synchronous rounds where in each round robots perform the following steps in order: (i) co-located robots may exchange messages (ii) robots may compute based on the available information (iii) robots may move through an edge to some adjacent node from the current node based on its computation in step (ii). We further assume that all the robots start the algorithm at the same time, i.e., from the same round. The time complexity of the algorithm is measured as the number of synchronous rounds required by the robots to complete the task. We also study the amount of memory required per robot to run the algorithm.

---

[1] This is known as the Face-to-Face communication model and has already been considered while studying problems related to mobile robots including exploration [11,12] and dispersion [1,13].

The Problem: Distance-2-Dispersion(D-2-D): Given a set of $k \geq 1$ robots placed arbitrarily in a port-labelled graph G with n nodes and m edges, the robots need to achieve a configuration by the end of the algorithm where each robot needs to settle at some node satisfying the following two conditions: (i) no two adjacent nodes can be occupied by settled robots, and (ii) a robot can settle in a node where there is already a settled robot only if no more unoccupied node is present for the robot to settle satisfying condition (i).

The conditions ensure that the distance between any pair of settled robots is at least 2 unless both are settled at the same node. Hence, the nodes with settled robots form an independent set of the graph. And with *enough* robots, we get a maximal independent set.

Our Contribution: We solve the D-2-D problem for rooted[2] initial configuration on arbitrary graphs in $2\Delta(8m - 3n + 3)$ rounds using $O(\log \Delta)$ memory[3] per robot in Sect. 3. All the settled robots terminate even without any global knowledge regarding any of the graph parameters m, n, or Δ. In Sect. 4, we provide a $\Omega(m\Delta)$ lower bound of the D-2-D problem on the number of rounds considering robots do not have more than $O(\log \Delta)$ memory. Also, if $k \geq n$, it is guaranteed that the nodes with settled robots form a maximal independent set, which can itself be an interesting topic to study in the domain of distributed computing with mobile robots.

Related Work: Dispersion is the most related problem to our problem and we consider a similar model that is considered to solve the dispersion problem. In fact, we formed this problem from the dispersion problem. Though in the case of some inputs, the nodes with settled robots form a maximal independent set, our problem is nowhere close to the distributed maximal independent set finding problem [14–22] and hence in this section, we restrict ourselves mainly to the discussion on the dispersion problem.

Augustine et al. introduced the dispersion problem in [1] for the rooted configuration. They proved the memory requirement by the robots for any deterministic algorithm to achieve dispersion on a graph is $\Omega(\log n)$. The lower bound for any algorithm to perform dispersion on any graph is $\Omega(D)$, where D is the diameter of the graph. For rooted graphs, with the knowledge of m, n, they gave an algorithm that requires $O(\log n)$ memory by the robots to complete dispersion in $O(m)$ rounds [1]. Kshemkalyani et al. [23] improved the lower bound of running time to $\Omega(k)$ where $k \leq n$. They developed an algorithm for a synchronous system that solves dispersion in $O(m)$ rounds using $O(k \log \Delta)$ bits at each robot. However, for an asynchronous system, they developed an algorithm that requires $O(max(\log k, \log \Delta))$ bits of memory with the time complexity $O((m - n)k)$. Later Kshemkalyani et al. [24] significantly improved the result and provided a deterministic algorithm for dispersion in arbitrary graphs in a synchronous setting that runs in $O(min(m, k\Delta) \cdot \log l)$ rounds, where $l \leq \frac{k}{2}$,

---

[2] A configuration where all the robots are initially placed on a single node.

[3] We mean $O(\log \Delta)$ additional memory, i.e., memory apart from what it requires to store its id.

using $O(\log n)$ bits of memory at each robot. Their intuitive idea was to run DFS traversals in parallel to minimize time. The robots required the knowledge of m, n, k, and Δ. Shintaku et al. then presented a dispersion algorithm that does not require such global knowledge [5]. Their algorithm solves the dispersion problem on arbitrary graphs in $O(min(m, k\Delta) \cdot \log l)$ rounds using $\Theta(\log(k+\Delta))$ bits of memory at each robot. Recently, Kshemkalyani et al. [13] provided an algorithm that is optimal in both time and memory in arbitrary anonymous graphs of constant degree. They presented an algorithm that solves dispersion in $O(min(m, k\Delta))$ time with $\Theta(\log(k + \Delta))$ bits at each robot improving the time bound of the best previously known algorithm by $O(\log l)$ where $l \leq \frac{k}{2}$ and matching asymptotically the single-source DFS traversal bounds [24]. They extend the idea of [24] by making the larger size DFS traversal to subsume the smaller size DFS thus avoiding the need of revisiting the nodes of subsumed traversal more than once.

D-2-D, in some sense, is also related to the problem of scattering or uniform distribution. Scattering has been worked mainly for grids [25] and rings [26,27] though with anonymous robots. Finally, as in some cases, our algorithm forms a maximal independent set, we cite the following study on forming a maximal independent set with movable entities, though it is done with stronger model assumptions. Vamshi et al. presented the problem of finding the maximal independent set (MIS) using myopic luminous robots [28] of an arbitrary connected graph where the robots have prior knowledge of Δ, $O(\log \Delta)$ bits of persistent memory and at least 3 hops visibility. The authors also used colors to represent different states and worked under semi-synchronous as well as asynchronous schedulers. On the contrary, our model is different, we do not use visibility or lights.

D-2-D vs Dispersion: The Challenges: In the previous works on the dispersion problem, the algorithms use the depth-first search (DFS) traversal with limited memory of the robots [1,4,13]. The key idea to achieve dispersion from any rooted configuration is that the group of unsettled robots continue a DFS traversal starting from the root by making the smallest id robot settle at vacant nodes. The settled robots remember the parent port and thus help the moving group of unsettled robots to backtrack during the DFS traversal. Also, the settled robots work as markers for the nodes where they are settled, i.e., if the group of unsettled robots visits a node with a settled robot, it can understand that it is in a cycle. Thus dispersion can be achieved with $O(\log \Delta)$ memory per robot and the time complexity is the same as of sequential DFS traversal. Firstly, since there is no settled robot present in the one-hop neighborhood of any settled robot, the information regarding the parent pointer of those neighboring nodes is difficult to be stored and subsequently used while backtracking. This may lead to high memory requirements. Secondly, the robots can settle at a node u if and only if there are no settled robots at any of the neighbors of u. As the maximum degree Δ can be large, this may lead to high time complexity.

2   Warm-Up: D-2-D with $O(\Delta \log \Delta)$ Memory per Robot

In this section, we provide an informal discussion on a straightforward solution of the rooted D-2-D without bothering about the memory requirement per robot or the time complexity. Our algorithm is based on the depth-first search traversal (albeit with some modification) that solves the dispersion problem as we discussed above in Sect. 1. Later in Sect. 3, we improve this solution.

As the group may need to backtrack from an unoccupied node in our D-2-D problem, it is required to store the parent pointers of the unoccupied nodes too. Note that all the neighboring nodes of any occupied node must be unoccupied. We instruct each settled robot to remember the parent ports of all its neighbors including itself. Basically, each settled robots work as a *virtually settled* robot at its neighbors. However, to store as well as to provide the stored parent pointers, each settled robot must meet the moving group of robots whenever the group reaches one of its neighboring nodes. To achieve this, each settled robot does a back-and-forth movement from its position to its neighboring nodes. To be more specific, let a robot r settle in round T at a node u of degree δ. It visits $u(0)$ in round $T + 1$, comes back to u in round $T + 2$, visits $u(1)$ in round $T + 3$, and so on. It visits $u(0)$ again after $u(\delta - 1)$ is visited. The settled robot r stops only when it meets the group of unsettled robots at some node, say $v = u(p)$, and at some round say T'. It stays with the group at $u(p)$ till the group leaves $u(p)$, say in round T''. Then r comes back to u in round $T'' + 1$ and again starts visiting its neighbors one by one as described earlier.

For simplicity, let us assume that all robots know Δ; in the next section, we show how we remove this assumption from our main algorithm. The algorithm instructs the moving group to wait for 2Δ rounds at each node v it visits. If v is occupied, then the settled robot must meet the group within 2 rounds; else if v is a neighbor of an occupied node, then the settled robot that is working as a virtually settled robot must meet the group within the 2Δ waiting time.

Now we provide the algorithm. If the group is in the forward exploration state, the following are the possibilities.

- The group meets at least one virtually settled robot and finds that none of the virtually settled robots who meet the group has the parent pointer for this node, the group understands that it is visiting this node for the first time and continues the DFS traversal in the forward exploration phase after providing the parent pointer to each of the virtually settled robots. This is possible as all the settled robots that meet this group wait till it leaves.
- The group meets at least one virtually settled robot and finds that at least one of them comes with the parent pointer for this node, the group understands that this node is explored earlier, and thus subsequently backtracks.
- The group finds that the node is occupied, it goes to the *backtrack* state and backtracks with the help of the parent pointer stored at the settled robot.
- The group sees no settled or virtually settled robots, then the minimum id robot from the group settles there.

If the group is in the backtracking state, it must meet at least one virtually settled robot or a settled robot at the node. The group checks if all the ports associated with this node are already explored or not, by looking at the parent pointer and the port through which it just backtracks to this node. The following are the decisions.

- If all ports are explored, it continues the backtracking.
- Else changes to the forward exploration state.

To store the parent pointer for each of the neighbors, each settled robot requires $O(\Delta \log \Delta)$ memory i.e., $\log \Delta$ memory per port number. This leads to high memory requirements and waiting for 2Δ rounds for the moving group at each newly explored node leads to a high run time of the algorithm. Both of these issues are mentioned when we discussed the challenges in Sect. 1. The run time of this algorithm becomes $2\Delta(4m - 2n + 2)$. This is because we just run the DFS traversal for dispersion that takes $4m - 2n + 2$ time as done in [1,24] assuming all the unoccupied neighbors of each occupied node are virtually occupied. Also, we keep all the necessary information with the settled robots. After completing the DFS traversal once, if some robots are left unsettled then they settle at the root node. Note that as the settled robots keep moving, it is desirable that the robots can terminate. However, here we do not discuss the termination of the algorithm, but it can be achieved in a similar way we do in Sect. 3 in our main algorithm.

3   D-2-D with Termination: $O(\log \Delta)$ Memory per Robot

In this section, we present an algorithm with improved memory requirement than the algorithm discussed in Sect. 2 and we include the termination of the robots without any global knowledge as well. The main idea is not to do the usual DFS traversal so that the path from the last settled robot to the node where the unsettled group is currently present, can be bounded. If the length of this path is high, then in the worst case, all the nodes in this path may remain unoccupied as all of them can be the neighbor of some particular occupied node v, and in this case, the robot that is settled at v needs to remember the parent pointer of all the unoccupied nodes present in that path. We restrict the depth of the traversal during forward exploration by 2 from the node where a robot settled last. Each settled robot may need to remember the parent pointer of the node where it is settled and the parent pointer of one of its one-hop neighbors, through which the group of unsettled robots continues the forward exploration. Based on this, robots achieve D-2-D and we call this stage 1 of the algorithm. As in our algorithm, the settled robots move back and forth, termination is required which we do in stage 2 of our algorithm. The idea for termination is the following. During stage 1, let a settled robot r meets the group of unsettled robots for P times. If the last settled robot r_L can return to the root and repeat stage 1 again, by acting as the group of unsettled robots, then we make that settled robot r meet r_L exactly P times during this repetition. When this happens, then r terminates. Now we are ready to provide a formal description.

Table 1. Description of variables

Variables	Descriptions
$r_i.parent$	This variable contains the parent port of the node u where r_i is settled in stage 1 or $act\_settled$ in stage 2. Else, $r_i.parent = -1$
$r_i.portentered$	The port through which robot r_i enters the current node. Initially $r_i.portentered = -1$ for all the robots
$r_i.virtualparent$	The parent port of $u(p)$ where p be the last port that was explored from the node where r_i is settled. Initially $r_i.virtualparent = -1$ for all the robots
$r_i.dist$	This variable is initialised to 0. Each unsettled robot r_i maintains the distance from the settled robot it last encountered during its traversal. According to our algorithm, $r_i.dist \leq 2$. For each settled robot, $r_i.dist = 0$ if it is at the node where it is settled, else $r_i.dist = 1$
$r_i.special$	A robot r_i settled at some node u, say, updates $r_i.special = 1$ only when the group of unsettled robots is at u with r_i and will move through one of the adjacent edges of u in the $explore$ state. For other settled robots, $r_i.special = 0$ and for any unsettled robot, $r_i.special = -1$
$r_i.settled$	Takes value 1 if r_i is a settled robot, else takes 0
$r_i.count$	If r_i is a settled robot in stage 1, this variable counts the number of times r_i meets the group of unsettled robots, else it does not modify its value
$r_i.stage$	This variable can take values 1 or 2 where $r_i.stage = 1$ indicates stage 1 of the algorithm whereas $r_i.stage = 2$ indicates stage 2
$r_i.act\_settled$	Takes value 1 if r_i settles in the stage 2, else takes value 0
$r_i.count'$	In the stage 2, if r_i is an $act\_settled$ robot, this variable counts the number of times r_i meets the robot r_L with $r_L.terminate = 1$
$r_i.terminate$	This variable is initially set to 0. When the robot with the largest id, say r_L settles at a node, and then returns to the root node, it sets $r_L.terminate = 1$

3.1   The Algorithm

Here we describe our algorithm that the robots can run with $O(\log \Delta)$ memory per robot to achieve rooted D-2-D and terminate in $2\Delta(8m - 3n + 3)$ rounds.

Consider an arbitrary graph G and let k robots be initially placed on a single node, say u, of G. Each robot r_i maintains variables defined in detail in Table 1. Apart from that, each unsettled robot maintains its state, which can be either $explore$ or $backtrack$. In the $explore$ state, it does forward exploration by moving through a computed port number from the current node, whereas in the $backtrack$ state, it learns the parent pointer from a settled robot and backtracks through that port. Robots also maintain a variable ϕ which is initialized to $\delta(u)$, where u is the root. When the group of unsettled robots reaches a new node, say

v, each robot in the group updates the value of ϕ with $max\{\delta(v), \phi\}$. However, settled robots do not modify ϕ once they are settled. Note that each robot in the group of unsettled robots has the same value of ϕ; also $\phi \leq \Delta$, the maximum degree of the graph. Our algorithm works in two stages, stage 1 and stage 2. In stage 1, robots achieve D-2-D and in stage 2, robots terminate. The group of unsettled robots runs the algorithm in phases, where each phase consists of 2ϕ rounds. Since each unsettled robot agrees on its ϕ value, the group starts and ends each phase at the same round.

Our algorithm starts by settling the minimum id unsettled robot, say r_1, at the root node u in the end of phase 1, i.e., at the 2ϕ-th round. The remaining unsettled robots move to the adjacent node via the incremented value of *portentered*. The settled robot r_1 updates its *special* value to 1 and moves with the group of unsettled robots as well. After reaching this node, the unsettled robots update ϕ and wait for 2ϕ rounds. As this is a rooted configuration and r_1 is the first robot to settle(which is currently present along with the group of unsettled robots), no other settled robot visits this group during the wait of 2ϕ rounds. The settled robot r_1 saves the parent pointer for the current node in the variable $r_1.virtualparent$, increments the value of $r_1.count$ variable updates the $r_1.special$ value to 0, and returns to the node u. However, the unsettled robots either move through the updated value of *portentered* or backtrack to the previous node in case the incremented value of *portentered* is the same as the *parent* value for the current node where the unsettled robots are present. This ends phase 2 for the group of unsettled robots. Observe that the group of unsettled robots moves only at the end of each phase. So each phase of unsettled robots corresponds to one edge traversal and each phase requires 2ϕ rounds. Settled robots do not bother with phases, they either wait with the group of unsettled robots and increase the *count* variable, or continue back and forth traversal. So, the time complexity of stage 1 of our algorithm depends on how many phases the group of unsettled robots works before the last robot, i.e., the largest id robot, say r_L, settles. Below, we start with the algorithm for the settled robots.

Algo_Settled: Algorithm for Each Settled Robot r_j in Stage 1

- If a settled robot r_j has the value *special* = 0, then it continues its visit to each of its neighbors one by one and keeps modifying $r_j.dist$ accordingly. As and when the r_j meets the group of unsettled robots, it increments the value of $r_j.count$ and waits with the group unless it leaves that node. Post that, the settled robot resumes its visit to each of its neighbors one by one.
- If a settled robot r_j has the value *special* = 1, it moves along with the group of unsettled robots in the next round to the neighboring node, and waits along with the group of unsettled robots. The settled robot r_j increments the value of $r_j.count$. During this waiting period, if any settled robot with id lower than $r_j.id$ visits then r_j does not store the parent pointer for this node and returns to its original position after the group leaves. However, if no settled robot with an id smaller than $r_j.id$ visits the group of unsettled robots then the settled robot r_j updates $r_j.virtualparent = r_j.portentered$. The robot r_j keeps updating its distance to 0/1 based on its position.

Next, we provide the algorithm for the unsettled robots.

Algo_Unsettled: Algorithm for Each Unsettled Robot r_i

- For $phase = 0$, after 2ϕ rounds, the minimum id robot, say r_j, settles at the current node and sets $r_j.parent = -1$. The remaining unsettled robots update $dist = 1$ move through $r_i.portentered = (r_i.portentered + 1) mod\delta$ according to initial values given in Table 1.

- For $phase > 0$, we have the following cases:

  - When $r_i.dist = 1$ and $state = explore$ at the beginning of a phase
    * If no settled robot with $special = 0$ visits the group of unsettled robots such that the visiting settled robot's id is lesser than the id of r_j with $r_j.special = 1$, then the group updates $r_i.portentered = (r_i.portentered + 1) mod\delta$. Note that whenever the group of unsettled robots has $r_i.dist = 1$ and $state = explore$, there is definitely a settled robot r_j present with the group having $r_j.special = 1$. If $r_i.portentered = r_j.virtualparent$, then the group of unsettled robots backtracks to the previous node after updating $r_i.dist = 0$. Else if $r_i.portentered \neq r_j.virtualparent$ then the group of unsettled robots leaves the node via the updated port number in the $explore$ state after updating $r_i.dist = 2$.
    * If at least one settled robot, with $special = 0$ and id lesser than id of r_j with $r_j.special = 1$ visits the group of unsettled robots, then the group backtracks via $r_i.portentered$ after changing $r_i.dist = 0$.
  - When $r_i.dist = 2$ and $state = explore$ at the beginning of a phase
    * If no settled robot visits the group of unsettled robots in 2ϕ rounds, then the lowest id robot from the group settles on this node and updates its $dist$ value to 0. Each unsettled robot updates $r_i.dist = 1$ and leaves the node via updated port number in $explore$ state.
    * If one or more than one settled robot visits the group of unsettled robots, each unsettled robot updates $r_i.dist = 1$, and the group backtracks via the $portentered$.
  - When r_i is at the root and there does not exist any unexplored port, r_i settles at the root. Also, if $r_i \neq r_L$, r_i terminates and hence does not take part in the algorithm anymore.

However, when the group of unsettled robots is in $state = backtrack$, the group of unsettled robots reaches a node that has been visited earlier. Thus, the node visited in $backtrack$ state has either a settled robot on it or any settled robot in its one-hop neighbor has stored the virtual parent for it. After backtracking to the current node, the group of unsettled robots decides to further explore or backtrack based on the following cases.

  - When $r_i.state = backtrack$ at the beginning of a phase

* If all the ports are already explored i.e. $(r_i.portentered + 1)mod\delta$ equals the $r_m.parentpointer$ where r_m is the settled robot on that node or $r_j.virtualparent$ where r_j is the settled robot which has stored the parent pointer for its neighbor. Recall that this information can be exchanged during the waiting time. In this case, the group of unsettled robots backtracks through $r_m.parentpointer$ or $r_j.virtualparent$ of the node after updating their *dist* variable.

* If the $(r_i.portentered + 1)mod\delta$ is not equal to the $r_i.parentpointer$ of the node then the unsettled robots change their *state* to *explore* and move through $r_i.portentered$ after updating their *dist* variable.

As and when the largest id robot, r_L settles, it understands a D-2-D configuration is achieved. It sets $r_L.stage = 2$ and moves to the root(if not already there) by following the parent pointer of each node. After reaching the root, it sets $r_L.terminate = 1$. Any robot r_j (except r_L) goes to stage 2 by updating $r_j.stage = 2$ as and when it meets another robot with $r_i.stage = 2$. First, we see the algorithm for the robots other than r_L in stage 2.

Algo_Terminate: Algorithm for $r_j(\neq r_L)$ with $r_j.terminate = 0$

Note that, each robot has initially set $r_j.terminate = 0$. Any such robot r_j runs Algo_Settled (or Algo_Unsettled) if it is a settled (or unsettled) robot unless it meets any robot r_i with $r_i.stage = 2$.

- If $r_j.stage = 1$ and r_j meets r_i with $r_i.stage = 2$ at some node v' other than its original position v then it updates $r_j.stage = 2$ and goes back to its original position, say v, if not already there, and waits till r_L arrives. When r_L arrives at v with $r_L.terminate = 1$, r_j also updates $r_j.act\_settled = 1$.
- If $r_j.stage = 1$ and r_j meets r_L with $r_L.stage = 2$ and $r_L.terminate = 1$ at its original position v, then r_j updates $r_j.act\_settled = 1$.
- If $r_j.act\_settled = 1$ and $r_j.special = 0$ then it continues the back-and-forth movement through all its neighbors and increments the value of $r_j.count'$ by 1 as and when it meets r_L. When $r_j.count$ becomes equal to $r_j.count'$, it terminates at its original position where it was settled.
- If $r_j.act\_settled = 1$ and $r_j.special = 1$ then it moves with the robot r_L to the neighboring node through the updated value of $r_L.portentered$ and waits with r_L. It increments the value of $r_j.count'$ by 1. Now two cases arise:
  • If no $act\_settled$ robot visits with id lower than $r_j.id$ then r_j sets $r_j.virtualparent = r_L.portentered$
  • Else move to the original settled position and set $r_j.special = 0$

Algo_Help_Terminate: Algorithm for r_L with $r_L.stage = 2$

If r_L is settled at some node other than the root, first it backtracks through the parent pointer to reach the root. If r_L settled at the root, it does not even need to backtrack. After reaching the root u, it updates $r_L.terminate = 1$, $\phi = \delta(u)$ and begins mimicking stage 1 by acting as the group of unsettled robots.

The robot r_L runs the same algorithm Algo_Unsettled. Accordingly $r_L.act\_settled$ remains 0 till r_L reaches its original position and settles where it settled at the end of stage 1. The decisions made in stage 1 by the group of unsettled robots were dependent on the visiting settled robots. Whereas now the same decisions are made based on the visiting act_settled robots.

This verifies the same path traversal by r_L as by the unsettled robots in stage 1. Now, when r_L has $r_L.dist = 2$ and $r_L.state = explore$ and during the wait of 2ϕ rounds, no act_settled robot visits that node, this indicates this is the original position where r_L was settled during stage 1 and hence it sets $r_L.act\_settled = 1$ and terminates. By this time, all the settled robots already have $count$ value matched with $count'$ value, and thus all the robots terminate.

An outline of a pseudo-code of the main algorithm is given as Algorithm 1. Figure 1 shows the run of stage 1 of our algorithm.

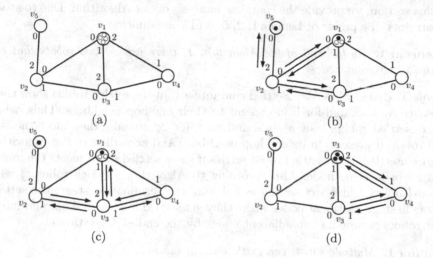

(a)   (b)   (c)   (d)

Fig. 1. (a) The initial configuration with four robots at v_1. (b) One robot, say r, settles at v_1 and updates $r.special = 1$. The remaining robots including the robot r moves to v_2 and wait for 2ϕ rounds. No robot settles at this node and thus moves to v_3 while r moves back to v_1 after storing 0 as the parent pointer of v_2 in $r.virtualparent$. After waiting for 2ϕ rounds, the unsettled robots backtracks and further explore the node v_5 where another robot r' settles. The unsettled robots backtrack to v_2 and further to v_1. Note that each time the settled robots meet the unsettled robots, they update their value of $r.count$ and $r'.count$. (c) Similarly, the unsettled robots now move to node v_3 and then to v_2. From v_2, it backtracks to v_3 and further explores v_4. Now the unsettled robots backtrack to v_3 and then to v_1. (d) Now the group moves through port 2 to explore v_4 and it further moves to explore v_3. It backtracks to v_4 and then further backtracks to v_1. As v_1 is the root and all the ports of v_1 are explored, the unsettled robots settle here. Also, among these two robots, the smaller id unsettled robot terminates and the larger id robot sets stage value to 2. At the end of this stage 1, the value of $r.count = 15$ while $r'.count = 2$.

Algorithm 1: D-2-D_with_Termination for robot r_i

---

if $r_i.settle = 0$ *and* $r_i.stage = 1$ **then**
| call Algo_Unsettled
else if $r_i.settle = 1$ *and* $r_i.stage = 1$ *and* $r_i \neq r_L$ **then**
| **if** r_i *did not meet any robot with* $r_j.stage = 2$ **then**
| | call Algo_Settled
| **else if** r_i *meets any robot with* $r_j.stage = 2$ **then**
| | call Algo_Terminate
else if $r_i = r_L$ *with* $r_L.settle = 1$ *and* $r_L.stage = 2$ **then**
| backtrack to the root node
| call Algo_Help_Terminate

3.2 Analysis of the Algorithm

In this section, we provide the complete analysis of our Algorithm. Due to space constraints, the proofs of Lemma 1, 2, 5, and 7 are omitted.

Theorem 1. *By the end of the Algorithm 1, there are no two robots that are settled at adjacent nodes.*

Proof. The Algorithm Algo_Settled guarantees that the settled robots show their presence by back-and-forth movement to their one-hop neighbors. Thus, when the unsettled robots visit a node and wait for 2ϕ rounds, they meet the settled robot, if present, in its one-hop neighbor. And according to the Algorithm Algo_Unsettled, no unsettled robot settles if some settled robot meets the unsettled robot in some node. Also according to Algorithm for each robot r_j with $r_j.settled = 1$ and $r_j.act\_settled = 1$ during the termination stage, the settled robots in stage 2 settle at nodes where they get settled in stage 1. This guarantees that robots occupy no two adjacent nodes by the end of Algorithm 1.

Lemma 1. *Multiple robots can settle only at the root.*

Lemma 2. *If multiple robots settle at the root in stage 1, then it is guaranteed that each node is visited by a group of unsettled robots at least once.*

Theorem 2. *By the end of the Algorithm 1, multiple robots settled at the root implies no vacant node left with none of its neighbors containing a settled robot.*

Proof. Let us suppose there is a vacant node u in the graph such that no settled robot is present in any of its one-hop neighbors in stage 1. Lemma 2 proves that node u is visited at least once. According to our algorithm Algo_Unsettled, when the group visited u, each of the robots r_j in the group must set $r_j.dist = 2$. During the waiting period, there were no settled robots in the neighbors of u to visit u. Hence the minimum id robot must have settled there. This contradicts the presence of such a node in the graph.

observation 1. *If multiple robots settle in the root, it follows from Theorem 1 and 2 that the nodes with settled robots form a maximal independent set.*

Theorem 3. *Algorithm 1 runs with $O(\log \Delta)$ memory per robot.*

Proof. The variables $r_i.state$, $r_i.stage$, $r_i.settled$, $r_i.act\_settled$ and $r_i.special$ requires 1 bit of memory while $r_i.dist$ requires 2 bits of memory. The variables $r_i.parent$, $r_i.portentered$ and $r_i.virtualparent$ requires $O(\log \Delta)$ bits of memory. The settled robot at a node v with $\delta(v) \leq \Delta$ can meet the group of unsettled robots at most $(\Delta + 1)$ nodes including node v and there can be at most $O(\Delta^2)$ associated edges with these nodes. Since the group of unsettled robots visits any edge at most 4 times, the variable $r_i.count$ can take the maximum value that is in $O(\Delta^2)$. Similarly, in stage 2 the $act\_settled$ robot at a node v with $\delta(v) \leq \Delta$ can meet r_L at $(\Delta + 1)$ nodes and thus, $r_i.count'$ can take maximum value that is in $O(\Delta^2)$. Therefore, $O(\log \Delta)$ memory is needed by the robots to store any information and thus to run the algorithm.

observation 2. *When the group of unsettled robots in stage 1 are in explore state and $r_i.dist = 1$ then there is exactly one settled robot present along with the group which has $r_i.special = 1$.*

Definition 1. *Tree Edge: An edge (u, v) is said to be a tree edge if the group of unsettled robots in stage 1 reaches v through (u, v) such that either the settled robot at node u (if exists) stores the parent pointer of the node v or the minimum id robot among the group of unsettled robots settles at v.*

Lemma 3. *Every tree edge is traversed exactly twice by the unsettled robots.*

Proof. Without loss of generality, according to Definition 1, let u have a settled robot. The tree edge (u, v) has either a settled robot at v, or a settled robot at u that stores the parent pointer for node v during the exploration of edge (u, v). This ensures that v is visited for the first time as we have its parent pointer stored. Thus, the edge (u, v) is traversed twice once in the *explore* state and the next in the *backtrack* state. As mentioned in Algorithm Algo_Settled, the parent pointer of node v is saved by robot r_u settled at node u only when no robot visits v with id $< r_u.id$. Hence the robots do not backtrack from v with the objective of exploring node v from another node with a lower id robot settled on it. This proves the edge (u, v) is traversed exactly two times.

Lemma 4. *A non-tree edge (any edge that is not a tree edge) is traversed at most four times by the group of unsettled robots.*

Proof. Let (u, v) be a non-tree edge. According to Definition 1, the robots backtrack from node v, and the parent pointer for v is not yet stored. Till this round, the edge (u, v) has been traversed twice. The robots reach v from the smallest id settled robot in its neighborhood to explore v later. At that time edge (v, u) is traversed again. Hence, every non-tree edge is traversed at most four times.

Lemma 5. *The graph induced by the tree edges is connected and cycle free.*

Lemma 6. *After the round when r_L settled at the end of stage 1, $r_i.count$ did not increase for any other robot r_i.*

Proof. Any settled robot increases $r_i.count$ only if it meets the group of unsettled robots r_j with $r_j.settle = 0$. After r_L got settled, there is no robot r_j with $r_j.settle = 0$ ever after. Hence the proof.

Lemma 7. *By the time stage 2 finishes, each robot terminates.*

Theorem 4. *The Algorithm 1 achieves D-2-D with termination in $2\Delta(8m - 3n + 3)$ rounds on arbitrary rooted graphs.*

Proof. It is clear from Lemma 3 and Lemma 4 that every edge is traversed at most 4 times except the tree edges. Also from Lemma 5, there can be at most $(n - 1)$ tree edges. So the total number of edge traversals is no more than $4(m - (n - 1)) + 2(n - 1) = 4m - 2n + 2$. After each edge traversal, the robots wait for 2ϕ rounds and $\phi \leq \Delta$. So at most $2\Delta(4m - 2n + 2)$ rounds are required for all the robots to settle. Thus Stage 1 is completed within $2\Delta(4m - 2n + 2)$ rounds. After the last robot settles, it may take at most $2\Delta(n - 1)$ rounds to reach the root node in the worst case. Now, the remaining part of stage 2 is a replica of stage 1 of our algorithm. Thus, it takes $2\Delta(8m - 3n + 3)$ rounds to achieve D-2-D with termination, where termination is ensured by Lemma 7.

4   Lower Bound

In this section, we discuss the lower bound on the number of rounds of the D-2-D problem considering robots do not have more than $O(\log \Delta)$ memory. We start by defining the view of a node to a robot.

Definition 2. *View: View of a node v to a robot is the information of whether there is a settled robot at any of its one-hop neighbors or not, including v.*

Next, we prove the theorem by constructing a class of graphs. The idea is that each graph in the class is a regular graph of degree $n - 1$ and has $2n$ nodes. We start with two robots, one of which settles first, and the other looks for a node to settle. The graphs are such that, unless the unsettled robot reaches two particular nodes, it will not be able to differentiate the graph with a clique. So, before reaching one of those nodes, if it decides to settle, that will lead to a wrong solution. We show that, with limited memory, finding one of those nodes requires at least $\Omega(m\Delta)$ rounds.

Theorem 5. *The lower bound on the number of rounds of D-2-D problem on arbitrary graphs is $\Omega(m\Delta)$ where robots have no more than $O(\log \Delta)$ memory.*

Proof. We prove this using a class of graphs where we show that there will be at least one graph for which the robots require at least $\frac{\Delta m}{12}$ many rounds to complete D-2-D. Let us consider two cliques of n vertices but with one edge missing from each of them. Let $v_1, v_2, ..., v_n$ be the vertices of the first clique Q_1 and $u_1, u_2, ..., u_n$ be the vertices of the second clique Q_2. Let $\overline{v_1 v_2}$ be the missing edge from the first clique and $\overline{u_1 u_2}$ be the missing edge from the second clique. We join v_1 with u_1 and v_2 with u_2. Now, the graph G has $2n$ nodes with $\Delta = n - 1$. Considering all possible different port-numbering of this graph gives us a graph class $\mathscr{G}$ which has cardinality equal to $[(n-1)!]^{2n}$. Let two robots r_1 and r_2 are initially present at v_j where $j \neq 1, 2$. Let us assume that there exists an algorithm $\mathscr{A}$ which solves D-2-D in time less than $\frac{m\Delta}{12}$. Let r_1 settle first and at node w. We can claim that there will be at least $\frac{|\mathscr{G}|}{2}$ graphs where, $w \notin \{v_1, v_2, u_1, u_2\}$. W.l.o.g. let w be some vertex of Q_1, say v_i. Let us denote $\frac{|\mathscr{G}|}{2}$ by N. Note that, even if r_1, r_2 try to work together, they can't achieve much as this is a zero storage algorithm and the robot's memory are $O(\log \Delta)$ only.

As the robots have $O(\log \Delta)$ memory, they can remember only constant many port numbers at a time. After r_1 is settled, we provide r_2 even more power by letting it know that there is a node to settle within the two-hop distance of v_i. The robot r_2 aims to explore all the $\Delta(\Delta - 1)$ many two-hop neighbors. There are enough graphs(in particular, $\frac{N}{4}$) wherein the robot r_2 needs to explore at least $\frac{\Delta(\Delta-1)}{2}$ many vertices before exploring u_1 or u_2. Unless it reaches u_1 or u_2 and has the view, r_2 can not distinguish any graph of our graph class from a clique of n nodes.

Let the sequence in which the nodes are explored is as follows $\{v_{i_1}, v_{i_2}, ..., v_{i_{\frac{\Delta(\Delta-1)}{2}}}\}$. When r_2 reaches v_{i_1}, it needs to know the view of the graph. If v_{i_1} is reached from v_i directly, then getting the view takes only one round as r_2 understands it is one-hop away from v_i. Else, if v_{i_1} is not reached directly from v_i, then it is easy to see that, in at least half of the graphs, r_2 needs at least $\frac{\Delta}{2}$ rounds to get the view. So, there exists enough instances (in particular at least $\frac{N}{4 \cdot 2}$) where r_2 requires $\frac{\Delta}{2}$ rounds to find the view. Similarly, after reaching v_{i_2} there exists at least $\frac{N}{4 \cdot 2^2}$ many graphs where $\frac{\Delta}{2}$ many rounds will be required to find the view of that node. In similar fashion, at $v_{i_{\frac{\Delta(\Delta-1)}{2}}}$ there exists at least $\frac{N}{4 \cdot 2^{\frac{\Delta(\Delta-1)}{2}}}$ many graphs. Now $\frac{N}{4 \cdot 2^{\frac{\Delta(\Delta-1)}{2}}}$ is a function of n and the value becomes more than 1 for all $n \geq 3$.

Hence, there is at least one graph where robot r_2 needs to spend at least $\frac{\Delta(\Delta-1)}{2} \cdot \frac{\Delta}{2}$ rounds to settle. For $n \geq 3$, $\Delta \geq \frac{M}{3}$ where $M = 2n$. Thus, $\frac{\Delta(\Delta-1)}{2} \cdot \frac{\Delta}{2} \geq \frac{M}{3} \cdot \frac{(\Delta-1)}{2} \cdot \frac{\Delta}{2} = m \cdot \frac{\Delta-1}{6} \geq \frac{m\Delta}{12}$. This proves there is at least one such instance in the class $\mathscr{G}$ where the robot r_2 requires $\frac{m\Delta}{12}$ many rounds to complete D-2-D, else both r_1 and r_2 settles in Q_1 (or Q_2, in case r_1 did settle at some node in Q_2) and this leads to wrong D-2-D. This completes the proof.

5 Conclusion and Future Work

We propose a variant of the dispersion problem and provide an algorithm that solves it for the rooted initial configuration with $O(\log \Delta)$ memory per robot and in $2\Delta(8m - 3n + 3)$ synchronous rounds. We also provide a $\Omega(m\Delta)$ lower bound of the problem on the number of rounds. In some cases, we guarantee to form a maximal independent set by the robots which can be of independent interest. It will be interesting to see how to solve the problem for arbitrary initial configuration of the robots.

Funding Information. Tanvir Kaur acknowledges the support of the Council of Scientific & Industrial Research (CSIR) during this work (Grant no. 09/1005(0048)/2020-EMR-I). This work was partially supported by the FIST program of the Department of Science and Technology, Government of India, Reference No. SR/FST/MS-I/2018/22(C).

References

1. John Augustine and William K. Moses Jr. Dispersion of mobile robots: a study of memory-time trade-offs. In: ICDCN, pp. 1:1–1:10 (2018)
2. Molla, A.R., Mondal, K., Moses Jr., W.K.: Byzantine dispersion on graphs. In: IPDPS, pp. 942–951. IEEE (2021)
3. Molla, A.R., Moses, W.K.: Dispersion of mobile robots: the power of randomness. In: Gopal, T.V., Watada, J. (eds.) TAMC 2019. LNCS, vol. 11436, pp. 481–500. Springer, Cham (2019). https://doi.org/10.1007/978-3-030-14812-6_30
4. Molla, A.R., Mondal, K., Moses, W.K., Jr.: Optimal dispersion on an anonymous ring in the presence of weak byzantine robots. Theor. Comput. Sci. **887**, 111–121 (2021)
5. Shintaku, T., Sudo, Y., Kakugawa, H., Masuzawa, T.: Efficient dispersion of mobile agents without global knowledge. In: Devismes, S., Mittal, N. (eds.) SSS 2020. LNCS, vol. 12514, pp. 280–294. Springer, Cham (2020). https://doi.org/10.1007/978-3-030-64348-5_22
6. Kshemkalyani, A.D., Molla, A.R., Sharma, G.: Dispersion of mobile robots using global communication. J. Parallel Distrib. Comput. **161**, 100–117 (2022)
7. Barun Gorain, Partha Sarathi Mandal, Kaushik Mondal, and Supantha Pandit. Collaborative dispersion by silent robots. In: Devismes, S., Petit, F., Altisen, K., Di Luna, G.A., Fernandez Anta, A. (eds.) SSS, vol. 13751, pp. 254–269. Springer, Cham (2022). https://doi.org/10.1007/978-3-031-21017-4_17
8. Das, A., Bose, K., Sau, B.: Memory optimal dispersion by anonymous mobile robots. In: Mudgal, A., Subramanian, C.R. (eds.) CALDAM 2021. LNCS, vol. 12601, pp. 426–439. Springer, Cham (2021). https://doi.org/10.1007/978-3-030-67899-9_34
9. Kshemkalyani, A.D., Molla, A.R., Sharma, G.: Dispersion of mobile robots on grids. In: Rahman, M.S., Sadakane, K., Sung, W.-K. (eds.) WALCOM 2020. LNCS, vol. 12049, pp. 183–197. Springer, Cham (2020). https://doi.org/10.1007/978-3-030-39881-1_16
10. Agarwalla, A., Augustine, J., Moses Jr., W.K., Sankar Madhav, K., Sridhar, A.K.: Deterministic dispersion of mobile robots in dynamic rings. In: ICDCN, pp. 19:1–19:4. ACM (2018)
11. Das, S.:: Graph explorations with mobile agents. In: Flocchini, P., Prencipe, G., Santoro, N. (eds) Distributed Computing by Mobile Entities. LNCS, vol. 11340, pp. 403–422. Springer, Cham (2019). https://doi.org/10.1007/978-3-030-11072-7_16
12. Dereniowski, D., Disser, Y., Kosowski, A., Pajak, D., Uznanski, P.: Fast collaborative graph exploration. Inf. Comput. **243**, 37–49 (2015)
13. Kshemkalyani, A.D., Sharma, G.: Near-optimal dispersion on arbitrary anonymous graphs. OPODIS 8:1–8:19 (2021)
14. Alon, N., Babai, L., Itai, A.: A fast and simple randomized parallel algorithm for the maximal independent set problem. J. Algorithms **7**(4), 567–583 (1986)

15. Barenboim, L., Elkin, M., Pettie, S., Schneider, J.: The locality of distributed symmetry breaking. J. ACM **63**(3), 20:1-20:45 (2016)
16. Elkin, M., Pettie, S., Su, H.-H.: $(2\Delta - 1)$-edge-coloring is much easier than maximal matching in the distributed setting. In: SODA, pp. 355–370 (2015)
17. Fischer, M., Noever, A.: Tight analysis of parallel randomized greedy MIS. In: SODA, pp. 2152–2160 (2018)
18. Ghaffari, M.: An improved distributed algorithm for maximal independent set. In: SODA, pp. 270–277 (2016)
19. Harris, D.G., Schneider, J., Su, H.-H.: Distributed $(\Delta + 1)$-coloring in sublogarithmic rounds. In: STOC, pp. 465–478 (2016)
20. Kuhn, F., Moscibroda, T., Wattenhofer, R.: Local computation: lower and upper bounds. J. ACM **63**(2), 17:1-17:44 (2016)
21. Lenzen, C., Wattenhofer, R.: MIS on trees. In: Proceedings of the 30th Annual ACM Symposium on Principles of Distributed Computing (PODC), pp. 41–48 (2011)
22. Luby, M.: A simple parallel algorithm for the maximal independent set problem. In: STOC, pp. 1–10 (1985)
23. Kshemkalyani, A.D., Ali, F.: Efficient dispersion of mobile robots on graphs. In: ICDCN, pp. 218–227 (2019)
24. Kshemkalyani, A.D., Molla, A.R., Sharma, G.: Fast dispersion of mobile robots on arbitrary graphs. In: ALGOSENSORS, pp. 23–40 (2019)
25. Barrière, L., Flocchini, P., Barrameda, E.M., Santoro, N.: Uniform scattering of autonomous mobile robots in a grid. In: IPDPS, pp. 1–8 (2009)
26. Elor, Y., Bruckstein, A.M.: Uniform multi-agent deployment on a ring. Theor. Comput. Sci. **412**(8–10), 783–795 (2011)
27. Shibata, M., Mega, T., Ooshita, F., Kakugawa, H., Masuzawa, T.: Uniform deployment of mobile agents in asynchronous rings. J. Parallel Distributed Comput. **119**, 92–106 (2018)
28. Pramanick, S., Samala, S.V., Pattanayak, D., Mandal, P.S.: Filling MIS vertices of a graph by myopic luminous robots. In: Molla, A.R., Sharma, G., Kumar, P., Rawat, S. (eds.) ICDCIT 2023. LNCS, vol. 13776, pp. 3–19. Springer, Cham (2023). https://doi.org/10.1007/978-3-031-24848-1_1

Author Index

Printed in the United States
by Baker & Taylor Publisher Services